The Early Settlement of Stamford, Connecticut 1641-1700

Including

Genealogies of the Stamford Families of the Seventeenth Century

History by

Jeanne Majdalany

Genealogies by

Edith M. Wicks and *Jeanne Majdalany*

HERITAGE BOOKS

2008

HERITAGE BOOKS
AN IMPRINT OF HERITAGE BOOKS, INC.

Books, CDs, and more—Worldwide

For our listing of thousands of titles see our website at
www.HeritageBooks.com

Published 2008 by
HERITAGE BOOKS, INC.
Publishing Division
100 Railroad Ave. #104
Westminster, Maryland 21157

Other books by the author:

Early Villages of Stamford, Connecticut: The Cove and Long Ridge
Jeanne Majdalany

Poems on Stone in Stamford, Connecticut
Jeanne Majdalany and Jean Mulkerin

International Standard Book Number: 978-1-55613-394-7

To the memory of

Virginia T. Davis

Whose inspiration, sense of fun,

and dedication to achievement

encouraged and delighted all who

worked with her

Contents

A pull-out map is located at the back of the book. This map combines three maps which outline the homelots of Stamford, 1641-1660, 1661-1680, and 1681-1700.

Preface

Stamford today is a metropolis, priding itself on being home to innumerable corporate headquarters. It is a vast sprawling city of buildings, all sizes, all shapes--dominoes, plazas, rectangles and squares of glass, of concrete, towers, and spires, all sandwiched together into odd land blocks determined by busy, powerful highways. What can be found of the Stamford of 1641?

Take a look from the air, for a few elements do exist. Mill River still runs to the west down to Long Island Sound, though its course is very different and its sides in the center of Stamford are bounded by stiff, man-made barriers. Noroton River, now a mere trickle of its former glory, bounds Stamford proper on the east. Between the two rivers runs the Main Street (Route 1, the Post Road, or the Stage Road) which was the Country Road of the earliest days. It is an interrupted highway now, no longer passing through the section between St. John's Episcopal Church and the cupola-topped Town Hall in the center of Stamford. Urban renewal chopped across it and even cemented over the town green, once subject of a deed stating it was to remain such in perpetuity. The contours of the land remain in some sections, the ridges to the north, for instance, and some of the smaller streams and some outlying sections of woods, but the central swamps and impeding rocks are mainly gone as men have striven through the years to make use of all land at their disposal.

This book has been written in an effort to recapture the Stamford of 1641-1700. My experience with its early history developed primarily during the bicentennial years of 1975 and 1976 when I was quite unexpectedly called by a stranger (Mrs. Virginia Davis) to see if I would be interested in doing research on Stamford's oldest houses to determine whether they were built prior to the American Revolution. I answered simply that I would love to--quite a shock to her as she didn't get that kind of answer from others she called.

Some of the many title-searches took weeks of careful delving into the Land Deed and the Town Meeting records (which Stamford is most fortunate to have from the earliest days). The research went on for many years actually, and during that time I became historian of the Stamford Historical Society. Thereafter, I was involved in all kinds of projects and later used some of the accrued information in three small books of local history: *The Early History of Long Ridge Village 1700-1800*, *The History of the Cove in Stamford, Connecticut*, and *Poems on Stone in Stamford, Connecticut.*

One day as I studied the Town Meeting Books for the year 1650, I became aware that I could try matching up the recorded descriptions of some of the house-owners' properties and thereby build a map of the original plan of Stamford. This project took a very long time, for it resembled assembling a jigsaw puzzle with a number of parts missing. A man's property boundaries would be given with a road as one of the four sides. It was a case of making rectangular pieces of paper for the lots and then trying to match the neighbors together. Fortunately, Stamford's main center remains so today with a recognizable north, east, south, and west axis. Also, a map by W.H. Holly of 1837 served as a guide, as well as a mock-up map representing 1806, both on record at the Stamford Town Hall.

Members of the Historical Society encouraged me to write a book on Stamford in the seventeenth century, as a result, saying that I knew more about it than anyone else. I too wanted to write a chronological study (a difficulty in that the Town Meeting Records are not all in chronological order and also the first three months of each year were then considered a part of the previous year). I wanted to depict the people themselves and the slow evolvement of the Stamford community, while recognizing, of course, that records are scanty at best and that hardly any manuscripts for that period exist today.

Research has taken me to the Connecticut State Library in Hartford, the Massachusetts Historical Society, the New Haven Historical Society, the Westchester Historical Society, the New York Historical Society, the Fairfield Historical Society, the Fairfield Probate Court, the New Canaan Historical Society, the Ferguson Library in Stamford, the Greenwich Library, and the Stamford Town Hall. Two books which have been helpful are *The History of Stamford* written in 1868 by E. B. Huntington, and Estelle F. Feinstein's *Stamford from Puritan to Patriot* (1976). However, both of these books cover far longer periods of Stamford's history and present the material in quite different ways with no close study of the actual settlers, their lives, or their contributions.

I am indebted to the following people for reading my material, providing ideas, and generally offering criticism: Edith Wicks, President of the Stamford Genealogical Society; Louise McLean, Historian of the Darien Historical Society; my two daughters, Carol Williams and Gail Heaslip; Jim Williams for measurement calculations for my map; Carolyn Comings, Richard and Barbara Cole, Betty and Robert Scribner, Jean Charles Sasportas, Paul Prindle, and, of course, members of the Stamford Historical Society, especially Ronald Marcus, Lois Dater, and Margaret Bowen. Even the most careful researcher is prone to make mistakes no matter how much effort to be accurate has been made. I apologize for any that may appear. Then, too, one always hopes new material will turn up--it is a tantalizing situation. Where else should one look? Would there be some old letters stashed away, for example, in England somewhere? I can only hope that this work will inspire others to enlarge the picture of Stamford's early families and that the individuals will come more fully to life than I have been able to make them.

LIST OF ILLUSTRATIONS

All photographs (pages 3, 6, 54, 58, 68, 88, 100, and 117) by Donald G. Piper

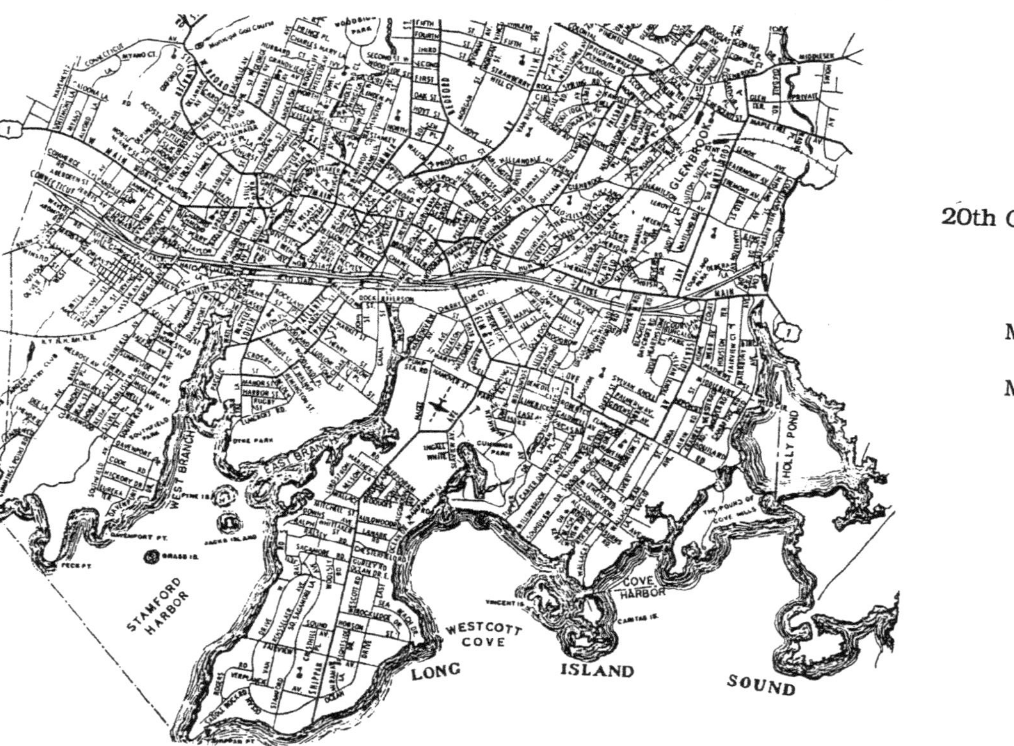

20th Century Stamford, CT

Map courtesy of

Martin Map Co.

Yonkers, NY

Chapter One: 1640-1649

On a day in the spring of 1641, when the weather seemed reasonably settled for some mildness and warmth, a body of men and boys gathered in the village. There was an expectant air about them as they shifted their muskets, tightened their bundles of tools, checked their few horses and oxen. These were Englishmen with their sons, Englishmen who had traveled far during the previous ten years.

They had left their homes in England, lured by the prospects of better opportunities in the New World - good lands, equality of status, and freedom from the Church of England. Everyone would have a chance to be himself, to grow, to succeed. And so they had arrived in Boston during the great migrations of the early 1630s. Some had settled into the developing villages nearby. Many went to Watertown; some to Charlestown. However, these areas near Boston were becoming overburdened; there were too many settlers for the available land to support them. Also, the theocratic government of Boston was becoming increasingly restrictive. Men became restive. In 1634 a wonderful new prospect was offered by some friendly Indians. One could find all the land one needed along the banks of a great river, the Connecticut, far to the southwest of Watertown. So these ever-moving Englishmen packed their few possessions and with their families made the arduous trek through forest, swamp, and threat of unknown Indian or wild beast to the soft, rolling richness of Pyquag, soon to be called Wethersfield. The two weeks of difficult travel were soon history as the settlers struggled to build their homes and cultivate lands anew. A few years passed; the village grew.

Now in 1641, it was time to move once again. It was hard for these English settlers to accept another uprooting. However, they were determined in their support of their pastor, the Reverend Richard Denton, and his close friend, Sergeant Matthew Mitchell. Both religious and political dissension had proved unsolvable in Wethersfield in spite of the intercession of several outside mediators. Consequently, in 1640, two respected leaders, Andrew Ward and Robert Coe, had represented the group in buying a large tract of unsettled land from the New Haven Colony. The price was thirty-three pounds to be paid in produce by each man proportionately as soon as possible.[1]

So, the score or so men, accompanied by their able-bodied sons, resolutely said good-bye to their wives and young ones. These were men who surely were well tested. They knew their strengths. They could face the hardships of travel through forest and mud; they could meet the Indian and come through. They could rely on their own muscle and the combined force of their friends to hew down trees, to build their shelters, to plant their vital crops, and generally to set up a viable community.

Toquams or Rippowam, the Indian names for the tract, was at a distance of some seventy-five miles directly southwest of Wethersfield along the northern shore of an inlet of the ocean, which was bounded to the south by Long Island. To get there would take a number of days of travel along the well-worn Indian trails; these had probably been enlarged during the preceding months as, according to agreement, Mr. Denton and his family were already in residence. Also, preliminary planning for the new settlement had taken place.

It is also possible that the long Connecticut River was deemed a better route to travel. This route had already been used for transporting goods between Boston and the upper river areas, and it wouldn't have been a hard trip to go west from Saybrook at its mouth to the good harbors of the proposed plantation. One of their number, Jeremiah Jagger, may even have had a serviceable boat and good navigational training, as later, in 1658, he was the owner of a trading vessel and lost his life in the West Indies. Then too, Matthew Mitchell, the wealthiest man of the group, had lived for awhile in Saybrook and could have been of help concerning the arrangements. While there, he had owned a shallop that was destroyed by the Indians.[2]

When the men arrived in their newly acquired territory, what exactly did they find? What was this virginal tract of land that was destined to become a permanent home for many of them? They were in luck. The lay of the land was beautiful. Much of it was open rolling land descending to the sea in irregular form, which allowed for harbors, safe havens for their boats. There were three large rivers and a series of ridges and valleys with small rivers in them, and the land was fertile for farming.

They set about organizing their new village. A little hill between two swamps was chosen as an ideal spot for their meetinghouse. It could be fortified to serve as a refuge for the families against marauding Indians. Nearby was the old Indian trail that

(30

The first of July 1640

Bought of Ponus Sagamore of Toquams and of Wascussue Saga-
-more of Shippan by mee Nathanael Turner of Quenepiocke all the
ground that belongs to both the abovesaid Sagamores: except a piece of
ground which the abovesaid Sagamore of Toquans reserved for his and the
rest of the said Indians to plant on all which ground being expressed by me-
-dows upland grass with the rivers and trees And in Consideration hereof I
the said Nathanael Turner am to give and bring or send to the abovesaid
Sagamores with in the space of one monthes twelve coats twelve howes
twelve hatchets twelve glasses twelve knives two kettles four fathom of
white wompum. all which land both We the said Sagamores do promise
faithfully to perform both for ourselves heirs Executors or assigns to the a-
-bove said Nathanael Turner of Quenepiocke to his heirs Executors or assig
And hereunto we have sett our marks in the presence of many of the said
Indians they fully consenting hereunto

Witnessed by us
William Wilkes
James

the mark of [mark] Ponus Sagamore
the mark of [mark] Wascussue Sagamore

Witnessed by two Indians
the mark of [mark] Owenoke Sagamore Ponus's Son
the mark of

linked various coastal points, and this could serve as the main road running generally east and west. In order to keep the meetinghouse a true center, roads were planned to the north and south. Logically then, these prospective thoroughfares were soon called East, West, North, and South. The west road led to a hill, again with large swamps bordering it, but by veering to the north and then south slightly, a way could be made to the swift-flowing Rippowam River. That location could serve admirably for the building of the necessary dam and attendant grist mill. Throughout the area there were a number of ponds and outcroppings of rock as well as numerous swamps so that when it came to laying out the house lots of one and a half to two acres, such impediments had to be taken into consideration. Matthew Mitchell and young Francis Bell were entrusted with this responsibility.[3] About the borders of this nucleus village was plenty of fairly level land for the communal pastures and the planting fields. Before long they received the prosaic names of North Field, East Field, and South Field, and Rocky Neck for the area directly to the south of the village center.

Spring and summer passed in hard work. In his 1641 logbook, a Dutch captain named DeVries noted that there were "Englishmen at the mouth of the Rippowam building houses."[4] Before long, the men were able to collect their families and move together to Rippowam. There must have been many troubled spirits as they said good-bye to their relatives and friends in Wethersfield, but because of the animosity that had developed there, a sense of relief and new hope must have been present, too. The women had packed their few possessions into chests and bundles. What they carried to their new homes was really very minimal - a few well-worn, homemade clothes, the essential bedding, spinning-wheel parts, a few pots, kettles, skillets, and woodenware; trammels, cob irons, and peels for their fireplaces; and the tools of various trades. A few animals must have gone along, but no one had more than two or three cows or horses, a few pigs, chickens, and sheep. Any remaining supplies of food were packed with care, as were seeds for future crops.

To turn now to a consideration of these settlers of Rippowam, they were as follows:

Robert Bates	Jeremiah Jagger	Samuel Sherman
Francis Bell	John Jessup	Vincent Simkins
Samuel Clark	Richard Law	Henry Smith
Robert Coe	Matthew Mitchell	Andrew Ward
Richard Crab	Thomas Morehouse	Thomas Weeks

(continued next page)

Settlers of Rippowam (continued)

Richard Denton	John Northend	John Whitmore
Jeffrey Ferris	Thurston Raynor	Edmund Wood
Daniel Finch	John Reynolds	Jeremiah Wood
Robert Fisher	John Seaman	Jonas Wood #
Richard Gildersleve		Jonas Wood #

Note: one Jonas Wood was from Halifax, England and the other from Owram, England.

Of these twenty-nine settlers, ten are of particular note, for they were the true progenitors of Stamford. The two who became the recognized leaders in the plantation were Richard Law, who moved with his wife Margaret and his three small children, and Francis Bell, who came with his young wife Rebecca. One hopes that she had an easy voyage by boat rather than going on foot, for in September she gave birth to their first child, Jonathan. He was the first child born in the settlement, and technically his birthplace was Rippowam. Two of the other eight settlers eventually moved on to Greenwich to the west, but they were very much involved in the local affairs. These were John Reynolds and Richard Crab. Jeffrey Ferris was vital to the community's development, and though he himself did move to Greenwich eventually, he gave homes in Stamford to two of his sons. The following men lived and died in Stamford, took part in town affairs, and left children to carry on: Jeremiah Jagger, Henry Smith, and Robert Bates. Daniel Finch, the oldest man in the group, later left Stamford for Fairfield, but his brother John and his sons remained to carry the Finch name onward to the present day.

It is hard for us today to recognize the grinding physical labor involved in the everyday living of our forebears of the seventeenth century. When one thinks of what it took to establish a community on land that was very little cultivated previously, one is amazed at what this group of perhaps eighty to a hundred workers was able to accomplish. The two years following their arrival in the summer of 1641 were full of intense activity. Undoubtedly they were years of hardship and deprivation as well.

Their first form of shelter was rather makeshift with only a single room, a clay-packed chimney, and probably a thatched roof. This gave way to a more permanent structure, built like those in Plymouth. It was still a single room with space above for a garret under the steeply pitched wood roof, but now a large chimney of stone took up most of one end. When possible, the house faced south for the warmth of the sun. Later still, a second room was added making the chimney a central one able to heat both hall [illegible] gr[illegible] out of [illegible]

was [illegible] but [illegible] [illegible]

and [illegible] [illegible] [illegible]

[illegible] [illegible] [illegible]

[illegible] the place [illegible]

[illegible] [illegible] [illegible]

[illegible] land [illegible] out [illegible]

First [illegible] names [illegible] [illegible] have [illegible]

under the name of [illegible] or [illegible] to [illegible] on land to Ripowam

To [illegible] [illegible] the designe of a [illegible] [illegible] [illegible]

Amongst Mr. [illegible] Denton to remove his familie [illegible] by the [illegible]

[illegible] the rest [illegible] familyes [illegible] by the last of November

12 months [illegible]

[illegible] Denton	Ri. Gildersleeve	Tho. Weekes	Sam. Sherman
Mr. Mitchell	Edm. Wood	Jon. Wood Jr.	Hen. Smith
			Vincent Simkins
Thur. Rayner	Jon. Wood	Jer. Jagger	Dan. Finch
Robt. Coe	Jer. Wood	Jo. [illegible]	Jo. Northend
And. Ward	Sam. Clarke	Jo. Seaman	

[illegible] the purchase of the place and [illegible] of it first [illegible]

[illegible] our friends [illegible] [illegible] [illegible] [illegible]

[illegible] at the same time that 100 bushells of [illegible]

[illegible] [illegible]

Mr. Mitchell

[illegible]	[illegible]	[illegible]	3 2	Jo. Northend	[illegible]
[illegible] Rayner	5 3	[illegible]	3 1	Jon. Wood Jr.	[illegible]
Mr. Denton	4 1	Jo. [illegible]	3 1	Sam. [illegible]	2
And. Ward	4 1	[illegible]	3 1	Jer. Wood	2 2
Ro. Coe	4 1	[illegible]	3 1	Sam. [illegible]	2 2
[illegible]	4 0	[illegible]	3 [illegible]	[illegible]	[illegible]
[illegible]	2 2	Dan. Finch	3 0	[illegible]	[illegible]
	[illegible]	21 [illegible]	[illegible]		[illegible]

[illegible] 100 bushels [illegible] 30 [illegible]

[illegible] afterwards [illegible] [illegible]

[illegible] at [illegible] in May [illegible]

The [illegible] October [illegible] having [illegible]

[illegible] [illegible] There was [illegible]

[illegible] Mr. Mitchell And. Ward [illegible]

[illegible] [illegible] of [illegible]

[illegible] [illegible] determine [illegible]

[illegible] [illegible] [illegible]

[illegible] order was taken

It was ordered That whereas every man may [illegible]

right before his lott to the midle of the streete to be his [illegible]

[illegible] for his owne use. If he [illegible] to [illegible]

[illegible] he [illegible] or any of them, he or [illegible] shall

[illegible] ground and [illegible] the way of them, and [illegible]

[illegible] of them to [illegible] for every [illegible] not [illegible]

[illegible] [illegible]

3

It was ordered [illegible] [illegible] [illegible] [illegible]

[illegible] [illegible] [illegible] and order [illegible]

[illegible] what [illegible] and consider what [illegible]

[illegible] not fit to be measured for land and to [illegible]

[illegible] [illegible] [illegible]

[illegible] [illegible] [illegible]

[illegible] [illegible]

(kitchen) and parlor. Windows were primitive arrangements at first and very small; the central door, a strong one. A fairly typical example of this early form of house still stands in Stamford. It is the Hoyt-Barnum house of 1699, situated on Bedford Street. This house is larger than the earlier houses would have been and has several additional features, such as a kitchen and a staircase to the rear of the two front rooms.

In her home at last, the woman would settle in to her usual onerous chores. Preparing food for the heavy meals the family needed took much time; then the cooking over the smoky hot fire demanded constant attention. Along with all this, the ever-increasing number of children required care. Washing and general cleanliness must have been hard to achieve at all. The wheels for wool and flax had to be kept turning, for clothes had to be produced, though leather and skins could serve for the more durable items of apparel. The children, of course, were assigned their daily duties just as soon as they were capable of work.

The man of the family would be busy with the other men as they worked together on the houses and barns, and on the never-ending building of fences. When one thinks of the work entailed just in sawing the necessary wood for all the various needs, one realizes how backbreaking it all must have been. Also, each man had to clear and plant a plot near the house for the family supply of vegetables. The common fields, too, had to be cleared and planted with Indian corn, peas, flax, and rye, and once planted, they had to be tended. The hay from the salt meadows was readily available, but it had to be gathered - a slow process. The need for provisions for the family, both for daily use and for storage for the winter, was a constant worry. Fish and meat were there for the catching, and wild fowl were plentiful - too plentiful at times when they descended on the grain fields. Wells had to be dug also.

One wonders when these busy new householders found time for all the necessary community projects, such as clearing the "paths" (future roads), building a strong meetinghouse large enough to contain the population, and since it also served as a fort, putting up a surrounding palisade against marauding Indians or other enemies.

Another community project was the establishment of a functional "landing place," as it was named, for their boats at the mouth of the principal river, the Rippowam. In those times the water route was the practical one for the moving of people and for the transportation of commodities. These new English arrivals expected to carry on trade with both New Haven and Boston. They depended on future shipments of necessary tools, seeds, animals, and household goods, often originating in England. In return they planned to export farm produce, skins, and wood, as did most of the new settlements that had developed outside Boston.

A major concern, too, was the construction of a dam across the river, which Matthew Mitchell and John Ogden agreed to build, along with the construction of the accompanying grist mill. The mill was built under the direction of Samuel Swayne, who had agreed to handle this matter but did not settle in Rippowam.[5] The mill, very unfortunately, met with disaster soon after it was completed; it was the victim of either flood or fire by the end of the year. Every landowner had to pitch in with hard-gained shillings (usually given in produce) to cover the expense of rebuilding, this time under the control of Thurston Raynor, a well-respected leader of comfortable means, and Richard Law, who bought the concern for seventy-four pounds and ten shillings.[6] At the same time each man had to contribute to the building and fortification of the "Captain's house." Captain John Underhill, a professional soldier, had agreed to move to Rippowam in order to train the men against any assault by the Indians or even by the Dutch, very uncertain neighbors on the west.[+] The training and serving as watchman also took a man's time.

On Sunday the chores were laid aside, and all assembled to hear the Word of God as expounded by Mr. Denton. He was very highly esteemed by Cotton Mather as a man of great soul and strong persuasive powers, though he was small of body and blind in one eye.[8] He was clearly a man of power and influence in the community. Mr. Denton did, of course, rule the church and the village in true Puritan tradition and could well have been irked when other political powers tried to dictate. The long Sunday attendance (most of the day) at his services was perhaps a release from the weekly drudgery, in spite of the hard benches and the bitter cold of winter. Besides, these people expected to be exhorted constantly to prove themselves good Christians. Short interludes in the services did provide a chance for socializing and a modicum of pleasure.

In the fall of 1641 various matters relating to town government were resolved. In October five men were chosen to handle local affairs; these were Mr. Denton, Matthew Mitchell, Andrew

----

+ The Dutch at this time were firmly established in the territory to be known later as New York, and they also had claims to much of later Connecticut, especially in the area directly to the west of Rippowam. A Dutch official in New York sent word to Holland complaining that "the English now have a village called Stamfort from which a man can reach the North River and return home on a summers day according to the knowledge acquired of the Indian paths."[7]

Ward, Thurston Raynor, and Richard Crab. A month later John Whitmore and Richard Law were added to the list of "townsmen," as they were called. The two delegates to the New Haven General Court (the term for the legislature) were Andrew Ward and Francis Bell, who were admitted to the court session on October 27 as freemen.[+]

At the same session Thurston Raynor was appointed to the dignified office of constable with the highly responsible job of being the final arbiter of local disputes and keeping the peace. Two other men were chosen for public office at the December town meeting.[9] These were Richard Gildersleve and Robert Bates, appointed as fence viewers for the following spring. Why was this so important? Large animals could not be allowed to roam along the public thoroughfares and near the homes nor could they be allowed to range through the planting fields. It was essential that each man build strong fences for the portions laid out to him as his responsibility. Any neglectful man would be fined.

Evidently, word soon traveled back to Wethersfield and to New Haven that the settlement of Rippowam was a success, for new families began arriving all that autumn of 1641. By the middle of December there were forty-two families in all, thirteen new ones having been accepted.[10] These were:

Henry Ackerley	Thomas Pop
Thomas Armitage	John Rockwell
Thomas Hyatt	Daniel Scofield
William Mead	John Smith, Sr.
John Ogden	John Smith, Jr.
James Pine	John Stevens

and John Coe, the son of Robert Coe,
who now needed his own home.

Several of these new home owners, such as William Mead, Daniel Scofield, and John Coe, received house lots on the west side of the village along the east bank of the river. Two of these men were the heads of large families, for the Scofields and the Stevenses exist in Stamford even today. In fact, later in Stamford's history there was an area in North Stamford known as Scofieldtown, just as there was a Belltown. Also, a ridge was named for

----

+ A freeman was an inhabitant who belonged to the church. By taking the Freeman's Oath, he was enabled to vote and to hold public office.

the Rockwells. Henry Ackerley and William Mead's sons moved on to Greenwich, and John Rockwell, after twenty-eight years in Stamford, moved further west to Rye.

By the following year, 1642, the little community was reasonably well established with homes, roads, a mill, and even by April the enclosed common fields. Relations with New Haven were amicable, though some men still owed produce for their shares of the tract of land. Matthew Mitchell and John Whitmore, now designated freemen, had to travel to New Haven to the court sessions spring and fall, and either they or the New Haven officials determined that the name of Rippowam be changed to Stamford; most likely it was the desire of the community and its leaders - Mitchell, Denton, Ward, and Raynor - who preferred a name they had been accustomed to in England. At that time, also, Andrew Ward was appointed constable, taking over from Thurston Raynor; each must have found the job of keeping the peace no small task amongst these people of strong views and outspoken independence (except, of course, in church matters where they were held in abeyance to their pastor and to the principles of the Puritan tradition).

That same fall new settlers were accepted, and several proved to be valuable members of the community. These new arrivals were:

John Finch (who joined his brother Daniel)
William Graves
John Holly#
Robert Husted
John Lum
John Miller
William Newman
Henry Pierson
Symon Seiring
George Slason#
Thomas Slason
James Swead
John Towne
John Underhill
Jonas Weed
Francis Yates#

Note: These three are names included in Huntington's list, pp. 25-26.

Seven of these families established themselves permanently in Stamford. John Finch brought four sons, who founded large families in both Stamford and Greenwich. John Holly, who was a man of some standing and had owned a mill in Newtown (Cambridge), Massachusetts,[11] played an active, vital role in Stamford's government and had many worthy descendants. Robert Husted established himself very soon in Greenwich where his family became renowned for their public service and position. William

Newman's sons did well in Stamford, and descendants built a prosperous mill on the northern part of the Rippowam, or Mill River. Thomas Slason is a bit of a mystery, as there is only one land deed to him, but his brother, George Slason, was active in town affairs almost immediately. The Slasons later settled to the east in what was to become Darien. The last was Jonas Weed, whose numerous children had numerous children, and one is tempted to use a pun on the word "weed" as the family expanded to the point where there were in its history fourteen or so Jonases alone! It is striking that so many of the respected names of Stamford's history are connected with this group that arrived in 1642.

Although the settlement had now expanded to approximately fifty-eight families, and the house lots were spreading out north and south and east especially, the people of Stamford were constantly uneasy. They knew they were ever vulnerable to Indian attack. The Pequot War of 1637 was an all-too-recent experience of the violence and savagery that could be engendered on both sides. Matthew Mitchell, for example, had suffered severely in it, losing most of his possessions, some of his employees, and his wife's son.[12] A good number of the other settlers had taken part or had had relatives fighting to decimate the Indians along the east coast lands. Now in Stamford, their tiny raw settlement, the English were constantly on the alert. The train band had to practice steadily to sharpen the men's military skills under the competent John Underhill. Defenses were essential, as was a strong watch system. Rumors were ever rife, and New Haven was too far away from its westernmost plantation to give any immediate support.

On the other hand, the men of Stamford made their agreements and were accepted by the sagamores of the area, who seem to have been leaders of small groups of Indians living peacefully by their planting fields. There were four of these sagamores: Ponus to the north, Piamikin to the east, Wascussue to the south, and Myano to the west.[13] The Indians, at first grateful for the fine gifts of axes, kettles, coats, knives, and small household items, really had little conception that they were losing their lands, for to them there was no ownership of Nature's bounty. Then, too, they were ready to help the white settler and give him of their produce when needed. They enjoyed satisfying their very natural curiosity by entering freely into the new village, and even were willing to work in return for small presents. It is clear from several references in the early records that the people of Stamford were used to having their Indian neighbors enter their streets. Richard Law didn't find it unusual, one would judge, when an Indian came to his house in the center of the village.[14] Indians were accepted as servants, and clearly, a certain amount of interaction did exist.

However, misunderstandings were bound to arise between two groups of such different cultures. The white men, believing themselves superior, were often arrogant and ready to take advantage of the Indians for personal gain. The Indians, in turn, not simplistic at all, knew when they were taken advantage of and would steal or kill in revenge. Actually, Stamford was very fortunate - there were few incidents. Much ill feeling, however, was generated among the Indians by the treatment meted out by the Dutch of New Netherlands. As has been noted, the Dutch laid claim to the land as far east as the Connecticut River where they maintained a fort at Hartford. In 1642 they had even persuaded the very early settlers in what was later to be called Greenwich to become a manor under their jurisdiction. In return, the settlers would receive protection from the rather numerous Indians that had become a true menace on the northwest. It was primarily the Dutch traders who aroused the deep hatred of the Indians by taking advantage of the Indian susceptibility to the power of rum and then running off with their valuable furs and other objects of trade. The Dutch governor grew more and more determined to exterminate as many Indians as possible with a view towards ending the on-going savage raids. When a Dutchman living near Stamford killed the sagamore Myano in self-defense, the Dutch recognized that they must wipe out his tribe or suffer severely. In 1643 a party of one hundred and twenty men landed in Greenwich and spent time fruitlessly searching for Indians in the northern woods. When they returned through Stamford, they found Captain Daniel Patrick of Greenwich at Captain Underhill's house. An altercation ensued as the Dutch accused Patrick of warning his Indian friends. When Patrick, spurning the Dutch, spat at one and turned away to leave Underhill's house, that soldier shot and killed him. Since Underhill was a close friend of Patrick, but also eager to support the Dutch, he must have found himself in an unfortunate situation. Shortly thereafter, four Stamford men offered to guide the Dutch to the Indian village where twenty Indians were found and killed.

Thomas Stevens and George Slason, as watchmen, had the responsibility of guarding the guilty Dutch soldier in the Underhill's house. He was kept in a chamber upstairs, the door of which was carefully locked. However, one night while the faithful watchmen were sitting by the fire at the foot of the stairs and the Underhills had retired to their quarters, the prisoner escaped and was seen no more. George Slason later told the New Haven court that he had disliked the window in the prisoner's room but that both the Underhills had assured him that it was safe. It rather looked as though the Underhills had abetted the prisoner. One can understand it in that Underhill's wife was Dutch; he had known the Dutch well in Europe during his early military career; and also, he was very firmly supportive of all those who were out to end the Indian menace. (His strong antagonism had reached a peak during the year that he became a hero in the Pequot War of 1637, and soon after his return to England then, he had even written a book about his experiences.) Did he recognize that Patrick was actually in the wrong and that the Dutch had suffered more from Patrick than is evident in the terse account?[15]

This dramatic series of events must have created much concern and gossip along the village streets of Stamford, but Underhill was deemed blameless. The Stamford men looked up to him as their leader, one who had proved himself time and again. They had asked him to come to Stamford, had given him a house and lands, and in the same year, 1643, they paid him a substantial salary for his services. The New Haven Colony itself was reluctant to become involved in protecting their little subsidiary on the west when it begged for some financial assistance, but did offer to lend Stamford twenty pounds so that Captain Underhill could build up his defenses. In this same year the valiant military leader took his place as a man of political importance in Stamford. He served as deputy to the New Haven court with Richard Gildersleve. Then upon Thurston Raynor's being appointed magistrate, he was chosen to be one of the group to aid in handling the more minor court affairs in Stamford.[16]

The establishment of the Stamford court gives evidence that Stamford was gaining some respect in New Haven and that its needs were growing. Not only were the Stamford people thereby given more freedom in handling their own affairs, but also having now a magistrate, they had a representative to serve at senatorial rank. The other men chosen to help Raynor were Matthew Mitchell, who had also been considered for the position, Robert Coe, and Andrew Ward.

On the other hand, since New Haven clearly wanted complete loyalty from the towns that were springing up under her control (perhaps hearing of some of the dissatisfaction that was developing under her strong rule), it was soon decreed that the governor should give the oath of loyalty to the men of Stamford.[17] This, it was felt, would bind those people more closely to their rather shakily-based government, lacking as it did a proper charter from the king of England.

An interesting case came before the Stamford court the following year. It involved Richard Crab, who thereby began his crusade against those in authority. His young Indian servant had misbehaved in public - perhaps he had urinated on a public street. Obviously, whatever it was, it wasn't a serious crime, but it was some crime of a moral nature. His master punished him for his misdeed. However, Thurston Raynor as magistrate insisted that the lad be publicly punished. Richard Crab would not accept the idea of two punishments, as he said his servant might well run away. The consequence was that the case was referred to New Haven, and Richard Crab was pronounced in the wrong. He had flouted authority; this could not be allowed. The upshot was that Crab had to pay Raynor a fine of five pounds. Since Crab was a rather fiery man, he must have done much grumbling. At least the boy seems to have been let off.[18]

Early in 1644 Captain Underhill saw his chance for conclusively subduing the Indians in the Greenwich area. The Dutch offered him good terms to work for them and he accepted. An expedition of three yachts and one hundred and thirty men set out from New Amsterdam under his leadership, and passing along Long Island Sound, they landed at Greenwich Point in an evening snowstorm. The next day they marched all day in a northwesterly direction to an Indian village. A fierce battle ensued with the Indian warriors. A Dutch officer wrote in his journal as follows: "In a brief space of time, one hundred and eighty were counted dead outside the houses. Presently none durst come forth, keeping themselves within the house, discharging arrows through the holes..." Van der Hil (or John Underhill) resolved to end the struggle by setting fire to the huts. "What was most wonderful is that among this vast collection of men, women and children, not one was heard to cry or to scream." Five hundred or more Indians perished. The English and the Dutch proved themselves as savage as any uncivilized group in history, but this massacre in their view was justified as it did definitively end the Indian power in that area.

"On the next day the party set out much refreshed in good order, so as to arrive at Stantfort in the evening...The English received our people in a very friendly manner affording them every comfort."[19] Stamford breathed a sigh of great relief and entertained a short-lived sympathy with the Dutch, who were, nevertheless, viewed throughout this period with deep suspicion, a suspicion brought about by their constant claim to half of Connecticut. Once the Dutch even made a quickly aborted foray against Stamford and Greenwich.

During this year of 1644 a really surprising event occurred. In a seemingly well-established little community all was not right. We have seen that there was certainly uneasiness over the Indians, but that was no longer of major significance. We can realize, too, that having to submit to the distant New Haven jurisdiction was often irksome and frustrating, but something greater than that friction was rankling. The three principal leaders, the Reverend Mr. Denton, Matthew Mitchell, and Thurston Raynor, presumably recognizing once again that differences were irreconcilable, decided to accept the proposal of the Dutch to resettle across Long Island Sound on a beautiful piece of land to be called Hempstead. Was it that the Dutch sounded like better rulers than the men in New Haven? Was it that Mr. Denton found himself and many of his followers at odds over religious matters? Or was it the lure of better and more lands? The desire to strike out afresh overcame all other considerations. Clearly these men with their families found it reasonably easy to uproot themselves once more; they were willing to go through all the arduous tasks involved in resettling. To us with our lavish homes and many possessions such moves seem preposterous, but their homes and possessions were otherwise. Then too, one could easily sail across the small, comparatively sheltered body of water to visit the friends left behind.

In all, about twenty-three families followed their religious leader to Long Island. Of the first twenty-nine settlers of Stamford, at least eleven left. These were: Samuel Clark, Robert Coe and his son John (who later returned to Greenwich), Richard Gildersleve, Matthew Mitchell, Thurston Raynor, Thomas Weeks, and the four Woods: Edmund, Jeremiah, and the two Jonases. Four others possibly went also: Robert Fisher, John Northend, John Seaman, and John Jessup. Of the second group of settlers, Thomas Armitage, John Ogden, and the two John Smiths went. Thomas Pop and James Pine may have gone also. Of the third group, Henry Pierson, Symon Seiring, and Francis Yates left with Denton, and John Lum, James Swead, and John Towne disappear from the Stamford scene. There were four others, according to E. B. Huntington, who evidently passed through Stamford but left no record. These were John Ellison, John Fordham, Robert Jackson, and John Karman.[20]

What a shake-up this must have caused in Stamford! A good third of their number had left homes, fields, town duties, and church. The church was the worst off, for there was now no religious leader in the community. This was devastating; a Puritan community without a ministering father was truly in dire straits.

The remaining men of influence, Andrew Ward, Richard Law, Francis Bell, and John Whitmore, must have gathered the community to deal with this emergency. Someone knew of a man in Boston, a young preacher of excellent standing named John

Bishop. He had been educated at Oxford. Doubtless, they little realized what an excellent choice they were making. John Bishop, who was in his early thirties at the time, gladly accepted Stamford's call and traveled on foot (so tradition claims),[21] carrying his Bible, with the two emissaries, Francis Bell and George Slason. He was to remain Stamford's religious mentor for the rest of his life, for fifty years - a long ministry, and not an easy one. Certainly he was a leader of dignity, learning, and moral strength in Stamford's church and community, extending an influence beyond the bounds of the settlement.

In the early summer of 1644 came another unpleasant incident with the Indians that must have made every woman in Stamford tremble for her safety. The Phelps family had recently settled to the north of the village, and one day an Indian chanced to notice the father leaving his home for a time. Here was his chance to strike out against the hated English. He entered the Phelps' home and buried a hatchet in Mrs. Phelps' head as she bent over her baby. Then he plundered the house. Fortunately, although deeply wounded, Mrs. Phelps was able to identify Busheag, who was already notorious, but unfortunately, she was never normal thereafter.[22]

The inhabitants of Stamford were really roused and appealed to both Hartford and New Haven for action. This time aid was forthcoming. Busheag's tribe was commanded to hand over the murderer. Busheag faced the court of New Haven and finally his death by the executioner's inept blows; he never evinced any reaction, in stoic Indian fashion.

This event served to break the spirit of the Indians to the north of Stamford. They were made to sign a treaty to keep the peace, and many of their number drifted away. From then on the people of Stamford felt more secure, even though their military leader had moved on to the Dutch and a home on Long Island. The Indian threat from both the west and from the north was now greatly reduced.

In reassessing the situation in Stamford after the departure of the large Long Island group, one finds that of the fifty-nine men that arrived in 1641 and 1642 there remained only twenty-eight. These founding men were remarkably hardy, for in spite of toil and turmoil, only one of their number died during these early years. John Miller, who had arrived in 1642, died that same year. His wife married Obadiah Seely shortly thereafter, and his three young sons, John, Jonathan, and Joseph grew up in the Seely household.[23]

Unfortunately, the recording of the community's vital statistics was largely neglected during the 1640s. One head-of-

Sr I receivd yor letter by Judah and this yesterday by yor man and have spoke
to Gov Hubbert at both times but I know noe safe meanes of conveyance of a lettr
till now beeing not wth in when Judah came and went. and I heard of yor
[illegible] feare of comming downe and hoped I might as now I may write and
send by some of yor people. Gov Hubbert is full in his tale about raising the price
the termes of the contract [illegible] well remembred. [illegible] of raising to [illegible]
was if the Indians did [illegible] raise it so much to yo. hee saith noe body will denie it
but the magistrates. all grant that. but saith hee they [illegible] for his own
ends would have had the price raised wth the Indians whereas hee having
such interest [illegible] might have had so much at ould price and Capt. Mason
saith hee thought hee might, and heering his unfaithfullness to the Countrie in those
trust & words appeared & mr Hooker said hee could not beleeve but so wise
a man as mr Pinchon knowe how to governe & had such power wth the Indians that hee
might have performed. els hee would not have promised and ingaged him selfe
on this man doth Gov. reason and so did they yo. know in the Court. and I beleeve
they will doe soe still. but I as fully beleeve that in yor owne conscience yor are
cleare and that yor arguments to an understanding man not prejudiced will cleare
it to yo. and that yo will not neede to his testimony nor would I advise yo to be at so
much charges nor do I doubt but wth the church of [illegible] yo will easilie come
of it if yo do the experience of some saith yor example will be but in vaine and
long & tedious travells in yor longest cause but in vaine. except yo could finde
other [illegible] apprehentions all will not doe. if yo could but have the approbation
of [illegible] and mr Moxon and yor neighbours satisfied I doe beleeve it would
be yor best to make hast into argument if yo may in all the ordinances and to
let other mens example stay yo. in the sight of con[illegible] [illegible] chargable debates
and delayes will bring out. they will keepe [illegible] and the cause will
degenerate and now [illegible] grow & as far [illegible] as at first
I would be glad if [illegible] settled on the Co[illegible] was out of England
now is good & [illegible] to be knowne for wee [illegible] by mr [illegible]
confirmed [illegible] he saith he doth beleeve it [illegible] by the fishing shipps at
afore by the desire [illegible] came in having laden [illegible] brought for newes
of it but they bring it full the [illegible] I came to yor man whoe I doubt as well as
I could. if this be soe there will come but some passengers over. and if not [illegible]
not [illegible] northward winds are so [illegible] and may [illegible] on the coast to fill
up & Long Iland and Delaware Bay [illegible] think of it I doubt I shall
not yet soe much spare time as to see yo. before I goe if I can I will for my
love would and [illegible] and yor [illegible] my love to [illegible] obliged [illegible] I do
acknowledge my selfe much beholding to yo and know not how to make [illegible]
yo. have beene abundant in love. my wife was now [illegible] those [illegible] yo
sent formerly because of the [illegible] but now shee may not
continue a good while in her course of [illegible] shee findes [illegible] by them they
worke kindly. and I hope do her much good & shee is very thankfull to yo. [illegible]
if shee had it to [illegible] her selfe & my selfe thankfull. god may give an opportunitie
and meanes together in the meane time [illegible] like to [illegible] much beholding
to yo. wth our love to yo [illegible] mrs Pinchon kindly remembred [illegible] & to mr Moxon
mr Smith & there wives and to Gov Hubbert. and so wth our dayly [illegible]
and [illegible] to god for yo [illegible]

Yor much indebted and loving
friend to his power

Math Mitchell

household death is recorded in 1646. That was the death of John Dibble, about whom nothing else is known except that he had two sons, Samuel and Zachariah, and a wife Sarah. She married William Graves the following year after the death of his wife Sarah. Wives were at a premium during those very hard times so that widows remained so for very short periods in most cases.

In 1645, however, a very noted death occurred. Matthew Mitchell, the renowned leader, the wealthiest man to come in 1641, the great friend and supporter of the Reverend Richard Denton, died of a lingering natural illness at the age of fifty-five. Although he had gone to Long Island with the group, he had returned to Stamford. Sadly, before his death he experienced one last tragedy. In 1636 his house in Concord had burned, and now again his house was hit by fire. Houses burned all too easily in those days when the hearth fire was in constant use. Matthew left a very simple will, in which he allotted forty pounds to his oldest son David if, as he said, "I live not to build for him myself to repair the building now and without which he hath not a due portion I say he to build with."[24]

It is sad to see how meager the inventory of his possessions is. He had only the essentials: bedding, chairs, two spinning wheels, a set of scales, a warming pan, and the necessary pots, kettles and bowls, and an old iron. He did have some pewter, some cooper's ware, and paints. Just as in most of the early inventories, his Bible is listed, but other books are merely "other books." For farming equipment, he had plow and cart appurtenances, thirty bushels of corn, some bees (for honey and wax), and cattle. His possessions were valued at Ŀ245, and the debts outstanding to him at Ŀ1,505, a considerable sum at that time.

His real estate holdings were not listed, but David, as the oldest son, did receive his father's lands in Stamford; the detailed record of 1650 lists David's small pieces in the various fields, which total forty-four acres "more or less" (a usual expression during the seventeenth century).[25] In America the inheritance rules had been modified. The English law of primogeniture had left too many younger sons without the wherewithal to make a living; therefore, many of these had turned to America to seek their fortunes. Since a man's estate, if broken up among perhaps many children, would no longer prove viable, it was determined in America that the oldest son should receive a double portion. The wife, if she outlived her husband, was given a dower of a third of the estate. Usually she received the house for her lifetime use unless she should remarry. Often the wife was given a third of the house and barn with use of the kitchen, the oven, and the well.

One wonders how the household really managed if there were enmity between the house-holding members!

Matthew Mitchell left one hundred pounds to his second son, Jonathan, who, by 1645, was already married and well established in his ministry in Hartford. His two older daughters had undoubtedly been well settled when they married, for they are not mentioned in Matthew's will. He left eighty pounds each for his two younger daughters and a very large sum, £1,700, to his wife - a departure from the normal procedure.

To turn now to other matters concerning Stamford at this time, there was a problem over boundaries. The boundaries of the original territory of Toquams or Rippowam were not really defined; it was merely "a plantation" to the west of the present town of Norwalk. Naturally, during the 1640s the settlers began expanding their planting and grazing fields towards the east along the coast. Soon friction arose with the peaceful Indians settled in the area between Pine Brook and Five Mile River, or Rowayton. The sagamore Piamikin wasn't averse to having the English there in return for some prized tobacco and four warm coats; so he deeded the land to the Stamford representatives, Richard Law and Andrew Ward. Four Indians witnessed the deed and made their scrawls for signatures, and Jeremiah Jagger and George Slason witnessed for Stamford. There was a provision that the white men were not to build houses there nor to have hogs as these might ruin the Indians' corn. Also cattle that were kept there should have a keeper. Any violations would be redressed.[26] As time went on, this treaty of 1645 was often ignored by the Stamford men, but it did serve later to determine the boundary with Norwalk. Poor Piamikin and his Indian friends, as so often happened, gradually lost to the encroaching white man.

In April of 1647 the court of Stamford was graced with the presence of the governor of New Haven, Theophilus Eaton, and Captain Attwood. Evidently, although this court was commissioned to handle only the minor crimes and disputes, there was enough dissension at this time to call for the higher authorities.

Once more Richard Crab was in difficulty over his Indian servant. He is called William, "a captive Indian," but whether he is the same one that misbehaved several years before cannot be known. In any case, William took advantage of everyone's being at the meetinghouse on the Sabbath to sneak into Jonas Weed's house. He stole a cloth gown, a gun, some wampum (much prized as currency by the Indians), a glass bottle with wine, and some other things. Evidently, there had been words over this between Weed and Crab, for Weed told the court that Crab had counter-accused by saying that Weed's daughter (was it Mary, Elizabeth, or

Dorcas?) probably drank the sack and hid all the things. Crab then denied that he had ever said such a thing. Since William did confess to the crime, Crab conceded that he had stolen money - about seven pounds in wampum and Dutch money. However, Weed had solid backing in the community, for others gave witness that the Indian had stolen considerably more, to the tune of thirty to forty pounds. One Henry (Smith or Ackerley; the last name is torn in the record) claimed that William had stolen a gun, powder, and bullets from him. Again William confessed and said he had gotten a friend, Piamacye, to fetch the gun away.

Clearly William was a *persona non grata* in the town, and with the august support of the Governor the court meted out stern punishment. The Indian was to be whipped publicly by the marshal and then sent out of the country and sold as a slave. Three men agreed to be responsible - Richard Law, John Whitmore, and "Mr. Ward."+ If the sale brought in extra money after expenses were paid, Crab was to have it. Some justice did come Crab's way.[27]

John Chapman also presented a case against Crab, a case which had been previously brought before the court. Crab's horse had caused considerable property damage and so the court voted to have the reimbursement to Chapman increased by ten shillings. At this point Crab rose up against Chapman, but the existing record tells little; it would be very enlightening to know the details. At some point the Reverend John Bishop had tried to handle the problem, for Crab said that Chapman had unduly wronged Mr. Bishop. After discussion in which the Governor added his weighty opinion, John Chapman agreed to make his peace with the minister at a suitable time.[28]

That these people were easily roused and inclined to hot tempers makes one remember the feisty disputes that threatened at times to swamp the Plymouth plantation. In the history *Of Plimouth Plantation*, Bradford often expresses his despair over the arguments that raged among his neighbors once the early rigors of actual settlement were over. The next two cases that came before the Stamford court in 1647 are of the same nature. A full account of what actually ensued would be fascinating.

John Coe brought a case against Daniel Finch in which he stated that Finch had disturbed the ordinance of God on the Sabbath. Perhaps he had attended to some work that he felt just

---

+ The term "Mr." was used for one who had college learning or was of very high standing in the community. It was, of course, always used for ministers.

had to be done. At any rate he was judged guilty and would have to give public satisfaction.[29]

The last case in this august court must have seemed lacking in importance even to the court members, for no outcome to the case is given; perhaps, though, Richard Law, who did the recording in his neat handwriting, just neglected to complete the entry. Goodwife Simkins (the wife of Vincent) came forward to complain about Goodwife Graves. Goodwife Graves, as we have seen, was formerly the wife of John Dibble, by whom she had had at least two sons. Since she had only just married William Graves, she may have felt somewhat insecure in the community. At any rate she is accused of claiming that her children were more holy than all the others' children because they were "naturally better born." Both Goodwife Ackerley and Goodwife Bourrns (an unidentified person) were witnesses to this inexcusable boast.[30]

The following year, 1648, several court cases involved drunkenness. One man, James Lareson, was accused of selling wine, and he agreed not to sell it retail any more. Did he import his wine as a business, or was it locally produced? Jonas Weed, as noted, had his small quantity of sack, and others, too, had wine available, for two recent arrivals in Stamford who had over-imbibed had to appear before the court. Both Robert Penoyer, who was to settle down and raise a family in Stamford, and Thomas Corkrye were guilty. Robert Penoyer's crime had been the worse, for he had abused Francis Holmes, the watchman, and had even wounded him in the face. Presumably he was sorry as he was sentenced to pay Holmes twenty shillings and the court the same amount. He was also bound for a year to good behavior with forfeit of ten pounds. Corkrye, who doesn't seem to have stayed on in Stamford, was accused of profaning the name of God in his drunkenness, as witnessed by the two town powers, Law and Bell; so he was sentenced to be whipped by the marshal John Holly and then to pay him two shillings and sixpence. It is hard to imagine a worthy citizen such as John Holly raising the whip against a fellow inhabitant, but it was a part of the job of marshal in those days. A good whipping did wonders.[31]

A crime of a different nature was committed by one William Gifford. It seems that he was much taken with the charms of Mark Menlow's daughter and thought her an easy prey. He made warm advances and offered her some enticing cherries and a pair of stockings to encourage her to an evil deed. Mother Menlow came to the rescue, and Gifford's game was up. The Stamford court not only ruled that he be publicly whipped but also that he be banished "out of the country." A fine of five pounds would be imposed if he were delinquent about this.[32]

It is hard today to keep in mind how strictly the Puritan ethic ruled a community. Anyone straying from the accepted path was held up to public scrutiny and scorn. What is also interesting to note is that even with the strictures imposed, men would still break loose, especially when a community had become reasonably well established and the truly time-consuming, backbreaking grind of daily life lessened. These cases reflect a certain unruliness bursting forth in Stamford in spite of the strong determining presences of John Bishop, Richard Law, Francis Bell, and John Holly.

Land ownership was a matter that often brought about quarrels, even as it still does today. One such case involved John Finch. He had his troubles at this time, for he had already been brought before the court by David Mitchell, who was trying to collect money, due to him or to his mother, that his father Matthew had lent Finch. Mark Menlow served as witness, and the court ruled that John Finch must pay the two pounds and five shillings plus "damages" of ten shillings.[33] What is interesting in that account is that there is a list of produce and values included. It is clear how Finch was expected to pay, therefore, and also how these basic staples were rated:

4s 6d bushel of wheat
3s 6d bushel of peas
2s 8d bushel of Indian corn
3 1/4's pork
6d butter

Note: Twelve pence (d) = one shilling, and
Twenty shillings (s) = one pound

Evidently pork and butter came in recognized sizes of container.

When Finch came to court over the land ownership problem, he came on a charge from Jeffrey Ferris that he had cut down a tree and carried it away, all without Ferris's permission. Of course it is quite possible that Finch was oblivious of the fact that the tree wasn't on common land. Robert Coe testified that he had laid out a road two rods wide at that point, and since the tree stood two rods beyond, it was definitely on Ferris's land. Finch would, therefore, have to give Ferris a hundred "clabbords" and pay the court expenses. Poor Finch really must have been straining economically that year.[34]

At the end of 1648 Stamford was racked once again by a real tragedy similar to the one that occurred four years earlier to the Phelps family. One of the staunchest citizens was John

Whitmore. By the time he, in his early fifties, had moved to Stamford with the first settlers, he had had five children by his first wife and then upon her death had married John Jessup's widow in Wethersfield. Presumably his household consisted of a mixture of young Whitmores and young Jessups. (This is probably why John Jessup was considered separately from the other first settlers; he was still very young but of age.) During Whitmore's seven years in Stamford, where he was known as "a peaceable inoffensive man not apt to quarrel or p(ro)vocke,"[35] he served steadily in a public capacity. He also was a well-established farmer.

One autumn morning he left his home in the center of Stamford to check on his livestock in the common fields to the west. Hours passed, and he did not return. His family, becoming anxious, organized a search party, but all the searchers' efforts were in vain. There was absolutely no sign of John Whitmore. Ann Ackerley, who had been earlier at the Whitmores' house and had seen Ponus's son, Taphance, there, noted that he was acting suspiciously, and John's household later recalled his odd manner also.

Stamford was distraught. The Indians were believed to be trustworthy and of no more menace, but it must be they. Insistent appeals were made to both New Haven and Hartford. Hartford reacted with immediate sympathy and a determination to go to war and sent envoys to New Haven to determine the action to take.

However, instead of war, Uncas, the great Indian chief and friend of the white man, was prevailed upon to deal directly with the Indians. His authority had effect. Thereafter, Taphance led the way into the woods to the remains of John Whitmore (this after a full three-month interim). He claimed that another Indian named Toquattoes had done the ghastly deed and departed from the area. The Stamford men, especially Edward Jessup, Richard Ambler, and John Mead, who had been at Law's house two days after the murder when the Indians had come to report, felt very strongly that Taphance and one of his men had really been involved directly. Also, the two Indians, when they led the white men to the woods, were truly scared, shaking and evasive.

There seems to have been no clear solution to the case and no definite punishment meted out although the New Haven court took over the case fourteen years later. They questioned Taphance, finally believing he was probably guilty in some respect, but seemingly not the actual murderer. Eventually they let him go. Concern about the whole affair clearly was fading with the passing of years.[36]

Since John Whitmore met death when he was in a most flourishing state as a householder and farmer, the inventory of his effects, which was taken in detail by Robert Husted and Jeffrey Ferris, serves as a beautiful example of what a man of Stamford owned in the middle 1600s, actually only seven years after the founding.

Because the items on the given inventory follow no logical order, they are arranged into categories in the following table.[37] After the house and land, livestock was a man's greatest asset. Farm equipment and kitchenware naturally make up the bulk of the list. One can imagine the typical lay-out of a home as something like what is shown on page 28, with additional sleeping space for children in the loft overhead. It is no wonder that when moving, people would have found the livestock the largest problem rather than the household furnishings.

The Inventory of John Whitmore's Estate
(arranged by categories)

	£	s	d
Real Estate			
House and land	60		
Furniture			
1 bed and bolsters	2	10	
1 bed and bolster		15	
1 bedstead		4	
1 chest		10	
1 rug		7	
2 chairs		1	-
2 small tables		5	-
a linen wheel		3	-
a woolen wheel			
Linens			
4 sheets	1	3	
1 pillow		6	

The Inventory of John Whitmore's Estate (continued)

	Ł	s	d
Kitchen Equipment			
1 kettle	1	12	
1 kettle		16	
1 pot & hooks		8	
1 iron kettle		9	
1 skillet		3	
(two items missing)		3	6
1 pair cob irons		9	-
1 fire pan & tongs		4	-
1 trammel		3	-
1 frying pan		2	-
a brewing "tube"		4	-
old tubs		1	-
1 pewter platter		1	-
2 spoons		-	-
a porringer & saucer		-	-
2 beallers		-	-
a form and cheese press		-	-
a churn, a butter		-	-
2 beer vessels & form		-	-
a trough & board		-	-
a pair of bellows		-	-
bowls and dishes		-	-
a pint pot			8
old iron		-	-
a grid iron		-	-
2 pewter platters		7	6
1 pewter platter		1	6
a trammel		3	-
Weapons			
a musket		18	-
a sword, scabbard & hangers	10	-	
Clothes			
1 suit of apparel		2	5
1 coat		2	5
(clothes he was wearing)			

The Inventory of John Whitmore's Estate (continued)

	Ŀ	s	d
Miscellaneous			
a lantern	-	3	-
a Bible		-	-
2 testaments		-	-
a book		4	-
3 pair of cards (for wool & linen)		3	-
Animals			
3 fat cattle	17	10	
2 cows	11		
2 heifers	11	10	
2 yearlings	6		
4 calves	6	8	
2 oxen	16		
3 swine	3		
1 sow	1	5	
13 young swine	5	4	
2 pigs		8	
1 heifer	3	5	
2 hogs	2	8	
1 old mare	6		
1 colt	4	10	
1 young mare	7	10	
1 hive of bees	-	-	-
Produce			
50 bushels (wheat?)	-	-	-
40 bushels peas		13	4
barley & oats	1		
17 loads of hay	6	16	-
hops		12	
(20) bushels Indian corn	2	10	
Farm Equipment			
a plow cutter		9	-
a harrow & 24 t_		-	-
a plow share		5	-
a plow		5	-
a cart, wheels & iron works	2	2	-
2 chains		16	
yokes, hooks & irons		7	6

The Inventory of John Whitmore's Estate (continued)

	£	s	d
Farm Equipment (continued)			
4 hogsheads		12	-
- of nails		8	-
a pair of shears			-
2 hammers		1	-
3 wedges		-	-
2 beetle rings		-	-
- saddle & stirrups			-
1 pair of scales		1	-
2 scythes		4	-
a trowel		-	-
perser & dowribe (?)		1	-
2 peas meaks (hooks)		-	-
2 horse locks	-	-	-
1 bag	-	-	-
1 scythe	-	-	-
hoop nibs & wedge	-	-	-
a saw	-	-	-
a hachet	3	-	
a hachet	4	6	
3 pails	-	-	-
2 ropes	-	-	-
a cart rope	-	-	-
a bolt, "coles" & ground cloth	3	-	
a half bushel		2	-
a winnowing cloth		-	-
1 quart pot		2	-
2 shackles 7 bolts		4	6
Total: approximately	£230		

- denotes missing numbers

What is surprising, once again, is that the house furniture is so remarkably scanty - only bedsteads, a couple of chairs, a chest, and two small tables.

It is with difficulty that we today can recognize what the actual living conditions were in the 1640s. Even the ordinary comforts that we take so much for granted were luxuries then. Having water close at hand, and also having hot water, required great effort so that clean kitchen equipment, clean clothing, and even clean bodies were major achievements. Sanitation was negli-

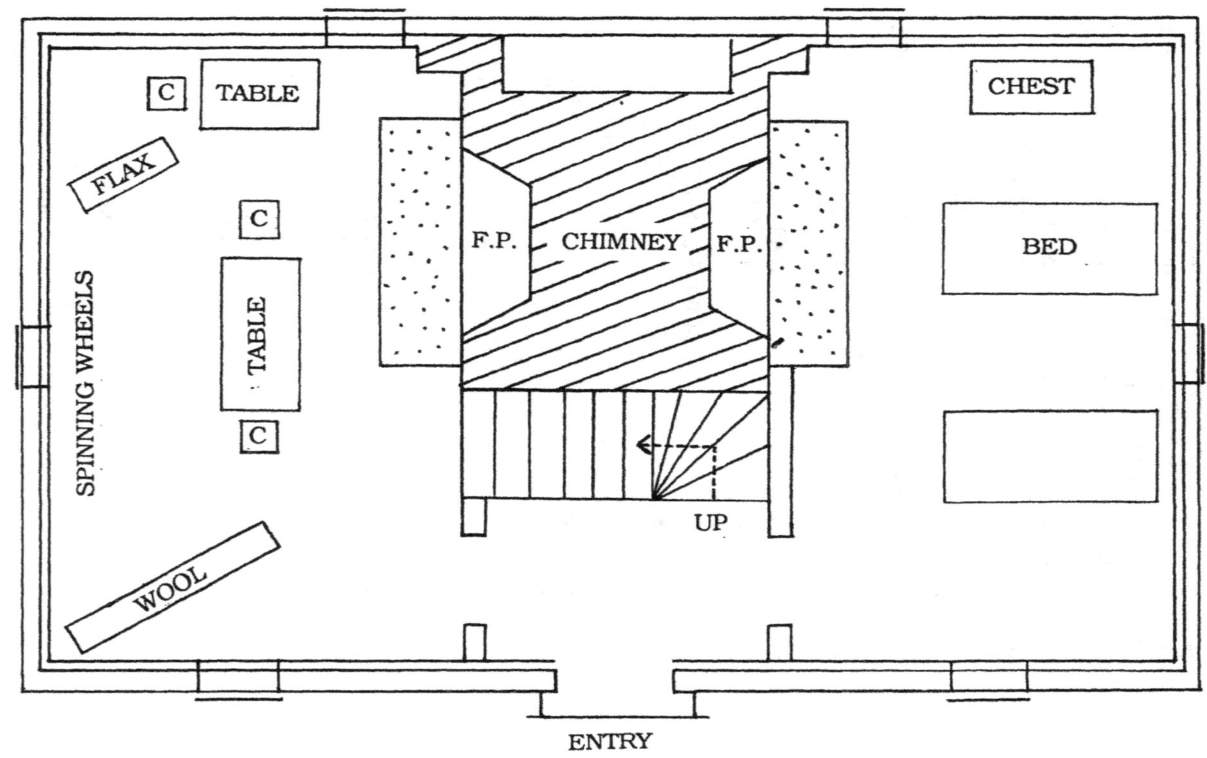
C
TABLE
CHEST
FLAX
C
F.P.
CHIMNEY
F.P.
BED
SPINNING WHEELS
TABLE
C
UP
WOOL
ENTRY

gible. In wintertime conditions with smoky homes, frigid weather, and squalling, fretful young ones must have been well-nigh unbearable. Sickness at times must have ravaged a family, with only homemade potions for medicine. Another real problem had to be faced constantly: vital possessions over a period of time would wear out or break and replacements often couldn't be found.

A few letters have come to light that allow glimpses of how these settlers struggled to keep going. The letters were written in 1648 and 1649 by Thomas Lyon and his first wife, who was the granddaughter of Governor Winthrop of Boston. Thomas seems to have been both an educated and a very pleasant man, for he writes warmly and naturally to his wife's grandfather; his wife also praises him in her letters. She was very unwell, beset by the harsh conditions of frontier life after the far easier conditions she had experienced both in England and in Boston. She died a few years later. In her letter of March 23, 1949 to her uncle, John Winthrop, Jr., she writes of her husband, "... he drinks water that I might drink beer (the standard drink as water was considered unacceptable) and eats Indian that I might eate white..." (or Indian corn flour as opposed to wheat). Thomas himself asked the governor if he could possibly send "a couple of sithes or a sickell or two against the harvest for here is none to be got." He also requests any second-hand clothing or linens, and later thanks Winthrop for the "gowne, petecote and savegards" (aprons) sent to his wife.[38]

Unfortunately, the New Haven records for the period 1649 to 1653 have been lost. Therefore, for that period whatever concerns that Stamford might have placed before the higher governmental authority will probably never be known. Stamford's own records, thanks to the diligence of Richard Law for the twenty-four years he acted as town clerk, are complete except for the crumbling of the edges of the earliest pages and a few torn spots. We are deeply dependent upon their accounts, meager as they often are. From 1650 on Richard Law must have felt somewhat freer in his daily life, because his accounts are fuller. The records of births, marriages, and deaths are carefully kept, and real estate dealings are more carefully documented. There a few other matters that are recorded just previous to 1650, such as two edicts that suggest a need for tightening the community. One of these forbade any family to accept outsiders into its home without permission of the town. This rule serves to remind us of the strong Puritan nature of the town at this time and the determination of those in power to control the people, particularly as to their religious strength. The other edict is an even stranger one: no one was to sell an English dog to the Indians.[39] What was the story behind this one?

Mark Menlow, a carpenter from Plymouth,[40] whose daughter had been so appealing to William Gifford, achieved true notoriety in 1649, for he ran up against court authority twice over. First, he was accused of handling the sale of a house deviously. He had bought it with lot and fencing from Elias Bayley, who often served as attorney. Then he sold it to one James Bears on the same terms that he had bought it. However, it was discovered that he had run off with the fence rails. Naturally, he wasn't able to get away with it. The court ruled that he had to return the rails and also pay the court expenses. Thomas Hyatt, Elias Bayley, and another (name missing) were to oversee the transaction.[41]

Evidently, Mark Menlow was a rather rough character, for he was soon slapped with other charges. He was accused of swearing "by God's blood, I think the devil's in it," "by God's wounds, I was bewitched," and over the selling of a chisel he had said, "before God he would get his pay." Then Henry Ackerley and Thomas Scofield brought up the fact that Menlow had previously been charged in some court with striking at an ox but hitting a man. Menlow was thereby deemed punishable by whipping and paying damages. This seems to have done it, for Mark and his family appear no more in Stamford's annals.[42]

The same year, 1649, trouble with the Indians arose again, only this time, interestingly enough, it was the Indians who were judged by the settlers to be in the right. Robert Husted and Jeffrey Ferris stated that James Steward had been appointed to care for the town oxen (no doubt this was in the ox pasture across Mill River). He was to receive twelve shillings the first week and a man to help him. Thereafter, he was to work alone for fourteen shillings. The hours must have been long and lonely, for James began to neglect his duty; he took time off to work on his own and also for other people. The inevitable happened: the oxen broke out. They ravaged the Indians' cornfields. The court determined, after the testimony of six other men, that Steward must pay the Indians twelve and a half bushels of corn and two and a half of peas, plus any other charges brought up. It is good to see that Stamford redressed the Indians' wrongs at this time.[43]

As the decade of the 1640s draws to a close in this account, it is well to review all that has happened to the group of settlers coming from England and then from the Boston area. Their subsequent move to a western frontier in southern New England involved moves totaling at least two hundred miles by land, involved gaining a right to the land from New Haven, and involved hacking out a suitable village center near a viable river and harbor. All this was achieved in a comparatively short time. The 29 to 71 families settled into their small, closely-set homes along paths set at a crossroads where the meetinghouse stood on its protective knoll. Leaders emerged as in any community. These were at first Mr. Denton (the minister), Captain Underhill (the military leader), Matthew Mitchell, Thurston Raynor, Richard Law, Andrew Ward, and Robert Coe. Both the church and the town government went into action, and a Puritan community, seemingly at peace with itself and with the neighboring Indians, became established. However, all was not at ease. A third of the settlers and most of the original leaders moved on for one reason or another. Those that remained found a new minister, John Bishop, and accepted a new group of leaders, namely, Richard Law (certainly the foremost one), Francis Bell, John Holly, and George Slason, all four of whom remained in positions of power for many years to come.

Chapter Two: 1650-1659

1650, the mid-century date, is a vital one for the study of the development of Stamford. It was then that the government, or at any rate Richard Law, decided that each man's land holdings should be recorded. Beginning with Thomas Morehouse, whose pieces of land were actually recorded in November of 1649, twenty-seven landowners were covered.[1] (John Bishop, whose lands are listed in a bill of sale in 1650, has been included in this number.) This ambitious project, however, was not completed, for one is able to determine that at least fifteen home-lot owners were not included. One surprising omission is Francis Bell. Perhaps he was the one primarily responsible for getting each man's listing; the one in charge is often neglectful about his own inclusion! Four other prominent men whose lands are not listed were Robert Bates, Jeremiah Jagger, Jeffrey Ferris, and Richard Ambler, who certainly had both houses and lands.

Because every piece of land recorded is carefully described by stating the owners of land to its sides, one can determine the names of those who owned land in Stamford. Each man had a number of pieces of land so that the total list is extensive. Take, for example, Thomas Morehouse's holdings:

2 home lots (with 2 houses) and 1 rood (1/4 acre) of meadow

Rocky Neck: 3 acres of upland
14 acres of upland
6 acres of meadow
7 acres of waste land
3 acres of waste land

Eastfield: 3 acres of upland
2 acres of upland
2 acres of upland

Northfield: 3 1/2 acres of upland
13 1/2 acres of upland
5 acres of upland
2 1/2 acres of upland

Southfield: 3 acres of meadow

It might be worth explaining at this juncture why the fields were broken up into such small portions. Mainly it was a leftover from the English medieval system. Each man was expected to get his fair share, and so the common fields were marked out as justly as possible. A man usually got his apportionment by means of a public drawing. Of course, as time went by, the desire to have large continuous tracts led to much buying and selling of these strips.

To return to the subject--if one studies all the bounds of the tracts, one comes up with a fairly accurate knowledge of all the actual owners of land. There are fifty-four men in all.[+] However, some of these people did not live in the village of Stamford. According to Spencer P. Mead in *History of the Town of Greenwich*, several of the Stamford men (such as Robert Husted, Richard Crab, and John Coe) had moved west to settle in Greenwich. Also, Robert Usher owned one plot of land but was not an inhabitant of Stamford until later. The one mystery person is John Rockwell, who settled in Stamford late in 1641. He never appears as an owner of any bounded land although in this same year of 1650 he is mentioned as a witness. Then later in 1669 his lands are described when he sells them; he seems to have had only a house and lot of three acres, and ten acres in Southfield at that time.

Now comes the exciting part! Because each home lot is given with its bounds, one is able to piece the lots together and make a map of where the inhabitants' homes were in early Stamford--the first map! It is like working out a jigsaw puzzle. Suddenly house lots that have not been recorded come to light because of the ones that have been recorded on either side. Sometimes the earlier owners of certain lots could only be determined in the light of later land deeds or by later wills. What does finally emerge is a picture of a vital nucleus of a village settled along the lines of the four streets and about the meetinghouse on its center little hill. This hill, bounded by two swamps, once was surrounded by a palisade and served as the fort. Probably Captain John Underhill's house was either within the compound or very close by. By 1650 the need for a central stronghold for the people of Stamford was slackening, especially as this same year Governor Stuyvesant of New Netherlands signed the Treaty of Hartford with the New England Confederation by which he gave up all Dutch claim to the Connecticut Valley and set the Dutch border at the west side of

----

+ See list in Appendix.

Greenwich Bay.[2] The meetinghouse itself, though, remained ever important for religious services and as a community center.

To the west of the meetinghouse plot was the home of the religious leader, first Richard Denton and then John Bishop. Grouped along the main street on both sides were the homes of the most important men. Matthew Mitchell's house was next to the minister's with Richard Law's opposite. Was Thurston Raynor's beyond Mitchell's? It seems probable. Across South Street on the corner was Francis Bell's home. To the west along the main street was another little hill, again set off by swamps. This hill became the public burying ground. Beyond it was the well-traveled road to the spot where Swayne had set up the first grist mill and where now Jeffrey Ferris had his mill complex complete with dam, head and tail races, the mill itself with its heavy grinding stones, and enough land along the sides of the river for both repairs and business expansion.

The original road south to the harbor was a continuation of West Street; before long, another road on the other side of the river led also to where the boats docked. Unfortunately, the records are silent about all the activity that must have gone on there. The other important road on the west side was that following the old Indian path that led to Greenwich. The bridge used to cross the river was named (and still is often called) Theale's Bridge because Nicholas Theale lived beside it on the north side of North Street.

Two important features of early Stamford can never be reconstructed accurately today on a map. The roads, as they developed, followed the easiest courses, avoiding miry bogs, rocks, etc., and they were very narrow by modern standards--two rods wide at first, later four rods. One can now only portray the general direction they followed. Secondly, the house lots cannot be drawn accurately. When they were given out, they were almost invariably stated to be one-and-a-half-acre tracts, but this proves to be a very loose designation indeed. When Bell and Mitchell were instructed to lay out the house lots, they were advised to take into consideration the lay of the land and to adjust the dimensions fairly in any way that they saw fit. Certainly they did not measure out the lots exactly in that busy year of 1641, and so the tracts really varied considerably, giving rise in the later land deeds to the prevalent term "more or less" as to actual acreage.

Consequently, this map of the house lots based on the records of 1650 is not accurate geographically speaking, but it does show where most of the inhabitants actually lived. Some pieces of land, such as those on the south side of the west end of North Street, don't show up in the records but may well have had houses on them. Sometimes men owned two or more lots, and sometimes a son by the same name, such as John Finch, may have gained a house lot; he then has a "II" after his name when that has been determined.

Naturally, there were constant shifts in the population and consequently in the ownership of the house lots. Although, as previously stated, fifty-four men owned land in Stamford, less than half that number, or about twenty-four settled in permanently. They established families who made up the backbone of Stamford's population development. These men were:

Richard Ambler	Edmond Lockwood
Robert Bates	William Newman
Francis Bell	Daniel Scofield
John Bishop	(and soon his brother
Clement Buxton	Richard)
Samuel Dean	Obadiah Seely
Jeffrey Ferris	George Slason
John Finch	Henry Smith
John Holly	Thomas Stevens
Jeremiah Jagger	John Waterbury
Nicholas Knap	Jonas Weed
Richard Law	

Plus three "men without land":
Francis Holmes, Simon Hoyt, and Robert Penoyer

During the 1650s five other men also settled in Stamford. These were: Stephen Clason, Joseph Garnsey, John Green, John Pettit, and Richard Webb.

Stamford in the early 1650s experienced severe friction, a tugging and pulling experienced by most of the towns in America as they struggled to move from tightly ruled governance by the few to the democratic forms of town government known today. Two systems of government--that of the powerful Puritan rule by respected town leaders and that of open town meeting in which most men could take part and influence decisions--vied with each other. Stamford's situation was exacerbated by the necessary allegiance to New Haven, which was not particularly zealous in meeting Stamford's needs. Slight grumblings could be heard before the 1650s, but when England was at war with Holland from 1652 to 1654 over naval rights in Europe, outspoken revolt was expressed in Stamford's town meetings. Once again, Stamford found herself in the vulnerable position of being the plantation closest to the Dutch in Manhattan and the western half of Long Island. Rumors were rife that the Dutch under Peter Stuyvesant were actively conniving with the Indians; as a consequence, the men of Stamford were forced to leave their daily all-demanding chores to set up constant watch and to practice the arts of war. Was it true, as some visiting Indians claimed, that the Dutch were planning a massive attack all along the coast, abetted by their ever-eager Captain Underhill? (It later turned out that he was actually concerned at this time with wiping out the Indians.) Stamford was made fully aware of the dangers when on April 29, 1653 a large boat docked at the waterside.[3] It was filled with women and children from Middelburg (Newtown), Long Island, where Edward Jessup, Robert Coe, and Richard Gildersleve, all formerly of Stamford, had become leaders.[4] They had judged it essential to prepare for action since they were living under Dutch jurisdiction and therefore could well be expeditiously massacred by the Dutch. One can't help wondering how this sudden influx of people was welcomed in Stamford. Were they absorbed into the already cramped households of the village or were they all settled into the fort and meetinghouse complex?

When New Haven was presented with Stamford's very real concerns, little help was forthcoming although the court did decide "out of tenderness" for Stamford "in these troublesome times" to abate Stamford's tax rate but not to offer soldiers or to pay Stamford's men.[5] Both New Haven and the New England Confederacy, based in Massachusetts, were in touch with each other over the possibilities for war, but they moved cautiously, preferring to deal with Stuyvesant directly by letter and citing bad weather during the winter as an excuse in delaying military action.[6] Stuyvesant disclaimed all intent of attacking the English settlers though it seems clear that he had actually formulated such plans, in the process of which he had totally alienated the valiant Captain Underhill.[7]

All during this time, Law, Bell, and Bishop, the very loyal leaders of faith and order in Stamford, found increasing difficulty in handling the town meetings. Righteous indignation spilled over. Why should Stamford alone have to bear the brunt of providing for the constant watch, both in time and money? Shouldn't New Haven provide some soldiers, some payment for the various expenses involved? Why should Stamford citizens knuckle under to New Haven and pay whatever yearly tax New Haven decreed? Was New Haven the ruler or was the government of England? Why couldn't men be accepted as freemen and vote in town matters without being members of the church? The church, they claimed, was a separate institution, as even the Connecticut Colony at Hartford recognized.

Three men became particularly vocal: John Chapman, a well-recognized man who was both a freeman and had previously been a deputy to New Haven; Robert Bassett, an impulsive person whose chief renown was as the drummer first in New Haven and then in Stamford; and Jeremiah Jagger, an enterprising merchant and ship owner. Words flew both against New Haven and against local authorities. What were Stamford men? They were no better than slaves or Indians, beasts of burden, under New Haven's yoke! Jeremiah even told off Francis Bell, shouting that he was a silly fellow to be set in authority! Others rose, egged on by the strong arguments against New Haven. William Newman and his elderly father, George Stuckey, Nicolas Theale, Richard Webb, and John Finch were soon to be mentioned in the New Haven records (8).

Bell and Law found the situation beyond their control and appealed to the magistrates of New Haven to come to Stamford. John Chapman, however, stated firmly that he wouldn't consider meeting with them; he wanted instead to go before the full court in New Haven so that the whole case could be aired. Nevertheless, the magistrates did hear the many grievances in Stamford and then sought to quiet the people by reading a recent letter from Parliament that supported the New Haven government as its local representative. Also, by reminding the men of Stamford of their oaths of allegiance to New Haven, the magistrates reinforced their authority.[9] At least Stamford's settlers' demands for soldiers and help with strengthening the meetinghouse defenses, their dissatisfaction with their tax rates, and their wish for free voting for their civil officers were now on record in New Haven.

Shortly thereafter, matters reached a dangerous state. Both Bassett and Chapman were traveling to the various coastal settlements plotting with others to take matters into their own hands. One day Bassett was accompanying Thomas Baxter, a firebrand who was developing plans to raise arms against the Dutch. They were apprehended by the authorities in Fairfield and because Bassett resisted, he was arrested along with Baxter. It was also discovered that he had some highly seditious material in his house, but somehow, when a search was made, the articles were not to be found. It was later said that they had been secretly moved to the house of Richard Webb.[10]

New Haven was disturbed by this attempt by individuals to flaunt her authority. Both Bassett and Chapman along with Jagger and the two Newmans were called to appear at the March, 1654, court session. The Baxter case was handled separately.

Once the men appeared before the full authority of the court at New Haven, they lost their spirit. As often happened in the early days in America, the time-honored bowing to those in power won out. The five men (Newman's father *in absentia*) admitted humbly that they were in the wrong and were very sorry. One wonders whether at heart they really were so abjectly sorry, but at least they were to cause no more trouble.

Bassett for his offensive connivance was put in prison after he was captured, but because the jail proved to be too cold, he was remanded to the marshal's house. The whole experience must have chastened him considerably. The New Haven Court was disposed to be lenient, rather surprising considering the fomenting nature of his actions. Probably, though, there was some sympathy with his desire to fight the Dutch. Bassett was given a fine of twenty pounds and a bond of a hundred; Jeremiah Jagger was given the same, though his fine was later abated. The Newmans were not fined but had a bond of twenty pounds imposed. John Chapman was given a fine of ten pounds and a bond of fifty.[11]

It is surprising that Bassett and Jagger received the same sentences, but how can we judge? It is feasible that, because Jagger had been very disruptive in town meetings and because Bassett had been sent to prison for awhile, their cases balanced out.

There were two major results of this whole unsettling situation. One was that the New Haven jurisdiction decided it must tighten its authority by requiring each plantation to administer the Oath of Fidelity to all men over the age of sixteen and to send in the lists. The other result was that, in spite of the outcome of the case itself, the whole episode served to lead men into thoughts of discontent and even rebellion against the establishment.

A year or two later Richard Law found himself in an increasingly bitter conflict with John Mead. Law recognized that the young man had been deeply infected by the views of Robert Bassett against all authority. The conflict began when Mead, seeking redress for some damage to his corn,[+] sought out Constable Law to support him. Law, realizing that the damage was slight and that a very poor man was responsible, advocated leniency as there was nothing the poor man could give but the clothes off his back.[12] Mead went off in a huff (although Law had offered him some money in payment) and continued to find fault with Law whenever possible, especially in town meeting. He also began talking against the authority of the church, saying that when Thomas Hunt joined the church in the near future, he still would be quite at liberty to lie or steal or drink as he wished! Both Richard Law and his son

----

+ "Corn" means grain

Jonathan heard some of his remarks. Law, approaching Mead's father in church and no doubt shaking his head, stated that there was too much forwardness in John and that Mead should counsel his sons more diligently.

The situation grew worse when John Mead began accusing Law of forging a document and saying that he was not fair in his dealings. In fact, Mead became so worked up that he went to the Reverend John Bishop with quite monstrous complaints about Law. Bishop listened patiently and said in effect, "Then do you mean that Law should hold no public office?" Yes, that was what Mead believed.[13] Evidently this young man was becoming unbearable; his rash words were being carried abroad and affecting Law's worthy reputation not only in Stamford but also in the neighboring plantations.

In May, 1656, John Mead rashly brought his case against Law to the court session in New Haven but failed to make any headway, though he did rouse Law to a display of temper. However, Law's careful explanations of every point Mead brought up, supported by such strong men as George Slason, John Waterbury (who also had an altercation with Mead), John Holly, and John Bishop, were convincing.

The Court of New Haven grew weary of the case that day and said that Mead was wasting its time with trivial arguments. He was put in prison but was released after he had written a letter full of repentance and after Bishop, Law, and Waterbury had requested his release.[14] The court declared that his was the worst case they'd had as he was both against the church and against Stamford's sole public officer. He didn't get off easily, for he had to show public repentance in Stamford, pay Law ten pounds for his trouble and expense, and also pay a fine of ten pounds to the Stamford government. In addition, he had to give the marshal twenty shillings for his services and give a bond of fifty pounds, together with his brother, for good behavior.[15]

A year or two later in 1657 this fractious young man married Hannah Potter of Stamford and thereafter seems to have become an acceptable citizen. He and Hannah produced eleven or more children. He was clearly a restless man, as both he and his brother Joseph moved away, first to Long Island and then to Greenwich where he remained to become in time a venerable, honored citizen. The Mead families of Greenwich prospered through the years like the Weeds, Bells, and Scofields of Stamford.

Greenwich during the 1650s was posing problems of its own. As we have seen, the residents there were divided in their loyalties. Some had depended on the Dutch; others, such as Richard Crab and Robert Husted, had considered themselves part of the Stamford community. There was no defining boundary between Stamford and Greenwich so that in the records there sometimes appears a phrase defining a man's home as near or in one or the other. One man's home so referred to was Abraham Frost's, which was despoiled by the Indians and his family kidnapped.[16]

Greenwich was not a well-knit community. In the eyes of the Stamford people, those settlers were an undisciplined lot. No doubt some men did move there from Stamford seeking a measure of freedom from public scrutiny. It was claimed that runaways were sheltered in Greenwich, drunkenness and illegal marriages were reported, and the righteous men of Stamford complained that the men of Greenwich pastured their animals as they pleased on the commons of Stamford.[17]

The deputies, Law and Bell, presented their grievances to the New Haven court, whose members agreed that Greenwich must be brought to heel. A letter was prepared, which Bell and Law delivered; it demanded a list of the male citizens. After ignoring the letter for as long as possible, the Greenwich men bowed to the inevitable, sent in their list in October 1656, and thereafter grudgingly accepted the fact that they were a part of Stamford and under New Haven's jurisdiction. The list of men living in Greenwich was a short one. Only twelve men appear on it:[18]

Angel Husted (the second son of Robert, who died in 1652 or in 1653)
Peter and Joseph Ferris (the young sons of Jeffrey, who was still alive and had a house in Stamford)
Richard Crab (the leader in that little community)
Henry Ackerley (who had sold his home in the center of Stamford in 1653)
Jonathan Reynolds (the son of John, who was still alive)
Laurence Turner
John Austin
Thomas Steadwell
Hanc Peterson
Henry Nicolson
Jan, a Dutchman, "commonly called Varlier"

Ostensibly then, Richard Law, the constable, and Francis Bell, newly made lieutenant and leader in all military affairs, would hold down the unruly members of their neighboring town while John Bishop would labor to regulate their religious lives.

In studying both Stamford's town meeting books and the New Haven records for the decade of the 1650s, one can glean bits of information about some individuals and about Stamford's concerns by looking carefully at what is given, sparse though the accounts are. For example, John and Joseph Mead had a sister, Martha, who was the cause of a rather spectacular case in court.

Martha seems to have been an epileptic. In 1653 she married John Richardson, about whom there is practically nothing in the records. He knew that she was pregnant before their marriage, and when the time came for her to give birth, he took her away to Roxbury, Massachusetts, to avoid scandal. The baby died a month thereafter. Who was the sneaky one who found out and leaked the news in Stamford? This wrongdoing was considered serious enough for New Haven to handle. Joseph Mead explained about her fits, and Martha herself said that when she was at her master's house, she happened to have a fit and came to find only Joseph Garnsey in the room. There was also a John Ross in the house. Martha claimed that she was taken advantage of while unconscious and therefore did not know the father. Several goodwives--Knap, Stuckey, Buxton, Webb, and Emory--testified as to her fits. They also admitted that she had lied about ever having had the baby.

The court didn't buy Martha's story. They considered it nonsense. The men concurred that a sexual act involved some reaction, particularly a reaction of pleasure. Punishment should have been a severe whipping, but since Martha was again pregnant, she was fined ten pounds, which, of course, her brother and her husband were responsible for. The death of the baby in Roxbury aroused suspicion, but Joseph said he would present proper documents to prove that the death was a natural one.[19]

Though this case is handled, or at least written up, in a very cut-and-dried fashion, one can draw questioning inferences from it. Martha was evidently a servant as she refers to being in her master's house. Were many girls so employed? Both her family and her husband wholeheartedly supported her. Was it to protect themselves, too, from scandal? Did they know the true facts, or did they honestly believe her? The full weight of Puritan law stands on this case, but once again, we see the court members ready to be lenient. We also get a glimpse of Martha's lady supporters, how they defended her, and also how they may have enjoyed their moment in an almost gossipy way.

The worst case in the records about Stamford concerned John Ferris, Jeffrey Ferris's son, who in 1657 was in his early twenties. John happened to be discovered by Henry Ackerley in an act of bestiality. The Biblical stories of Sodom and Gomorrah were strongly alive in the minds of the Puritans, and any person indulging in such acts must come face to face with his evildoing in order to be saved. Treatment could be extremely harsh; in fact, in the laws of the New Haven Plantation all acts of this nature were punishable by death. The court ruled, after hearing all the lurid details, that John was to be whipped in New Haven, and then when he was fit again from that, he was to be whipped publicly in Stamford. He was sentenced to pay twenty pounds for the expenses, to be kept in prison until surety was given, and, worst of all, to wear a halter about his neck at all times.[20] Poor Jeffrey Ferris must have been so humiliated by his son's behavior. After two years of this John begged the court to have the halter removed, and this was granted. He moved away from Stamford a few years later, married, and lived into his eighties. Such a traumatic experience must have weighed heavily on him always.

A third case, which also occurred in 1657, involved a number of men, and it dragged on for several years. One gains a little knowledge of the men's characters and of some of the aspects of the daily life of these people. The original case concerned a mare that belonged to Edward Jessup, who left two mares behind when he and his mother, Mrs. Whitmore, moved to Middelburg, Long Island. He had made Joseph Mead, who was known to all for his care and knowledge of horses, responsible for them. Since all the horses seem to have been turned out into the woods in those days, they could only be identified definitively by the owners' special brand marks on them.

According to the plaintiff for Jessup, Richard Crab had taken one of the mares, and, offering part ownership to Abraham Frost, had arranged for the tail to be docked (his mark). When Crab had originally taken the mare, she had a colt that was born with a star on its forehead, according to young Daniel Simkins. The court decided that the mare was undoubtedly Jessup's, required Crab to pay forty shillings plus any other expenses, and to hold the mare for a year in case Jessup did want it back, at which time he would pay Crab for its care.[21]

A year later, George Slason found a horse methodically demolishing an acre of his peas. He was quite unable to drive it off. Three men came to his rescue and managed to secure it in his barn. Clearly this half-grown colt was a stray as it had no markings on it. Joseph Mead, when called in, thought it might be Crab's, but when he and Crab went to Slason's barn, Crab said it wasn't one of his. Slason, therefore, "cried the horse" twice in town meetings and then again on training day, at which time Robert Usher claimed it for Jessup but offered no proof. The court told Slason to mark the horse S/S, which he did and after some time returned it to the woods.[22] To confuse matters a bit more, one time when Joseph Mead was in the woods with John Bates,

Robert's son, tending to some horses, they found another young horse that was Crab's and so marked. Joseph asked John if he could tell any difference between this one and the one in Slason's barn. John said no, he couldn't.

In October of 1659 Usher brought the case to court after trying to claim the horse through Francis Bell in Stamford. Once again the court heard all sides and then agreed that the horse could go to Usher on behalf of Jessup provided he paid forty shillings and charges and waited a year and a half for any further action.[23]

George Slason, who seems to have been a very level-headed man, told the court that it wasn't right for stray horses to be able to get into men's fields. Mead said people's fences should be stronger. However, it was determined that absentee owners (David Mitchell, Edward Jessup, and Joseph Mead himself) should take their horses and also should pay the tax rates for their horses for as long as they did remain in Stamford.[24]

And so ended the complicated horse problems in which a good number of men were involved and a considerable amount of time spent. In the end new rules were established, and the horse-ownership quandaries were resolved.

Slowly from the meager writings of the period one recognizes the small body of the leading citizens of the community, and these leaders continued to hold their positions. John Bishop regulated the religious and moral concerns, well supported by Richard Law, Francis Bell, George Slason, and John Waterbury. The town government was carried on for a good twenty years by Richard Law, Francis Bell, John Holly, and George Slason. They must have been honored not only as men of intelligence and some degree of learning but also as just and understanding men.

In 1655 Richard Law took the shoemaker, William Newman, now no longer in opposition to the government, with him to make a more binding agreement with the peaceful Indians to the north of the village. (Newman had also accompanied Law and Slason earlier when they were studying the lands of Piamikin to the east and considering their merits before making the treaty of 1645.) Ponus, the sagamore of Toquams, and his oldest son Onax represented the Indians. Today at the corner of Ponus Street and Davenport Ridge Road, near the line of the Merritt Parkway, stands an erect stone, marking where Ponus's home once was.+

+ This is now in New Canaan.

A treaty was drawn up. In return for four coats, the Indians confirmed that Stamford should be defined as the plot of land approximately sixteen miles north from the seaside and eight miles east-west, excepting for a two-mile strip at the north to be used solely for grazing.[25] Unfortunately, the bounds were marked by means of initials on white oak trees - not very permanent markers. No doubt, Law was seeking thereby to strengthen the case against Greenwich, and he, also, being a sound businessman, wished the bounds of Stamford to be absolutely clear in the eyes of New Haven.

It is interesting to note that William Newman gained some renown of his own on a quite different matter. Upon leaving England, he had carried along a special shoe-measuring instrument, which proved to be the only one in the New Haven Plantation. In 1659 when controversy arose as to how to standardize shoe sizes, the New Haven Court asked him to present his form so that a uniform standard in the colony could be set.[26]

In the late 1650s Stamford became involved in a situation that was engaging the attention of a number of settlements in the coastal areas. The New World was facing a quiet intrusion by people of an unacceptable new religious sect. Only ten years after the tenets of the Society of Friends were presented by George Fox in England, Quakers, as they were derisively called, began appearing in America. In the summer of 1657 a boatload of Quakers arrived on Long Island and quickly left for the New England colonies. Richard Gildersleve, once of Stamford and now sheriff in Hempstead, was particularly distressed by the appearance of "heresy" in the Island.[27] Times were changing, however, and so were some attitudes. In Flushing, Long Island, for example, the people joined forces to issue their Flushing Remonstrance, which stated that they saw no reason for prohibiting Quakers from settling; they thus took issue with Stuyvesant's dicta on the matter. A certain number of those who found the power of both the church and the strong-armed rule of the few galling admired the loose freedom of the Quaker beliefs.

It is not surprising, therefore, to find that Richard Crab in Greenwich opened his heart and mind and even his house to the Quakers. In spite of the recent New Haven law forbidding the presence of Quakers, he was discovered to be harboring a visiting Quaker, Thomas Marshall. He also was collecting Quaker tracts.

Consequently, the marshal, Daniel Scofield, fortified by three of Stamford's leaders, Bell, Slason, and Officer Waterbury, marched over to Greenwich to arrest Thomas Marshall. Quite naturally, they met with resistance at Crab's house. It turned out to be more of a situation than they could have foreseen. Goodwife

Crab wasn't having anyone march into her house to arrest a guest! She rushed in and barred the inside door to the room where Marshall was; her husband had to take a hand to get it opened. Crab was primarily concerned with seeing if the warrant were really in order. His wife meantime rained emotional invectives, raising her hands and eyes heavenward as she accused the Stamford men of taking people's lands (a reference to the forced joining of Greenwich to Stamford) and stealing into people's homes. The more the men, including the peace-loving George Slason, tried to deal with her, the worse she became. Why should she go to the Stamford meetings? The priest was the "priest of Baal" and "preached for hire." She called Francis Bell everything she could dream up: he was a traitor, a liar, a villain, a rogue, and a rascal, and his posterity would suffer (fortunately it didn't). Bell answered that he hoped she wasn't a witch--a really dire threat in those days when women could be put to death as witches. Slason tried to persuade her to return to the Stamford church, but he hardly was choosing a wise moment in which to persuade her. She replied that she never would. Bell said that her religion was of thee's and thou's, at which point Richard Crab interposed, saying that her religion was as good as Bell's.[28]

All in all, the altercation went on for almost an hour until Goodwife Crab called for a drink, and the group dispersed, evidently fearing that she would merely be fortified for more violence. Interestingly, two men appear to have been watching from the sidelines. These were William Oliver, the son-in-law of Henry Ackerley, and Jonathan Reynolds, John's son; they later gave testimony in court. Strangely, nothing further is said of Thomas Marshall, the main cause of all the trouble. It is presumed that he was sent speedily out of the plantation or else he himself decided to leave while he could.

On May 31, 1658 Richard Crab appeared in court, but his wife refused to. This was the day on which John Waterbury died, but the others were there to present plenty of evidence against the Crabs. The court had little sympathy with the sturdy freethinker and noted, particularly, his complete absence of effort to curb his wife. He tried explaining how she had been a very upstanding religious lady in England, but this only made her more culpable as her fall from grace was all the worse. Crab himself was cited as a troublemaker and for his failure to go to meetings. He stated that he planned to leave Greenwich soon to which the response was that they "feared a remove was far easier for him than a reformation"![29] The upshot was that he was fined thirty pounds and had a hundred-pound bond placed on him. He also had to make public acknowledgment in Stamford of his wrong treatment of Francis

Bell in particular. Two years later Crab was again to be arrested and brought to court, but by that time he had "removed" and John Mead had bought up all his lands.

The worst feature of all the Crab disturbance was the effect it had on the worthy John Bishop, who was finding his calling almost unbearable. He was very saddened by the falling-off of the young people from the time-honored respect for the Puritan religion and found his mission increasingly burdened. Richard Crab had promoted the flouting of authority among the young people, who had never known the strictures of life in England and were growing up in an increasingly free atmosphere. Richard Crab had even taken a maiden into his home, and then against the wishes of her parents had led her away from their orthodox religious views.[30] Bishop felt that he had lost his former persuasive powers and was even so discouraged that he said he was considering leaving Stamford altogether. Men of authority were later sent to Stamford to give him support in meeting the vexing problems.[31]

In the late 1650s a time of sadness, sickness, and bereavement beset the citizens of Stamford. Some epidemic struck. Was it malaria? Today one associates malaria with the warm regions of the world and considers it of little importance, thanks to methods of control and modern medicine. It is a disease which strikes its victims with dreadful shaking chills and high fever followed by dry relentless heat and finally by profuse sweating. The attack recurs, and the victim's whole system is greatly debilitated.

In the New Haven accounts there is a reference to the dreadful illness which attacked the colony in 1658-1659. Mr. Davenport is quoted as writing of the effects of the disease as "gripings, fluxes, agues, fevers, giddiness, much sleepiness and burning."[32] It is a surprise to learn that malaria did exist in New England; however, areas in Europe and in England suffered from it, too. The anopheles mosquito frequented the salt marshes along the seacoast and any other swampy areas.

The Stamford records are silent about any disease but instead are devoted to recording the inventories for this period. It is only when noting the number of people who died in 1657 and 1658, primarily during the summer months, that one recognizes an unusual situation.[33] Only two men are recorded as dying in 1655: Robert Rugg (about whom little is known) and the once outspoken John Chapman. In 1656 eight people died, five of them in September, according to the records. Then in 1657, seventeen people died, and in 1658, fifteen more died. It is quite true that some of these deaths may well have resulted from other causes, such as childbirth among the women. Henry Ackerley was an elderly man in his seventies and was one of the few men during these two years to make out a will. Jeremiah Jagger's young daughter died in December of 1657, clearly not of malaria at that time of the year. Jeremy himself died at sea in 1658, but whether he contracted disease before he left Stamford cannot be known. When one notices the close groupings of the death dates, one does suspect an epidemic. Also eight of the twelve men were in their thirties and forties, really in their prime.

Deaths in 1657:

April 6 Clement Buxton	August 7 Jonathan Simkins
May 31 child of John Rockwell	August 21 _______ Buxton
June 18 wife of Gregory Taylor	August 21 Sarah Reynolds
June 24 John Austin	August 25 Obadiah Seeley
July 1 Simon Hoyt	Sept. 5 John Finch
July 21 Samuel Austin	Sept. 7 Debrow (Deborah?) Pettit
July 24 Gregory Taylor	Sept. 14 Mary Green
July 27 Mary, John Pettit's wife	Sept. 19 Philippa Mead, William's wife

Deaths in 1658:

May 25 Mary Crissy	June 19 Nicholas Theale
May 31 Jeffrey Ferris (son)	June 21 Eleanor Brown
May 31 John Waterbury	June 21 Peter Brown
June 13 Habakuk Seely	July 21 Ebenezer Brown
June 16 Eleanor Knap	August 14 Jeremiah Jagger
June 17 Henry Ackerley	August 16 Samuel Smith
June 17 Mary Eliot	October 10 Mary Smith
June 19 Thomas Stevens	

Malaria is not an inevitably fatal disease, but it is a devastating one. A community stricken by it would be sadly debilitated for a considerable period of time. Those people who were laid low but recovered would be subject to recurrent attacks and left with lingering weakness.

The inventories for the twelve men who died serve both collectively and individually to reveal many aspects of the lives of these early settlers. Collectively they give us an understanding of their economy, based as it was principally on farming. The relative values of land, livestock, and produce are presented. Also, a clear list of what was essential both to the home and to the farm can be deduced. The estates ranged in value from Jeremiah Jagger's £472 and John Waterbury's £383 to John Austin's and Gregory Taylors' £78 and £45, respectively.[34] Unfortunately, a number of the pages have been torn away so that in Peter Brown's and Clement Buxton's inventories the values cannot be assessed conclusively.

In each man's inventory a house and land were accounted for. Land for obvious reasons was not expensive, nor was a house. Obadiah Seely's list states that his house and four acres were worth twenty pounds, and five and a half acres of meadow, thirty pounds. John Waterbury's land and home were prized at eighty pounds. The average was thirty pounds.

Next in importance was a man's livestock. Every one of these men had cattle, and they were carefully judged as to value. Most cows were worth three pounds, but some were as high as five: steers ranged in value from two to five pounds; and heifers were two or three pounds and yearlings only a pound each. A single bull was listed (worth three pounds), and that was Jeremiah Jagger's. These twelve men had a total of one hundred and thirteen cattle.

Horses and oxen were not very plentiful. The best horse was worth ten pounds. Jagger had nine (three of them colts), Waterbury had six, Simon Hoyt four (two of which were colts), and Peter Brown and Nicolas Theale each had one. One would judge, therefore, that these men did not travel much by land anyway. Oxen for pulling the plows, hauling wood, and carrying out the heavy work of farming were of great worth, each mature ox being valued at seven pounds; John Waterbury had four, as did Henry Ackerley. Finch, Buxton, Hoyt, Stevens, and Theale had a pair apiece.

Pigs were common to every household and were a cheap provider of various forms of meat, lard, and even skin and hair. They were reasonably peaceful and demanded little care. In Stamford they roamed at large where in the woods they could live on mast, young shoots, etc. On the village thoroughfares they served as garbage collectors, eating almost anything left from the garden produce and the dinner table. They reproduced prolifically so that each man on his list had a viable number, ranging from four to Peter Brown's twenty-six. They were worth less than a pound apiece. One hesitates to imagine what a walk along Stamford's wandering roadways might have entailed!

At this time sheep were not widely owned; in fact among these twelve men only John Waterbury was raising them. He had six rams and eight ewes with lambs. Jeremiah Jagger had two ewes and a wether lamb (young ram).

The only other asset listed of similar nature was bees, which were easy to care for and produced both honey and wax. Henry Ackerley had three skips of bees; Clement Buxton and Nicolas Theale, two each.

If one may be allowed to judge from what one sees today of the early life in Plymouth, one can be pretty safe in stating that each household had its share of chickens--so common that they are ignored entirely on the inventories.

When one considers the major crops used in a community, wheat, corn, and peas were the essentials. In a listing of twelve men's assets only, the supplies of grain given are not really indicative of anything since so much would depend on the time of the year in which a man died. Wheat was valued at four and a half shillings a bushel, peas at three and a half, and Indian corn (often listed as "india corn" or even "indy corn" but never as "corn") at two and a half shillings. Other forms of produce listed are flax (for linen), hemp (for rope), and tobacco or "tobacca." Only four men were growing flax; Buxton alone had hemp; and Simon Hoyt and John Austin had considerable supplies of tobacco.

What is very interesting to learn is what equipment was needed in farming life. It certainly seems primitive in the light of today's massive machinery. These were the essentials:

plow and irons	yoke
cart and wheels	chain
hoe	rope
scythe	saw
sickle	axe and/or hatchet
shovel and spade	wedges
fork	beetle rings
peas hook	hammer

Other tools, etc. that these men owned were as follows. Those marked with a # symbol were found on only one man's list.

stillyards	tow combs
scales	tubs, hogsheads, casks,
seed box or lip	barrels
bolts and shackles	bags
wheelbarrow#	horse lock and fetters#
trowel#	bridle
pick	saddle
scissors#	

Several men, such as Henry Ackerley, John Austin, and Simon Hoyt, were carpenters, or furniture makers, or coopers. Simon Hoyt had a mill and both turnersware and coopersware, plus a marking iron. They owned such tools as:

chisels	compasses
augurs	cotters
adzes	wimbles
mallets	rabetting plow#
gimlets	nails
persers (piercers)	bits
gouges	pincers
planes	

Aside from farm equipment, a man's prize possessions were, of course, his gun and sword, which no man went without. The men of Stamford had muskets, carbines, fowling guns, and John Waterbury also had a pistol. John Austin had a rapier. Accessories were powder and powder horns, bullets, lead, and bullet molds.

The home furnishings were still very sparse in spite of the passing of ten years since the listing of John Whitmore's possessions. Bed and bedding, three or four sheets, blankets and pillow beres (or cases), a table, a few chairs and a form (or bench), a cupboard, some chests, a churn, and the necessary flax and spinning wheels made up the furniture for the most part. There were some different items: John Waterbury had a cheese press and a trundle bed. Clement Buxton owned a desk, a cradle, and a settle bed, and Gregory Taylor had a loom.

Cooking and eating articles in all households ranged from a few pieces of pewter (ranging in value from ten shillings to Waterbury's forty-four pounds) to the common woodenware and earthenware. There were some brass pots and kettles in addition to the usual iron ones. Frying pans and skillets were vital as were spoons, bowls, platters, trays, meat troughs, sieves, and a basket or two. Most homes had trammels to hang pots on, fire tongs, and a peel to pull the bread from the oven.

One finds very few pieces of apparel on the lists. Most men owned a cloth suit, a hat, a long coat, and a leather jacket. Other items mentioned were a pair of boots, a pair of shoes, one or two pairs of stockings, britches, a shirt or two, and some shirtbands. Of course, each man would normally have been buried in his good set of clothes, and Jeremiah Jagger would have taken clothes with him on his journey. Once again John Waterbury outshines all the rest as he had four suits, two of cloth and two of stuff. He also had a stuff troop coat, six shirts, and two pairs of drawers. Jeremiah Jagger owned two doublets and two waistcoats, plus a cloak, a pair of gloves, and some handkerchiefs.

As mentioned earlier, one does get brief insights into the lives and personalities of these men from their inventories. What one gleans from them along with what one sees of the men in the records can be pulled together into rather interesting little pictures.

John Waterbury, who was about thirty-eight when he died, was a man of varied interests. He had first owned a house lot of the usual one and a half acre size on the south side of North Street, but when Thomas Morehouse moved to Fairfield and left his two-houselot holding on South Street, John Waterbury moved into that spacious home, which had rich meadowland to the rear. He went into farming in a thorough way, with his sheep giving him an added dimension.

Trade with the Indians seems to have engaged him also, as he had twenty-five pounds of beaver skins and wampum equal to a pound in value.[+] His home furnishings were certainly more lavish than most, for he owned such things as a looking glass, a case of glassware, a dozen napkins and several tablecloths, a cheese press, ten pounds of candles, and some books. He also had supplies of various kinds of material: shagg (rough wool), serge, calico, broadcloth, bed ticking, and fustian (a cloth of wool and linen). In addition to keeping abreast of the farming, he had many domestic concerns with children ranging in age from about seventeen years to eight. During the 1650s he was increasingly involved in community affairs, culminating, as we have seen, in 1657 when he was a delegate to New Haven and handled the Crab case with Richard Law.

Jeremiah Jagger was a merchant of considerable means. He stocked many items for the farmers and six and a half pounds of powder for the men's guns. He carried household supplies, such as a barrel of ginger, sugar, forty pounds of tallow, two and a half pounds of beef. He also had on hand a handsome supply of material goods--holland, serge, linen, red kersey (a fine wool tweed), plain kersey, cloth, stuff, and say (a rough wool material). He also offered finished items like sheets, pillowcases, tablecloths, napkins, and a variety of small items. Just as Waterbury did, he had a supply of beaver skins and four pounds' worth of wampum.

+ Wampum varied in value: six white ones equalled one pence, and three black or blue ones equalled the same.

It is hard to separate his personal belongings from his marketable items. Did he have seventy-two pounds of pewter and ninety-seven pounds of brass for his own use only? Were the reed and slayer for weaving on hand for sale?

Jeremiah was fifty-two at the time of his death with a very young family of three boys, his daughter having died the year before when only three months old. He, too, was a man of enterprise, for he had fought with distinction against the Indians in the Pequot War.[35] As we have seen, this seafaring merchant spoke out against the restricting forces in Stamford and New Haven, but he was basically a good, well-respected citizen in Stamford, taking his part in negotiations when called upon.

Elizabeth, his wife, took steps immediately after his death. She arranged to have her son John apprenticed in New Haven.[36] He was about fifteen in 1659 and probably had already been helping his father in his business as a merchant where containers of all kinds for the various goods were essential. John was to be an apprentice to John Winston, a cooper in New Haven, for six years. Many boys in these early times did serve as apprentices in order to learn a trade if their fathers were unable to teach them. However, this case seemingly is the only one for Stamford to be formally documented in the town records. John was to be a loyal servant in every way to Winston; he was to avoid unlawful games, taverns or alehouses in return for which he was to be instructed in both "sette-worke" (piece work) and "keyne-worke." He also was to be given lodging, meat, drink, apparel, and washing. At the end of the six years John was to be sent out with suitable apparel.[37] Twice John Jagger appears thereafter in the New Haven town meeting records for acting-up in the ways of young men on their own. In 1663 he was brought before the meeting for playing at cards. When asked what he had done with the cards, he said that as they were old, he had thrown them "in the creek." He was let off with a warning.[38] The following year he was cited with other young men for quarreling in the meetinghouse while John Davenport, Sr. was preaching. Stricter supervision of that section of the meetinghouse was advocated.[39]

Both Henry Ackerley and John Austin were carpenters, judging by the number of woodworking tools in their inventories. They lived in Greenwich, Henry having lived a number of years previously in the center of Stamford. Henry and Ann had had just one child, Mary, who had married Vincent Simkins. The young Daniel Simkins, Henry's only grandchild, received a large portion of Henry's tools, his weapons, and his clothes. By the time Henry died in his late sixties or early seventies, Mary had lost both her

[illegible] mak my
[illegible] said [illegible] name [illegible]
[illegible] as afores[aid] to [illegible] & the
[illegible] [illegible] now [illegible]
[illegible] as I [illegible]
[illegible] my [illegible] adding [illegible]
[illegible] [illegible] and [illegible]
[illegible] or to [illegible] [illegible] Smiking
[illegible] monthly [illegible] to [illegible]
[illegible] comes to age [illegible]
[illegible] to [illegible] An Accordy or [illegible]
[illegible] his young man before [illegible]
[illegible] to the [illegible] An Accordy [illegible]
[illegible] payment my heire An Accordy or her assigns [illegible]
[illegible] or [illegible] both meat or [illegible]
Smikings [illegible] leave to the [illegible] of my heire An [illegible]
[illegible] comes to age
[illegible] Accordy doe give out of my Estate unto mary
[illegible] (now living with me) [illegible]
to be paid at [illegible] of age [illegible]
[illegible] enjoye [illegible] twenty pounds [illegible] my [illegible]
[illegible] as [illegible] or her assigns [illegible]
[illegible] Stayes with my heire An Accordy [illegible]
[illegible] or if my heire [illegible]
[illegible] will leave it to [illegible]
comes to age his legacy [illegible] to my heire [illegible]
assignes
Further more I give unto my [illegible]
[illegible] a sword [illegible] long [illegible] all my [illegible]
[illegible] after my Decease [illegible] all my [illegible]
This is my Last & [illegible] will [illegible] from my [illegible]
this 17 June 1658 in the presence of [illegible]

[illegible] mark [illegible]

The names of the witnesses & [illegible]
marks transcribed
Frances Homes mark FH
William Oliver mark W
Rich: Homes mark RH
Frances Browne

Testified upon oath by [illegible]
William Oliver [illegible]
[illegible] Frances [illegible]

first husband and a son Jonathan, and had remarried. Living with the Ackerleys was an adopted daughter, Mary Dickason, who was still in her teens.

John Austin was not so well off as Ackerley, his estate totaling only seventy-eight pounds. He had a wife Katherine (or "Catern"), a son Samuel, who died a month after his father, and probably two other sons and a daughter. No furniture except for bedding and three chests is listed; so presumably Catherine had brought some of her possessions to the household. It looks as though John supplied the community with tobacco as he had not only a number of hogsheads of tobacco but also a tobacco wheel with bowls and trays. He also had one odd item: an otter skin.

Peter Brown was well supplied generally and had plenty of beef, tallow, butter, and salt. He made provision in his will for his wife and his son Thomas to go on living together, Thomas being about twenty at this time. Since both Peter and his wife Elizabeth as well as one child, Ebenezer, all died in these two years, this must have been a sorry home. Thomas had a great deal upon his shoulders.

Clement Buxton, as one can see from the 1650 map, had a very small house lot on West Street. He had shoe-making gear and owned both leather and some clothes made of leather. He is the only man listed as having a desk and also a wheelbarrow. Naturally, he too depended on farming for his livelihood, and his flax was turned into linen thread on his two linen wheels. He also grew hops and hemp. Surprisingly, he owned four Bibles and some other books; unfortunately, the books are never listed by name in these early inventories. Clement, who was married to Unice, had a son Clement and two daughters. There may have been another child, who died the summer after the father.

John Finch, who was in his late sixties, had first lived on the north side of North Street. In 1653 he sold that house and bought Ackerley's house on East Street, undoubtedly with a thought for his older son, who had been married the year before. His two younger children, Isaac and Martha, were both married the year after his death, and young John continued to live in the house. Finch's inventory is a thoroughly typical one except for the extent of his debts.

Simon Hoyt, the great progenitor of the many Hoyts in southern Connecticut, had moved four times since arriving in America and had had two wives by whom he had twelve children. He was a man of about sixty-seven when he died, and his older children were well settled in places other than Stamford. His six younger sons and daughters were aged twenty to twelve or thirteen. Strangely, his inventory lists only a home lot and a mill. No house is mentioned--was this merely an oversight? It seems probable. Noticeable in his list are coopersware and turnersware, in addition to eighty pounds of "tobaca." This estate was evaluated at £225.

The inventories of Obadiah Seely and Thomas Stevens reveal estates of approximately the same value--a little over £100. Obadiah had a large number of carpentry tools, and Thomas had a douse box and the only pair of scissors listed. Otherwise their inventories are unremarkable. Obadiah, who had a double house-lot south of Waterbury's on South Street, had married Mary, the widow of John Miller. They presumably, therefore, had a household of young boys--Miller's three plus their own Obadiah, Cornelius, Jonas and Habakuk, who died less than a year after his father. Thomas Stevens also had a household of boys. There were five, plus one girl. Thomas made provision for them in his will, giving his wife control for as long as she remained single. Both the Seely and Stevens names continue through Stamford's history.

Gregory Taylor and his wife Achsa died a month apart. Two years earlier they had been in ill health. Taylor had testified in a court case that they had been on a boat between Fairfield and Stamford and his wife had been sick all night. He also that year asked to be relieved from service of watching and training as he was unwell.[40] Gregory's inventory includes all their possessions. Achsa had a green apron and a scarf and a pair of "bodies." There were also two red caps. Their house was worth only eighteen pounds, and the total estate was ninety pounds six shillings according to the town meeting records. However, in the New Haven records his value is listed as forty-eight pounds, fourteen shillings, and sixpence. Could he have had many debts that at first weren't listed? Interestingly, they owned a loom and also two linen wheels, plus many linen sheets. Did they make a business of linen products?

According to very early records concerning the Taylors, they did have two children, and the supposition is that they died young. However, it is possible that they were girls, whose marriages weren't recorded. Was John Waterbury's wife, Rose, their child? The Taylors' estate proceedings were handled by both the Waterburys--an unusual circumstance since women seldom played a part.[41] Also, the records mention that Waterbury had recently lost both father and mother.[42] There often was no distinction between one's own parents and one's in-laws. The estate was disputed by Henry Jackson. Was his wife the other child?

Nicolas Theale, who lived next to the river on North Street and so gave his name to the bridge there, was a true farmer, judging by his inventory. He owned four oxen, on a part with

Waterbury and Ackerley, and a full complement of cattle and wine; he had two hives of bees and grew hemp. He and his wife Elizabeth had only two children: Joseph, who became a leader in Stamford affairs, and Elizabeth, who was married the year after her father's death to William Ratcliffe of Greenwich.

To conclude this study of the twelve men who died in 1657 and 1658, a fascinating situation concerning the women who were widowed should be noted. It has often been recognized that women were at a premium in this new land. In the first place, many more young men migrated than did young women. Secondly, childbirth took its toll on women so that family men were most eager to find new wives to run the households and care for what children were in them. In the two years of 1657 and 1658 twelve women were suddenly deprived of their mates, but they were not left without support for very long. From today's standpoint, they were remarried all too quickly, but from both the man's and the woman's points of view, marriage was a necessity. Another factor that played a part in the remarriage of widows was economic. A widow normally received a dower of one third of her husband's estate; this often could prove a valuable asset to a man on the look-out for a wife of means. Of these twelve women all but three were remarried; of the three that did not remarry, one was Achsa Taylor, who died, and one was Ann Ackerley who was in her early seventies. She was given a home on West Street by Edmund Lockwood.

Katherine Austin married William Hubbard of Greenwich.

Unice Buxton had a quite traumatic time. After Clement died, she married Peter Brown as his second wife in 1658 only to have him die almost immediately thereafter. She then the following year married Nicolas Knap, who took on her three Buxton children as well.

Martha Finch, John's second wife, married John Green in 1658.

Susannah Hoyt, Simon's second wife, married Robert Bates as his third wife.

Elizabeth Jagger married Robert Usher as his second wife.

Mary Seely, who had previously been the widow of John Miller, evidently did not remarry.

Ann Stevens married Francis Holmes as his second wife, but she herself died in another year.

Elizabeth Theale married Thomas Uffit (or Ufford) in 1660.

Rose Waterbury married Joseph Garnsey in 1659. (Was he by any chance working in John Waterbury's homestead where Martha Mead, the girl who got pregnant, could have been also?)

[illegible] An [illegible] [illegible]

[illegible]

[illegible] that [illegible] [illegible] agreement [illegible]

[illegible] [illegible] in order to marriage [illegible]

[illegible] respectively as the providence of God may [illegible]

[illegible] [illegible] the [illegible] Henry having [illegible]

[illegible] according to their former agreement [illegible] to [illegible]

[illegible] assignes [illegible] this present writing is to testify [illegible]

[illegible] [illegible] & demands of [illegible] any [illegible]

[illegible] [illegible] paid & satisfied so much [illegible]

[illegible] [illegible] between him & her of [illegible]

[illegible] by mutuall agreement between them [illegible]

[illegible] [illegible] legacy to her children [illegible] by [illegible]

with the seven pounds more to be paid to her [illegible]

[illegible] assignes, the three pounds above mentioned [illegible]

[illegible] her former husband's will to be paid by way of [illegible]

Executor in her former husband's will that is to [illegible]

Rebeca: Ruth & Abraham — & the seven pounds [illegible]

[illegible] for [illegible] In case the sayd An [illegible]

(by the providence of god) before her husband [illegible]

be paid to her Children [illegible] if [illegible] said [illegible]

the said Ane husband shall by the providence of god

the sayd An his wife [illegible] sayd [illegible] to have [illegible]

above said seven pounds [illegible] one third parte of all [illegible]

[illegible] estate [illegible] for the [illegible]

severally set to our hands this 21 January 1664

[illegible] of witnesses

Richard [illegible]

Daniel [illegible]

the mark [illegible] of Henry Smith

the mark [illegible] Smith

It is appropriate now to consider the young people who were growing up in the New World in a small community far from the old country. Their lives were far easier than those of many of their parents who had experienced such numerous vexations, hardships, and limited economic opportunities.

By the mid-1650s there were over a hundred children growing up in Stamford. Unfortunately the birth dates of girls were often unrecorded, so that out of an approximate list of one hundred and sixteen there is a disproportionate number of boys--seventy to forty-six. Actual numbers, therefore, have little bearing.

Parents tended to name their children the time-honored Biblical names, and if one child of the chosen name died, the next one born of that sex would be given the same name; it is difficult, consequently, to determine some of the birth dates. Very often the oldest child of each sex would be named for the appropriate parent or grandparent. There could be several cousins with identical names. Successive John Waterburys, John Pettits, and John Weeds appear on the genealogical charts. The choice of names was really very limited. For example, there are only fourteen girls' names, with Sarah, Mary, and Hannah the favorites. For the boys there is more variety--twenty-eight Johns (by far the favorite) followed by Joseph, Jonathan, Samuel, and Daniel. One is struck by the number of names for boys that begin with J: John, Joseph, Jonathan, Jacob, Jeremiah, Joshua, James, Jonas, Jeffrey, Jesse, Josiah, Jabez, Jared, Joel, Jotham. Only about eight boys' names stand out as individual: Clement, Obadiah, Eleazer, Cornelius, Caleb, Hachaliah, Habakuk, and Increase. Among the girls Lydia, Unice (or Unica), Achsa, Rose, and Dorcas are unusual.

Given the fact that the Puritans prized good learning, thought was given to the education of children as soon as possible after the plantation was firmly established. The Puritan leaders required that families teach their children to read in order to learn the principles of their religion fully. At first, though, in Stamford children escaped any real learning except in the necessary skills for survival. Some boys were undoubtedly given rudiments of reading and arithmetic within the home or with someone singled out as able in learning and with a bit of spare time. Girls, of course, were taught their domestic chores by their mothers. As time went on, it was becoming increasingly evident that the standard of education in America was deteriorating. John Bishop, for example, later deplored the fact that his sons had grown up with no real learning.[43] In studying the records of this period in Stamford, one is surprised to note the number of such men as Daniel Scofield, Robert Bates, Angel Husted, Henry Smith, William Potter,

John Holmes, and Thomas Stevens who signed legal documents with their "mark" only. However, one must be careful, for it is possible that signing in such fashion was merely a custom, not indicative of illiteracy.

In 1656 the New Haven Court decreed that every plantation within its jurisdiction must establish a school.[44] Richard Mills, who was in Stamford by 1653, may well have been Stamford's first recognized school teacher. The first reference to him as a schoolteacher, however, was five years later when he was cited as the teacher of Daniel Simkins, a boy of over fifteen.[45] Interestingly, Richard Mills was a restive man like so many others at that time, for he moved to Newtown, Long Island, in 1661 where he was honored as the first schoolteacher there and given the town-house by Peter Stuyvesant. A year or two later, having moved to Westchester, he acted as scribe.[46] Thereafter he was imprisoned by Stuyvesant as a traitor to the Dutch and was only released when he begged to be, on the grounds of being "ancient and weakly" and agreeing to go to Virginia.[47]

One wonders whether during the 1650s and 1660s there was any organized teaching in Stamford after the departure of Richard Mills, for the records are silent, unfortunately. In any case, the second generation was now coming to the fore, trained largely by experience. As the 1660s approached, many were already considered adult, for they had passed their sixteenth birthdays.

Two decades had now passed, Stamford was a reasonably settled, viable community. The young men and women now becoming prominent could only remember their early days within the village. The tales of their parents alone linked them to the past experiences in other, better established places. Even the older generation remembered their earlier lives more dimly and sensed real pride in all they had accomplished for themselves and their descendants in the plantation of Stamford.

Chapter Three: 1660-1669

Across the sea in the mother country the English government was largely concerned with internal problems. All during the period after the execution of Charles I in 1649, the newly established Commonwealth and later the Protectorate were dominated by the powerful figure of Oliver Cromwell. He was primarily occupied in setting up a workable new form of government which would wipe out many of the institutions of England's former monarchy. In addition, Cromwell was a strong Puritan, determined to remove the rich trappings of the Church.

Therefore, during the 1650s the American colonies were far freer than before to go their own ways without interference. Oddly, many men, especially the clergy, regretted the loss of their king and looked askance at the radical procedures of England's Puritans. Actually, Boston's form of religion was now more conservative than that of England!

Suddenly though, events occurred that brought a sad change to the New Haven Colony, and surprise and shock to Stamford. Oliver Cromwell died in 1658. Then after a short wavering period, England invited Charles II, son of Charles I, to return from exile in Europe. He returned to England in the spring of 1660, was greeted tumultuously, and England settled back to enjoy once more its monarchical form of government, not to be broken to this day.

A few of the colonial governments realized that, although they were quite legitimate in local eyes, they were not legitimate in the king's eyes. They lacked the royal charter. Both the Connecticut plantation based in Hartford and the New Haven one made all haste to remedy this situation. John Winthrop, Jr., the governor of the Connecticut Colony, was sent to England to gain a royal charter, but the leaders of New Haven, unfortunately for them as it turned out, did not send their own man. They relied instead on Winthrop to see to their rights. It has not been established, however, that Winthrop received word of this responsibility.[1] He surely knew later that he had sold New Haven down the drain!

In October of 1662 the Connecticut Colony received its royal charter, a charter which far exceeded expectations. The Colony was to cover the territory from Massachusetts on the north to the sea on the south, and from the Narragansett River on the east (thus including a chunk of Rhode Island) to the South Sea on the west (a rather ambiguous determination!). New Haven was stunned. What should be done? Surely there had been an oversight somewhere. Was the Connecticut Colony at fault? Or John Winthrop? Or did the king fail to realize that he had neglected to take New Haven's bounds into account? New Haven set out to rectify the situation. A committee was appointed, of which the estimable Richard Law was a member, to draft letters both to Connecticut and to the king. Due emphasis was laid on the legitimacy of New Haven as an established, recognized government. Law, who in 1661 had approached Stuyvesant in an effort to buy lands along the Delaware River for New Haven, considered along with others a new possibility: New Haven might reestablish itself on lands well to the west.[2]

What was the general reaction of the people of Stamford? It was natural that most of the inhabitants of Stamford were delighted by the course of events. New Haven would no longer be a distant "landlord" meddling in local affairs nor would she demand high yearly tax rates, setting them as she pleased. Since the government at Hartford had not nurtured Stamford from infancy, it could be expected to welcome the new plantation on an equal basis. The people of Greenwich were delighted too; now they had an excellent chance of being recognized as inhabitants of a separate town. However, the men were wary, or at any rate in no hurry to be accepted as freemen of the Connecticut Colony. Only nine men were proposed during the first two years of 1662-1663.[3] These, including three from Greenwich, were:

John Green	Peter Ferris
Richard Hardy	Thomas Hunt
Joseph Mead#	Robert Husted#
Richard Webb	John Reynolds#
Joseph Theale	

# indicates Greenwich men

One man who was particularly pleased by the turn of events was Francis Brown. He had been called by the New Haven Court twice since 1659. The first case concerned a young boy named Edward House, who had been sent by his father in England and indentured to learn the trade of brickmaker. Evidently Brown was responsible for him. Can one conclude, therefore, that Brown himself was a brickmaker? In any case, the indenture period ended, but Brown passed the boy on to a certain Samuel Plum of Branford, Connecticut. In 1660 the New Haven Court determined that Brown was in the wrong. He was instructed to pay ten pounds for the boy's use so that he could return to England. He also had to pay ten shillings to the court and to Samuel Plum eight pounds in wheat and peas, plus fifty shillings in wampum.[4]

The second case concerned an exchange of horses with a man named John Archer. Archer had found that the horse he had bought from Brown was sick and had to be dragged along on a journey to Norwalk. He didn't want the beast. When the case came to court, it was decided that within four months Brown would "get up" all his horses so that Archer could choose another. Then if Archer couldn't find one to satisfy him, Brown would pay him twelve pounds worth of wheat and peas. The court did conclude that Brown hadn't really been guilty of wrongdoing.[5]

Francis Brown must have been a stoutly thoughtful individual. Early in 1662 he had decided to present several propositions to the New Haven Court: 1) there should be equal liberty for all to choose persons for public office; 2) there should be equal rates for the plantations and all should bear equally the charge of transport; 3) there should be a colony school (i.e. college). The court members listened to him patiently but took action on the last suggestion only, referring the matter to a committee. Brown said he wanted the court in Stamford, which had been set up under Law and Bell in 1661 to handle minor cases, to handle all these concerns. Again his ideas met with no enthusiasm.[6]

Therefore, how elated Francis Brown must have been when he learned that Connecticut Colony was to be Stamford's governing power! He and Stamford's other disaffected persons - William Newman, Richard Webb, Robert Usher (who had married Elizabeth Jagger, the widow of Jeremiah) - along with other more quiet objectors and certainly a growing number of the new generation saw a bright future ahead under Hartford. What a relief it would be to have more universal vote in town affairs at last!

In 1662 the Connecticut Assembly appointed its first official for Stamford with what seemed to be undue haste. Robert Usher was chosen to be constable.[7] New Haven was intensely annoyed and sent a letter of remonstrance after its May meeting. The letter had no effect. And who was appointed the following year? Francis Brown! New Haven was incensed; the Court had found him a very troublesome person. Clearly he was a rebel. In one letter sent to Hartford in 1664 he was complained about as follows: When a "declaration based on his majesty's commands 'was set up in public places' to be seen and read of all, that all might obey it, it was at Stamford, violently plucked downe, by Browne your constable, and with reproachful speeches rejected...."[8] New Haven informed the General Assembly of Connecticut that they should either remove Brown entirely from the New Haven Colony (insisting still that it was the governing power) or expect New Haven to take action against him. This proved an empty threat.

Two years passed in acrimonious exchanges. New Haven went on governing. The Stamford deputies, Law and Bell (and George Slason once in 1663), tried to carry on. However, New Haven's dying struggles weakened until at the end of 1664 she gave in to Connecticut.

The strong upholders of faith and tradition were left hanging in air. Francis Bell seems hereafter to have been involved in only local and personal affairs, playing no part in colony affairs. John Bishop, abandoned by his much needed support from New Haven, must have felt that Christian godliness was doomed since now men could manage town affairs without belonging to the church. Perhaps, though, in his wisdom he saw that his mission would be eased; his responsibility would be narrowed, and the political friction removed. Richard Law, whose associations with many men had been built over the years of political experience, swallowed the bitter pill. He swallowed it reluctantly as is evident in a letter he wrote to Mr. Davenport in New Haven. He commented on the sad situation in Stamford and the "turbulent carriages of some...inhabitants."[9]

Fortunately for Stamford, he continued to be recognized and accepted by the Connecticut Assembly as a just and astute leader. However, he clearly had reservations and did not bother to become a freeman in Connecticut for several years. In 1664 he gave up his position of town clerk, a position he had held over the twenty-four years. He also that year was concerned with family affairs. His only son, Jonathan, married Sarah Clark of Milford where the young couple decided to live. Richard was devastated as he had expected his son to carry on the family tradition and holdings in Stamford. Fortunately, about this time Jonathan and John Selleck, young sons of the well-established David Selleck of Boston, appeared on the scene. Jonathan began his long career in Stamford by opening an ordinary or tavern (an important institution in those times),[10] and before long Richard's two daughters, Abigail and Sarah, were married to the two brothers.

Hartford saw fit to hand over to Richard Law magisterial power so that he could carry on as usual on the local scene in Stamford. He then became also the first Commissioner, in charge of the court affairs in the new county of Fairfield - a position he was to hold for twenty-one years until his death. How many arduous trips he must have made between Stamford and Fairfield!

The Colony of Connecticut had acted just in time to gather in both Greenwich and Stamford. In an act of generosity, Charles II gave his brother James the proprietorship of a huge tract of land between the Connecticut and Delaware rivers, which included New Netherland. An English fleet appeared off New Amsterdam in the summer of 1664, and the Dutch immediately surrendered. The Colony of Connecticut was thereafter strengthened by an edict giving control of Long Island to her as part of her land north of the sea itself.[11] New Haven, judging Connecticut the better of the two options confronting her, chose to submit to Connecticut over New York and joined formally in December of 1664.

Stamford found her position one of increasing independence and security. There are very few of the small court cases recorded thereafter, and the town meeting accounts deal with purely local town matters. External threats were minimal for Stamford. One does note in the colony records a reference to Indians. It seems they made a habit of walking the streets in the various settlements when they wished to get liquor at night. This was now forbidden. Various commodities also were forbidden to the Indians, such as cider, strong drink, boats (except canoes), horses, and even mastiffs, which were valuable against wolves.[12] Generally, though, for Stamford the Indians were not a problem, merely a nuisance at times.

Some of the local needs were met through the town meetings in 1664 and 1665; these matters were primarily agricultural in nature, though certain officials to serve the town and the colony were chosen by vote. Richard Law and John Green were elected to be delegates to Hartford; Peter Ferris was made constable, a yearly position; and the usual men of prestige, Law, Bell, and Holly, were given the responsibility of determining the rates for the town, Mr. Bishop, and the "country" or colony. Another appointed official was John Holly, previously responsible for collecting the excise on liquors and probably still doing so; he was now put in charge of recording the horse marks and brands. A minor official, who went about beating his drum and probably enjoyed the task on pleasant days, was the warner. In 1664 William Oliver received sixteen shillings a year for alerting the populace of meetings. The next year it was Joshua Hait, who was paid twenty shillings.[13]

Evidently the men of the town were recognizing the need for stronger organization in local affairs; the care of livestock and land received increasing attention in the town meetings. Cowkeepers were given specific charge of the cows and calves only. The oxkeeper was to care for oxen, dry cattle, and older heifers. Soon this arrangement proved unsatisfactory; it was found expedient to hire a dry herdsman, and the animals were divided up differently.

The care of the various fields was of major concern. Early in the season the planting fields had to be prepared. Each man who had a right in the field (the proprietor) had to put his section of the fencing in order or be fined. The cattle and swine that had been allowed to roam and graze over the spent fields had to be claimed and ousted, and any still found within after the fences were repaired were to be impounded.

Fence viewers were appointed; in 1664 these were Cornelius Jones, the widow Seely, George Slason, Samuel Holly, Joseph Garnsey, and John Holly. The two Hollys were probably the young sons of John, Sr. The surveyors, who were responsible for keeping the highways and bridges in good repair, were Richard Ambler, Robert Usher, John Green, and one other whose name is missing. Richard Ambler was chosen twice to help in lay-out work - once with William Newman and once with Newman and George Slason, all fully responsible men.[14]

A sign that the village was growing and changes were needed came in the spring of 1666. Since rounding up particular horses in the woods proved to be time-consuming and sometimes even fruitless, the proprietors decided to turn part of the Eastfield into a horse pasture, thereby making it common land. It took a year to prepare the area. In April 1667 all men who wished to put horses (no mares) therein gave in their names and took the responsibility for building the necessary fence. The total number of horses was sixty-two - six men only putting in two.[15] When one studies the list, an interesting point evolves: every landowner of the first generation is represented except William Potter, Richard Webb, John Rockwell, and Cornelius Jones. These four either had no horses or planned to use other arrangements. The twenty-three horse owners were:

Richard Ambler
Robert Bates
Francis Bell
Francis Brown
Stephen Clason
William Crissey
Samuel Dean
Joseph Garnsey
John Green
Richard Hardy
John Holly
Francis Holmes
Nicholas Knap
Richard Law
Edmund Lockwood
William Newman
Daniel Scofield
Richard Scofield
George Slason
Henry Smith
Robert Usher
Richard Webb
Jonas Weed

Thirty men of the second generation appear on the list. These are:

John Bates#	Thomas Lawrence#
Jonathan Bell	John Miller#
Clement Buxton#	Jonathan Miller#
Samuel Dibble	Daniel Newman
Zachariah Dibble#	John Pettit
Peter Ferris	Obadiah Seely#
Isaac Finch	John Selleck
Samuel Finch#	Jonathan Selleck
Samuel Holly	Daniel Simkins#
John Holmes#	John Slason#
Stephen Holmes#	Eleazer Slason#
Joshua Hoyt	Obadiah Stevens#
Samuel Hoyt#	Joseph Theale
John Jagger#	John Weed
Caleb Knap#	Daniel Weed#

# denotes those who are referred to later

Only three new landowners (and horse owners) appear - Thomas Stedwell, John Thompson, a gunsmith, and Daniel Westcott, who later became a prominent citizen.

The community was really still very small with a total of thirty-three family groups represented. There was also a mix of other persons in Stamford, from the Rev. Bishop to young servants and numerous hired help or passersby.

The men must have been kept quite busy each spring repairing fences, for part of the peninsula of Shippan had to be fenced for the cattle. Then, too, the ox pasture west of Mill River and near the Landing Place at the mouth required good fencing.

Since a portion of Eastfield had been taken for the horse pasture (much of it, incidentally, low-lying land and probably not too productive), a new field had to be found. The young men were undoubtedly clamoring for rights to fields like their fathers'. In December of 1667 it was determined that the town worthies, Richard Law, John Holly, Richard Ambler, and George Slason, accompanied by Richard's son John, and Edmund Lockwood, should set out to explore the bounds of Stamford for a new field or fields.[16] Evidently they met with success, for two weeks later the first four men plus Francis Bell, Francis Brown, and John Pettit were designated to order the field. The town would pay for the surveying. Presumably this field was Newfield, well north of the center of town and represented today in such names as Newfield Avenue and Newfield School.

Fairfield November [illegible] 1666   Entered [illegible] Law [illegible]

Know all men by these presents that I Richard Law of Stamford [illegible] for severall respects, out of a fatherly affection towards my son Jonathan Law, and in consideration [illegible] to my owne, being intended in order to marriage [illegible] that I said Richard Law of Stamford [illegible] freely make over & absolutely give [illegible] possession of all my housing and land in Stamford with all appurtenance belonging to it, only a third [illegible] of the said housing & land for the use of my loving wife Margaret Law during her naturall life & then all the said housing & land to return to my son Jonathan Law [illegible]. Also the said Richard Law doe reserve liberty of sale of the house & home lott [illegible] called that of [illegible] lott, also I doe hereby binde my self to paye unto my son Jonathan Law one hundred pounds to be paid within [illegible] yeares time, and for the truth hereof I have hereunto subscribed my owne hand in the presence of witnesses

signed Richard Law

Benjamin Hoyt

George Clark

postscript entered

For further explaination of what is above writen that the above said Richard Law doe declare that it was & is my minde that the above said housing & lands shall be to my son Jonathan Law & to his heirs for ever after the decease of me & my wife Margaret Law, and that the hundred pounds shall be paid by me or my [illegible] to my son Jonathan Law [illegible] 1666 [illegible] witness whereof I have hereunto set my hand this [illegible] day of [illegible] 1666

signed Richard Law

signed by us

James Bishop

Samuel [illegible]

[illegible]

Mostly second-generation men received rights in this new field, although the names of three older men, Samuel Dean, Richard Scofield, and Henry Smith, are on the list. The starred names on the previously given list of the horse pasture group are those who received rights. Daniel Scofield, Jr. and other young men now of age were added: Benjamin Hoyt, Jeremiah Jagger, Moses Knap, Joseph Miller, John Scofield, John Smith, Daniel Smith, Ephraim Stevens, and Jonas Weed. Two recent settlers, William Clemence and John Gold, were also given rights. In all, thirty-three men could use the new field.

In the late 1660s considerable areas of land in various directions from Stamford village were cleared for use. Since the Indians were no longer living in the part of Shippan originally allotted to them, that land could be utilized. In fact, John Jagger was soon given a piece there that actually was termed the Indian land.[17] Rocky Neck, south of Cornelius Jones' and Obadiah Seely's house lots, was to be cleared of brush and made useful land by every able-bodied man in Stamford.[18] New meadows were to be laid out to the proprietors, both the fresh meadows (north of the Country Road and west of the Noroton River) and Runkenheag (in what is now Darien). Fencing was to be agreed upon later. Even the Noroton Islands were to be utilized; John Rockwell was given the right to mow the grass there for as long as he lived in Stamford or until they were laid out.[19]

The men of Stamford also reconsidered the actual bounds of their territory. To the north, the Indians, who weren't averse to stealing hogs when possible, were called forth to sign a new agreement in 1668. Taphance, the son of Ponus, and Powahay, the son of Onax, agreed to the original terms set in 1655. In addition, they had to accept the jurisdiction of Stamford, to limit their numbers to their immediate families, plus "an old woman called Nowattonamanssqua" (Was this Noroton man's squaw?), and to agree to fence their twenty-acre planting field.[20] The Indians were clearly being squeezed out.

Although Greenwich on the west had been established as a separate plantation by the Connecticut General Assembly, no dividing line was established. Law, Bell, Holly, and Newman met with the men of Greenwich in 1669 to draw the mutual boundary line, a line later disputed by Greenwich but which stood.[21]

In addition to the laying-out of lands and determining boundaries, certain buildings came under scrutiny at this time. The old meetinghouse, which had served so many purposes since its erection in 1641-1642, was deemed too small. In 1669 it was decided that a new one of stone should be built, and half a year later a committee was formed to find workmen to do the job. It was then stated that timber could be used instead of stone if necessary. Shortly thereafter the whole plan was repealed and the decision made that the old meetinghouse be repaired only.[22] However, this decision did prove to be temporary.

Another concern was the town grist mill. Nothing about its functioning appears in the records from the early 1650s, when Jeffrey Ferris was running it, until 1664. Jeffrey had four sons, who probably helped him, or he may have turned the whole concern over to Richard Webb. Webb bought a house lot next to the Stamford mill in 1651. It wasn't until 1664, however, that the corn mill and its lands were turned over to Webb.[23] Evidently, as in the case of the meetinghouse, the mill needed repairs; Webb was instructed to put it in order within the year.

In 1667 Richard Webb, about forty-four years of age, certified that John Ogden, the well-known builder, had had considerable expense in moving to Stamford and in working on the mill. Two years later, the town recorded its covenant with Richard to take on the mill and agreed to consider putting in weights and scales at a later date. He was to have the mill lot plus the strip running north to Theale's Bridge.[24]

Evidently the Landing Place was growing as mercantile business expanded. This is evinced by John Selleck's request for a house lot and a warehouse there.[25] Both he and his brother Jonathan were prospering as merchants. They seem to have handled their business as a team, John running the shipping and Jonathan remaining in Stamford where he took charge of their operations and, as time passed, became more and more involved in town affairs. Both were men of enterprise, and they became men of wealth with extensive landed estates. They were fortunate, too, in having the guidance of their father-in-law, Richard Law. However, maritime dealings could be risky. In 1667 they sustained a great loss, as cited in the Colonial Records of Connecticut, so that the sum of three pounds ten shillings was deducted from their tax.[26]

One other building need is mentioned in the town records during this period. In 1669 the town members voted to have an ordinary (tavern) built for the convenience of strangers. The man who ran it would receive five pounds a year. Also, a piece of land next to the ordinary would be fenced for the strangers' horses.[27] People were traveling more and needed special consideration. The Connecticut Assembly had become aware of problems involving strangers; they often proved to be disturbers of the peace, particularly young men no longer under parental control, who might drift into a town, work for awhile, and then move on. A law in 1667 gave each town the right to punish any unruly stranger by fining him or placing him in the stocks for an hour.[28] Then in 1669 the Assembly, bowing at last to sensible judgment, decreed that those of differing religious beliefs might be accepted in the Connecticut plantation as long as they were well behaved.[29] At the same time some of the deputies became concerned about the tendency of some lively people to ride at full speed along the town streets with little regard for people or livestock. The Assembly, therefore, limited horse speed in the towns to an "ordinary and easy hand gallop"[30] - slightly different from the speed of traffic on the I-95 today!

The Connecticut Colony government divided the colony into four judicial counties. The cases from Stamford, Greenwich, and Rye were handled, therefore, in Fairfield, the county seat. Law, and later John Holly with him, were the commissioners chosen by Hartford to represent the three towns. Very unfortunately, the early records of this Fairfield Court have been lost so that we are deprived of possibly valuable glimpses into the personal concerns of the Stamford residents.

Small court cases continued to be handled by the individual towns. In Stamford these dealt mainly with drunkenness and swearing. The normal fee of eight to ten shillings was incurred by Francis Holmes and two young men, Obadiah Seely and Ebenezer Jones, for over-imbibing. Robert Penoyer in his cups aboard a ship challenged Obadiah to fight and even struck him. He was also charged with using "roughunall words."[31] Both John Miller and Eleazer Slawson were present and served as witnesses. Robert received a stiffer fee of thirty shillings and being bound for ten pounds, as this was not his first offense. The same year, 1665, he received another fine when he was found drunk by Thomas Lawrence (the young stepson of Francis Brown) and Isaac Finch.[32] Cornelius Jones (was this the father or the son?) seems to have had a severe drinking problem. One night he crossed South Street from his house to the widow Seely's. She and her two sons, Obadiah and Cornelius, were startled to find him drunk and without his britches! As this was his second offense of drunkenness and a severe one at that, he was fined one pound. Three days later Cornelius Jones, Sr. was fined for being drunk in Rye when with the builder John Ogden and his wife. The following year he abused his wife and proceeded to disturb the whole neighborhood one night. John Holly, who lived near him, objected to this behavior.[33]

One man was caught working on the Sabbath, and four were fined for swearing; these were incidental cases. One can't help reflecting on how some of our highly-placed national officials today would have been treated for their swearing!

Two more serious cases happened in 1667. Six young men, Edward Traherne, Joseph Studwell, Humphrey Hill, Cornelius Jones, Jonas Seely, and Samuel Hoyt (nicknamed "Coneticut") engaged in wrestling outside the meetinghouse on a Sunday. They also threw stones into the swamp. Some even took tobacco! All this was a severe violation of the Sabbath, but since it was their first offense, they were let off easy. They had to stand before the public for an hour and be whipped once on their backs so that the stripes would show.[34]

The other case seems to be one of pure stupidity. Humphrey Hill was again involved. He stole some wheat from his master and gave it to Samuel Dibble, who bought liquor with it. A drinking party then ensued. It took place after the limiting hour of nine o'clock at William Crissey's house and included Samuel Emery, the brothers Obadiah and Jonas Seely, and John Marshall. They were all fined two shillings sixpence. The perpetrators had to pay twenty shillings each and also had to pay back the master. William Crissey, because he had entertained servants and children in the night, was fined ten shillings.[35]

Certainly, though none of these cases is earth-shattering, collectively they do serve to show how tightly the community was held together by its Puritan standards. What more serious kinds of cases were brought before the higher court of Fairfield? Were there many involving Stamford people? How did Stamford fare in relation to Greenwich, Rye, Norwalk, and Fairfield? We cannot know; nor, on the other hand, is it probable that we shall learn of the heartwarming events that may have happened to the people of Stamford during this decade. Individuals must have been known for their helpful ways, their unusual talents, and their noteworthy accomplishments.

Chapter Four: 1670-1679

1670. It is time to reflect. Thirty years have passed since the little group in Wethersfield put their faith and hope into making a new home in the unsettled, far western land along the coast of Long Island Sound. How many of these first adventuresome settlers remained after thirty years? Of the men who arrived in 1641 and 1642 there were nine: Robert Bates, Francis Bell, John Holly, Richard Law, William Newman, Daniel Scofield, George Slason, Henry Smith, and Jonas Weed. During the ensuing decade four of these pioneers, Bates, Newman, Scofield, and Weed, died. The remaining four even in their advanced years continued to lead active lives. Bell, Holly, Law, and Slason were the leaders in Stamford, guiding constantly in all the variety of community concerns. It is a wonder that their many obligations over the years allowed them sufficient freedom to care for their livelihoods and their families.

Later arrivals in Stamford who were also members of the first generation of settlers numbered eighteen. Most of these men, too, appear over and over in the town records as they were called upon for duties befitting responsible citizens. These were:

Richard Ambler	John Gold	Edmund Lockwood
Rev. John Bishop	John Green	Richard Mills
Francis Brown	Richard Hardy	Robert Penoyer
Stephen Clason	Francis Holmes	William Potter
Samuel Dean	Cornelius Jones	Richard Scofield
Joseph Garnsey	Nicolas Knap	Richard Webb

Stamford had proved itself as a fine place to settle. The climate was healthful; the land good for farming; and the location on the protected Sound was an enviable one, situated as it was between New York and Boston, between New York and New Haven, and between points south, such as Long Island, and Hartford. By 1670 life in Stamford was quite stable and generally pleasing.

The second generation was bringing great changes to the whole structure of Stamford's society. The young men were now in their twenties and thirties. Jonathan Bell, the first child born in Stamford in 1641, was by 1670 a man of twenty-nine with a wife and several children. During the 1660s and 1670s these young men appear increasingly in the town records as fence viewers, surveyors, town drummer, and pounders, only gradually rising in the case of a chosen few to become worthy townsmen.

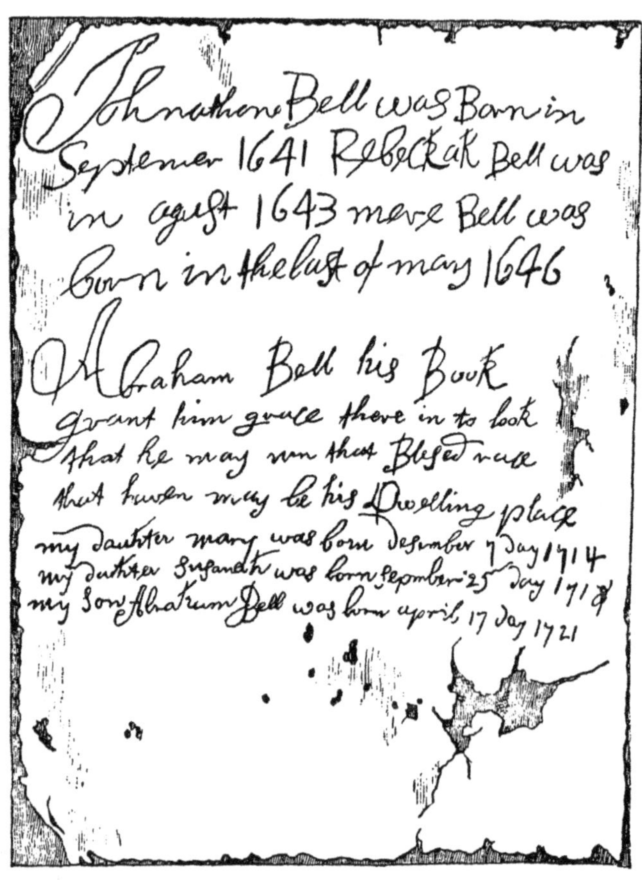

Johnathon Bell was Born in
Septemer 1641 Rebeckak Bell was
in agust 1643 mere Bell was
Born in the last of may 1646

Abraham Bell his Book
grant him grace there in to look
that he may win that Blesed race
that heven may be his Dwelling place
my dauhter mary was born desember 7 day 1714
my dauhter Susanah was born Sepmber 25 day 1718
my Son Abraham Bell was born april 17 day 1721

Many young men, whose fathers were unable to provide them with house lots, requested them at the town meetings; they were given the usual layout of an acre an a half. Stamford began expanding eastward to the Noroton River, north up the extension of North Street (or the path to Bedford as it was called), and westward on the other side of Mill River. A first son usually did inherit the father's homestead, but sometimes it was the youngest son who, still with his mother, was left the family home.

The second-generation sons of Stamford who were of age in the 1670s are as follows:

Abraham Ambler
John Bates
Jonathan Bell
Stephen Bishop
Joseph Bishop
Joseph Brown
Clement Buxton
Jonathan Clason
Nathaniel Cross
John Cross
Samuel Dibble
Peter Ferris
Isaac Finch
Samuel Finch
John Finch
Abraham Finch
Joseph Green
Benjamin Green
Samuel Holly
John Holly
Increase Holly
John Holmes
Stephen Holmes
Joshya Hoyt
Samuel Hoyt
Benjamin Hoyt
Jeremiah Jagger
John Jagger
Stephen Jagger
Ebenezer Jones
Cornelius Jones
Joseph Jones
Caleb Knap
Moses Knap
Thomas Lawrence
Jonathan Miller
John Miller
Joseph Miller
Daniel Newman
Thomas Newman
William Penoyer
John Pettit
Daniel Scofield
John Scofield
Joseph Scofield
Obadiah Seely
Cornelius Seely
Daniel Simkins
John Slason
Eleazer Slason
John Smith
Daniel Smith
Ephraim Stevens
Obadiah Stevens
Benjamin Stevens
Joseph Stevens
Joseph Theale
John Waterbury
Jonathan Waterbury
David Waterbury
Joseph Webb
Joshua Webb
John Weed
Daniel Weed
Jonas Weed
Samuel Weed
Jonathan Selleck#
John Selleck#

Law's sons-in-law

The newly emerging leaders during the 1670s were Abraham Ambler, John Bates, Jonathan Bell, Isaac Finch, Joshua and Samuel Hoyt, Eleazer Slason, Joseph Theale, Daniel Weed, and Jonathan and John Selleck.

One wishes that a richer, more intimate knowledge could be gained of this group of people, people who for the most part largely lived their lives within the bounds of Stamford. At this time most fathers were well able to provide their offspring with the essentials of living. Land was easily come by, farm animals reasonably abundant, access to goods from outside quite available so that a young man could readily make his way, albeit as a farmer in most cases. Very few men indeed moved away from Stamford at this time (unless, like Jonathan Law, one happened to marry a girl from elsewhere and found better prospects in her community). Young men married in their early twenties and chose slightly younger mates, many aged eighteen. Through what we consider gross oversight, the young ladies' last names were deemed of little importance and so many are lost to history. Of the sixty-nine young men listed, twenty-three married unknowns. (Some of the wives are referred to merely by such common names as Mary, Sarah, Abigail, Elizabeth, and Hannah.) Thirty-six men married local girls who are known by name, and ten married girls from other places. It is clear, naturally, that most of the men found their wives within the community, some choosing from the ever-present number of young widows. Stamford was, very understandably, therefore, a tight-knit society with a web of family ties.

During the 1660s and the 1670s the number of newcomers was small, and most of them did not remain. The list below contains the known men who did come during these years; those who remained are marked with a #. Undoubtedly, there were others whose names do not appear in the town records.

Jeremiah Andrews#
Richard Ayres#
Matthew Bellamy
William Clark
William Clemence#
William Crissy#
John Emery
Joseph Hilliard
Cornelius Hunt
Eliphalet Jones
Peter June#
Jonathan Kilborn
Thomas Studwell
William Sturdevant
John Thompson
William Ward
Nicolas Webster#
Daniel Westcott#
John Westcott

As the village of Stamford grew larger with new house lots extending along the winding streets or "paths," ever new building needs were becoming apparent. What were they to do about the crowded meetinghouse? Where could people rest between church services? What about a town school?

It was decided that the old meetinghouse on the center common could no longer serve. Joshua Hoyt was put in charge; he was to see that the old building was taken apart carefully and a new one built on the same spot. After considering building it of stone and erecting a square structure of thirty-five feet, the men decided to make it forty-five feet long, thirty-five feet wide, and twelve feet high abating three feet. John Jagger was to pay the mason thirty pounds for the work in return for land given him by the town. Then someone had a better idea. It was determined that a square building of thirty-eight feet would be large enough. The height would remain at twelve feet and a "turret" would be constructed on top. Since this whole operation was of singular importance to the whole population, five of the ablest citizens were to oversee the work as a committee. These were Law, Holly, Bell, Ambler, and Newman.[1]

Two years later in 1673 the new meetinghouse was ready for use. A committee was formed to arrange the seating of the men, which was done by order of age, dignity, and the tax rate each man paid - a method which undoubtedly avoided endless bickering but which seems rather arbitrary to us. The women were also seated by decision of a committee on the other side of the meetinghouse. It wouldn't be hard for us to seat the first row ourselves!

The old timbers were not to be wasted, though. A proper central school must be built, for although men like Richard Mills had been teaching the young, there was no standard educational policy, and it was realized that too many children were growing up without proper basic training. Therefore, the schoolmaster was to use the old wood to build a schoolroom ten to twelve feet square.[2] This was presumed large enough for the forms and benches and the wiggly little ones of diverse ages. Though in 1670 Matthew Bellamy was first chosen to be schoolmaster, a year later the town decided to hire a Mr. Rider. Very shortly thereafter, in 1672, he was not found acceptable any longer.[3] Did Mr. Bellamy continue then? In any case, a general schoolmaster was given authority, the "piety" schools were abolished, and parents were made responsible for paying the schoolmaster. Children who were sent to neighbors to learn to knit or sew were excepted, however.[4] The school itself was built southwest of the meetinghouse on the town plot or green. With both the meetinghouse and the school in this village center, a closeness of community activity was assured. And right nearby lived the three major leaders, Francis Bell to the southeast, Richard Law to the south, and John Bishop to the northwest.

Two new buildings were established during these years that would prove of great benefit to the community. A town house in those days had a special meaning. It was a shelter or gathering spot intended primarily for those people who had to come a considerable distance to church on the Sabbath and who needed a resting place between the morning and afternoon services. As time went on, it began to accommodate travelers. Thomas Lawrence gave over some of his land on the corner of West Street and the road to the mill (an inner piece), and the town house was built there by Joshua Hoyt, Daniel Weed, and Stephen Clason. A lot across the street along the river to the North Street bridge was to be fenced by the town and used for the horses.[5] As need for refreshment in the town house was recognized, Daniel Westcott was given the franchise to live there and run an ordinary. He was to receive a bed, furniture, and a loan of five pounds for the first year.[6] Daniel Weed also wanted to open an ordinary at this time, and the town gave him permission to run one for two years; it was to be west of Mill River next to Stephen Clason's lot.[7]

Joshua Hoyt was certainly establishing himself as master carpenter or builder. (Simon Hoyt, his father, it may be remembered, had a mill on his land on East Street, but if it was a saw mill, it must have been very small - or was it only a cider mill?) Joshua's major need as a carpenter was for well-dressed lumber; so in 1678 he took on a major project. He agreed to establish a sawmill "at the head of the salt" on Five-Mile River, the boundary with Norwalk on the east. Joshua was to build the mill within the next two years, and for timber he could take trees on the common land. The inhabitants of Stamford were to be served first and were given a special rate - sixpence off the rate for one hundred plank boards. Also, the town could have slabs for the fetching. Evidently, some men were concerned about a monopoly on timber; so the town declared that any man could have timber from the common land if it had lain for four months on the ground.[8] At first thought, one might consider that a sawmill built so far from the village center would prove unprofitable, but Joshua saw the need for building materials for the new homes stretching eastwards. He also saw two real assets - tidal power for a mill and plenty of virgin woodland.

Stamford's town government during the 1670s became increasingly involved in matters of the use of its land. Not only was the population expanding, but also at times the crop yield was poor. For example, in 1669 the Connecticut records mention a very bad harvest. Great damage was caused by "blasting and catmillows" (what catmillows actually were is left to our imaginations).[9] Consequently, a day of fasting and prayer was called for in March of 1670. In Stamford it is to be noted that the three major fields, Northfield, Eastfield, and Southfield, continued to be used for grain and allowed to be pasturage for animals during the winter months, primarily because of the value of fertilizer. More and more young men were made responsible as fence viewers, surveyors, and pounders for these three fields and later for the new field or Newfield to the north, and Rocky Neck, which was laid out to the proprietors in 1670. Because of the need for more agricultural land at this time, Stamford decided also to lay out all its fresh meadows so that each proprietor could use his portion to advantage.[10] The laying out of new fields to the east continued the widening spread of land use.

Indian lands were being taken over. As we have seen, John Jagger was given part of their past holdings on Shippan. Mr. Holly took over the lands of Taphose to the north. They had been so neglected that he would have to repair the broken fencing.[11] There were Indians still living in the uplands between Stony Brook and Five Mile River. Various problems arose concerning them; consequently, a committee of nine men was appointed to meet with them - doubtless to the Indians' disadvantage. The boundary lines in the Rowayton area to the east were to be determined also and the Norwalk markers removed when wrong.[12]

The Connecticut Colony government stressed the need to have the boundaries of each plantation clearly demarcated and was behind the effort to buy all land possible from the Indians. Stamford men under John Holly were detailed to run the lines of Norwalk, Stamford, Greenwich, and Rye, and Richard Law was appointed to study the settlement of a new plantation north of Norwalk.[13] Law and Holly continued to be commissioners, and Law and Lt. Jonathan Selleck were the two deputies, as was John Green upon occasion.

In June of 1672 a letter was received from Charles II announcing the opening of new hostilities with the Dutch. The threat of Dutch presence again in neighboring New York was cause for real concern in Stamford, a concern that was justified in August when the enemy actually did sail into New York and reestablish her power there. Soon thereafter one of the Sellecks' vessels, which was engaged in going to Long Island for lumber, was seized by the Dutch.[14] Captain John was taken prisoner but released. The ship was held, however. Hartford was incensed by this act and sent a strong letter to the Dutch commander-in-chief of the fleet in Hudson's River.[15] The response from the Dutch was merely that the ship belonged to their enemy and so taking it was justified. Connecticut sent out a call for the establishment of dragoons and train bands. Fairfield was to supply one hundred and twenty dragoons of which twenty-four were to come from Stamford. Each man was to be supplied with a sword and a belt, a musket or carbine, a shot pouch and bullets for it, one pound of powder, and three pounds of bullets. He was also to have a horse and a "half-pick" (pike). Muster masters were to be appointed, and a standing Council of War was established in Hartford.[16]

In December panic set in among the coastal towns, and a formal letter was sent by Stamford, Greenwich and Rye, drafted by Law and Selleck, to Hartford for advice on how to strengthen their defenses. Daniel Westcott agreed to carry it to Hartford, for which trip he was to receive fifteen shillings.[17] No response to this letter has been recorded, but it was undoubtedly a reassuring one with suggestions on fortifying the most vulnerable approaches to the towns and offering the full support of the Colony. Finally, in May of 1674 Hartford received word that a peace treaty had been signed in Europe. Mr. Jonathan Selleck and a Mr. Samuel Martin were appointed to carry the news to New York.[18]

The war in Europe between the English and the Dutch lasted a little less than two years (1672-1674), from March to February, and in America from the end of June to the middle of May. The English returned to New York under Major Edmund Andros, who proved to be a stiff-minded person eager to enlarge his domain. Again Jonathan Selleck was sent forth with others to determine very clearly a boundary line, the line between New York and Connecticut, stretching from Mamaroneck to Hudson's River.[19] This act, however, did not dampen Andros' determination to gain for New York all the land west of the Connecticut River. Connecticut had to be on guard.

Meanwhile during these years of the early 1670s both Stamford and Hartford did not neglect the ordinary needs of their people. Agriculture was the basis of life in the Connecticut Colony. In 1673 Connecticut rejoiced in its summer of good crops and fruits and proclaimed (as so often happened in the New England colonies) a day of general thanksgiving.[20] Sheep became part of the assembly's deliberations because it was noted that the stock was becoming inferior. Hereafter the rams were to be kept separate from the ewes from August to October, and the animals were to be held in flocks of a hundred with two or three men in charge of them[21]. A reference is made in the Stamford records to goats, not mentioned previously.[22] The following year the rule was laid down that horses over two years old should be gelded if kept in the common pastures. It was also ordered that each plantation should have its own hayward.[23] Since Stamford had long had fence viewers and pounders, these handled the duties for which a hayward was responsible.

Connecticut was also concerned about the produce coming from its plantations. Evidently there had been too many instances of bad grain and bad pork. Meat particularly must have been a problem without refrigeration. (Salt, of course, was the customary answer to that.) Hartford ruled that each community should have one man in charge of checking the barrels. Also, it was time to regulate prices, to set standards. Wheat was set at four shillings a bushel, peas at three, and Indian corn at two shillings sixpence. Pork was valued at three pounds a barrel.[24] These, clearly, were the vital commodities.

At the same time the Court took up the matter of what the towns should pay for a representative's stay in Hartford. It was determined that a man should be paid seventeen shillings for his expenses, for his horse ten shillings; a man's meal was set at sixpence, and a horse at grass fourpence or the same for half a peck of oats or hay.[25]

When it comes to studying what the Connecticut law court cases were at this time, one finds little reference to Stamford since the subsidiary Fairfield Court was functioning efficiently.

It is interesting to note, however, the kinds of cases that were handled, as these reflect the whole colony's concerns. Mostly, they dealt with crimes of fornication, adultery, sodomy, theft or cheating, land disputes, the wrongdoings of Indians, and a few cases of murder, with an axe often the weapon. Since the early laws had omitted the crime of incest, this was made punishable by death in 1673. The same year it was ruled that every household in the Colony should have the new book of the laws, for which they were to pay twelve pence, or one and a half pecks of wheat or two shillings worth of peas.[26]

Back in Stamford Mr. Bishop at this time was feeling his age and his twenty years of service to the community, including as it did caring for the families of both Stamford and Greenwich. There was at this time a kind of free-lance minister living in the Greenwich area named the Reverend Eliphalet Jones. As he was well liked there and perhaps because he did offer a threat to Stamford's authority, he was prevailed upon to live in Stamford where he was given land and a house lot.[27] Mr. Bishop and Mr. Jones shared the ministerial duties for about four years, but then Mr. Jones left. Was Mr. Bishop intransigent, or did Mr. Jones have a roving spirit? Anyway, thereafter, Stamford returned to the sole ministry of Bishop for the following eighteen years until the year of his death. Mr. Bishop must have been pleased when in

1674 the Assembly in Hartford recognized his untiring service by granting him 200 acres.[28] With two young sons now of age to be householders he must have particularly welcomed this gift, which came at the same time these sons were given house lots of their own.

One event must have come as a shock to Mr. Bishop, however. In 1675 word came from Hartford that Quakers were no longer to be ostracized.[29] So long as they lived peaceably, they were to be accepted into the communities. How Mrs. Crab would have rejoiced and raised her voice in triumph if she had remained in Stamford! John Bishop, the sturdy Puritan, must have had renewed moments of torment of soul when such changes, so contrary to his early teachings, were adopted. A reflection of concern about some of these changes was voiced by Hartford in 1676 when the government urged the people to look to their young. The Sabbath must be observed; education must be improved by use of good literature, the scriptures, and the teaching of sound morals. We see these attitudes strongly reflected in John Bishop's letters to his friend Increase Mather in Boston. In a letter of 1677 he writes about the new settlements springing up to the west "where may be many young ones grown and growing up, that never lived under the means & scarce even heard sermon in all their lives, some of them." He also voices concern about his own four sons "...none of them brought up to learning, to my great grief, though two of them in a good forwardness long since, but our Latin scole failing, and my estate too feeble to send them forth, their progress also failed." He still had hopes of sending Benjamin, his youngest, to Boston later on.[30]

Hartford was further concerned about the problem of too much drinking. Fancy clothing also was cause for regulation; the tailors were advised to make sober clothing devoid of gold or silver lace, silk ribbons, fancy buttons, and lavish scarves. Lastly, to control the communities Hartford ruled that any boarders or sojourners in the towns were to be housed only in good moral homes.[31]

Suddenly in the middle 1670s all of Connecticut was drawn into a war. This war is known to history as King Philip's War. Who was King Philip? He was an Indian, the son of Plymouth's friendly Massasoit. He became increasingly aware of the white man's power over land and law. Constant friction with the white man finally caused the tribes, principally along the east coast from Maine to Rhode Island and eastern Connecticut, to join in a great confederacy and go on the warpath in 1675. It was a determined and desperate effort on the part of the Indians to oust the white newcomers. A sign of what was evolving is seen in the Connecticut records. Earlier, Indians had been forbidden liquor, were limited as to what arms they could buy, were punished by twelve days of labor for drunkenness, and were forced to honor the Sabbath. Then in 1675 word went out that the Indian was an enemy unless recognized as truly friendly. No arms at all were to be sold to the Indians.[32] Also no grain, meal, or bread was to be exported without special license as the colony in its support for the war would need all available. This, of course, affected not only Indians but trade in general.[33]

The New England Confederation + called for its member colonies to muster their soldiers. Stamford already had her trained young men, who were prepared to withstand Sir Edmund Andros should he move from New York in a bid to take western Connecticut. Tales of the savagery of the Indians burning homes and killing English families must have stirred up horror in the Stamford households. Jonathan Selleck, now captain, gathered his men and went forth to meet the "common enemy"; he was made captain for Fairfield County, also.[34] At least twenty-two men went to Fairfield and then east to New London by boat or by horse.[35] They saw service for a time in Rhode Island. These young men were:

Abraham Ambler	Thomas Newman
Joseph Bishop	William Penoyer
Benjamin Green	Joseph Scofield
Increase Holly	Jonas Seely
Samuel Hoyt	Obadiah Seely
John Jagger	Benjamin Stevens
Cornelius Jones	David Waterbury
Joseph Jones	John Waterbury
Moses Knap	Daniel Westcott
Thomas Lawrence	

The other military officers, Lt. Jonathan Bell and Ensign Francis Brown, may well have stayed to protect the homefront. Bates and Lt. Bell, Sr., were given the responsibility of strengthening the fortifications along with John Green, Peter Ferris, and Daniel Weed. Most essential was the town stockade, which in March of 1676 was still unfinished.[36]

+ The New England Confederation was established in 1643 and consisted of representatives from the Massachusetts Bay, New Haven, and Hartford. It served especially in times of war to insure united action.

John Thompson, a gunsmith, had been in town, but in 1673 Nathaniel Cross, who had spent much of his youth in Stamford, was sent for to take on repairing arms in Stamford. Possibly he was in Windsor at that time. He was evidently quite willing, for later he was given a house lot and land provided he stay for seven years.[37]

Of the soldiers who took part in the fighting, David Waterbury seems to have shown particular leadership qualities, for he became a lieutenant some years later. Daniel Westcott became a sergeant.[38] Two of the soldiers died in 1676 - Joseph Scofield and Cornelius Jones. Joseph was killed in the war, and Cornelius may have died as a consequence of being a soldier, though this is only surmise. The men were in their twenties and early thirties, their captain being only thirty-five.

It is of interest to note that there were questions about the cause of this war. John Bishop asked his friend Mather to explain "about the original of this unhappy war, how it began, & whether our English were wholly innocent on that account." He stated that it had "proved very difficult, dissatisfying, & uncomfortable to conscientious parents and other Relations to send out their children, & other dear relations unto the war, where many were slain, & all in danger of their lives," if the cause were not justifiable and honorable.[39] He wanted to know the facts. Was he given a satisfactory answer?

Fortunately for Stamford the war was soon over, and the men returned by the end of 1676 to be given grants of land for their service. The town itself could relax: it had a new strong stockade; all its fortifications were in order, and more significantly, the Indian menace in New England was broken for all time. It had been a very bloody war, and a number of towns had been devastated, but not in southwestern Connecticut.

The Stamford town meeting records for the next three years - 1677 to 1680 - reflect a burgeoning growth in adult population and consequently great expansion in land use. Signs were already pointing towards the problem faced by all the early New England towns. Young people could be accommodated only so far, and then the quest would begin for better opportunities in the virgin lands to the northwest and west. The very size of the families meant that a father of many could hardly provide the wherewithal for all of his young. Actually those families that happened to have only two or three children in them were often the ones to prosper. The Bateses had only two children: John, who did very well, and Mary, who married Abraham Ambler, also an only son with one sister; he too became a very well respected leader in the community. Jonathan Bell (with only two sisters) grew up to take over his father's position of importance. Of Richard Law's three children, his son, as we know, did not remain in Stamford, but his two daughters, married to the two Selleck brothers, certainly had enviable positions and well-furnished households. Joseph Theale, son of Nicolas, who also had only one sister, rose to leadership and represented Stamford time and again in the Connecticut Assembly.

During the next twenty years the government of Stamford did its best to accommodate the growing needs for house lots, meadows, and fields. Seventeen (possibly eighteen) house lots were allotted between 1677 and 1680, Stamford bearing in mind Hartford's edict that people should settle close to each other. The new house lots were either west of Mill River or east towards Noroton Hill. Both swamps and more productive land were given out often in return for particular services. Swamps were of value both for the marsh grass and reeds, and for possible farm acreage once drained. Shoresmag Swamp, a little north of East Street and east of North Street extension was given to Joshua Hoyt, Daniel Simkins, Richard Ayres, and Samuel and Abraham Finch, all of whom lived on its borders.[40] The two brothers Samuel and Daniel Weed requested a swamp west of Mill River. Round Swamp (near Shoresmag or Shore Swamp) went to young Obadiah Seely. Service involved being responsible for the various gates used for entering the three center fields and Rocky Neck. Also the floodgate on the river above Northfield had to be monitored.

Several men were given large pieces of land. Richard Law received a tract near the Landing Place from "the going over to Bassett's Island east."[41] Jonathan Selleck (for his service as a soldier) was given land on the west side of the Landing Place beginning at the brook called Hardy's Hole (had Richard Hardy owned it or had he had some adventure there?) and running to the Southfield fence.[42] Mr. Bishop was given eight acres of the common land. Abraham Ambler received land at the east end of town between his own land and that of William Penoyer; he was to allow a driftway down to the Horsepasture.[43] Eleazer Slason got three acres on the west side of Northfield where he was to allow for a highway one and a half rods wide going up to "Clabord Hill".[44]

There are several references to the roads and to efforts to improve them. The Country Road beyond Mill River to the west was to be surveyed and improved. A foot bridge was to be built over Mill River for the benefit of those living on the further side. Another road was run down the west side of Long Neck or Open Neck (in present-day Darien). A common highway was to be established at the east end of town going down to the plains in Eastfield to meet the highway there. (This was probably the road bordering Noroton Cove.)[45]

Sometimes changes in men's boundaries were made to allow for better routes. A set of bars was placed in a strategic place where a side road entered, and it was maintained by a local landowner there.

Since much land was being apportioned at this time and it was recognized by many that landowners, when given the opportunity, would stretch their holdings onto those lands designated as common, firmer laws were passed. In 1678 it was agreed that the land from the bridge by the mill to Hardy's Hole, bordered north by the cowpath and east by the river, was not to be disposed of without the consent of the proprietors.[46] Another tract known as the Sequest common land was laid out across the north of the village from the Noroton River by the Country Road to the great rock at the Mianus River. It passed above the North Field and by Peter Ferris' wolf pit. (Wolves were a constant menace to livestock, and several men had established pits; the trapping of wolves could be profitable as they were subject to a bounty.) The Sequest was to remain common forever and any infringement on its boundaries would be subject to a fine at twenty pounds per acre.[47] Setting up such an area so close to the village appears to us today as remarkably shortsighted; with all the expansion east and west, it would be inevitable that Stamford would expand northwards in a matter of time.

Lastly, more fields and meadows were laid out to the proprietors. At first only those men who had original home lots, or their heirs, were termed proprietors. Later, men who had eight pounds or more in real estate were accepted. A home lot was valued at one pound ten pence so that a man would have to have accrued considerably more acreage than just his home lot to qualify.[48]

In 1677 a list was made of the "meadow men"[49] who had drawn lots for various meadows, such as the newly cleared lands in Runkenheage to the far east or possibly for the land comprising the Oxpasture on the west. Both this land and the Horsepasture were laid out at this time. Fifty lots were drawn, as detailed in the following table.

Lots Drawn in 1677

1. Benjamin Hoyt	26. William Crissy
2. Francis Brown	27. Daniel Weed, Jonas & wd. & Samuel
3. John Holmes	28. John Bates

Lots Drawn in 1677 (continued)

4. William Potter

5. Peter Ferris

6. Mr. Holly

7. Cornelius Jones

8. John Miller

9. Joshua Hoyt

10. George Slason

11. ____

12. Samuel Finch

13. Joseph Garnsey

14. Stephen Clason

15. John Slason

16. Edmund Lockwood

17. ____ ten

18. Jonathan Waterbury

19. ____

20. Seelys & Jonathan Miller

21. Mr. Bishop

22. John Waterbury

23. Wd. Knap

24. ____ lason

25. Isaac Finch

29. John Green

30. David Waterbury

31. Hardy, Austin ?

32. Joseph Theale

33. Daniel Scofield

34. Smiths

35. Daniel & Thomas Newman

36. Samuel Dean

37. Richard Scofield

38. ____

39. widdow ____

40. ____

41. Obadiah Stevens

42. Samuel Hoyt

43. Lt. Bell

44. ____

45. ____ Scofield

46. Stephen Holmes

47. ____ Penoyer

48. ____

49. Thomas Lawrence

50. ____ Ambler

It is unfortunate that twelve names are missing from this list because of the damaged Town Meeting book, but most of them can be readily supplied. John and Jonathan Selleck acted as a team in their land dealings and so were probably on the list as No. 11. No. 17 was probably Clement Buxton; No. 24 Eleazer Slason and No. 50 Richard Ambler. No. 47 was Robert (or his son, William) or Thomas Penoyer. Other names that are missing are: Richard Law, Samuel Holly, John Gold, John and Jeremiah Jagger, and William Clemence. Widow Knap was Caleb's widow and widow _____ could have been either John Pettit's or Richard Webb's wife.

From all of this one can judge, therefore, that there must have been between fifty-five and sixty households in Stamford at this time. This figure allows for the men who were either poor or newly married. If one also allows for an average of five members per family, this would bring the population of Stamford by 1680 to three hundred people. What a close, extended-family community this must have been with so many siblings, cousins, and step relationships. Naturally all the men knew each other well as they banded together in diverse groups to work as soldiers, field clearers, repairers of roads, builders. Town meetings must have been lively with the participants voicing their views as friends, and even as foes. They would have known each other's attitudes well.

And the women, though largely busy within the home at the never-remitting household tasks, would have cared for each other's children, borrowed necessary items, and joined little groups for sociability and gossip. Little that went on escaped their eyes.

One tends to forget that these people lived far more in the outdoors than we do today. They also were far more affected by natural phenomena: earthquakes and thunderstorms could presage ominous events to come. In 1678 John Bishop wrote:

> "As touching the Earthquake lately in these parts, I can speak to that as being sensible thereof, & many others in this Town, and other Townes also perceived the same; though more westward of us it was more perceived, & more eastward, lesse. It was on an evening after the Sabbath viz. 12m. 3. 77. Likewise on 4m. 20, 78, a like noise was heard here by myselfe & many others, who took it to be an Earthquake, rather than thunder, considering circumstances, though the terrae-mocon not so perceptible. On the last day, same month, here was a violent storme of hail in several plantacons, one west & others east of us, that did much damage as its said, & I do verily believe, though I forbear to mencon the quantity of that

hail & the effects of it, because I canot fully believe all that's said of it. At Stamford it was only a storme of wind & rain, & that but short." He goes on to speak of a "plentiful, sober & soaking rain, that sweetly refreshed the earth & revived its dying product."[50]

This was after a period of drought. Clearly Bishop himself took these events in his stride, but the weaker members of society must have run together in distress and fear.

One very shocking event that set many tongues clicking happened in 1676. Its impact resounded even to Hartford. Boston, too, learned of it as described by John Bishop to Increase Mather. "An horrid murder committed among us, here at Stamford. A brother killing his own dear sister, a very good woman that loved him dearly, but was ill requited, killed her with an ax, mauling & mashing her head to many pieces, in a barbarous & bloody maner."[51] This man was Benjamin Tuttle, who was twenty-eight at the time. His sister Sarah had married George Slason's oldest son John and was the mother of four, ranging in age from twelve to four. The case was referred to the Court of Assistants in Hartford, and Benjamin was sentenced to death by hanging.[52] Probably today the young man would be pronounced mentally deranged - if one can judge by his treatment of Sarah's corpse.

Another case that came before the Hartford Court was one concerning divorce. There were few such cases. However, Sarah Waterbury, who had married Zachariah Dibble in 1666, wished to "break the conjugal tie" in 1672. She evidently presented a strong case with good witnesses as she claimed that not only was Zachariah guilty of "cruelly beating and pinching her" but also he had deserted her for several years. The divorce was granted.[53]

Several well-established families suffered losses during this decade of the 1670s. It is surprising to read in one of John Bishop's letters of the rampant sickness in 1676. He stated "we have been all down, & some of us dangerously sick, but graciously restored [except for his wife]. We buried 6 [?] in one week in our little town; neer 20 this spring; about an 100 sick at once; besides sundry slain in the war."[54] One wonders about this latter statement as only two possible soldiers who met their deaths were previously noted; however, others from Greenwich may have met the same fate.

When Rebecca Bishop died in 1679, the Reverend John mentioned his loss very succinctly to Increase Mather: "It hath pleased Him who is the disposer of all, to lay me under bereavemt of my dear yoke-fellow, a great breach upon my poor family, myself & children. But it is the Lord, & that calls to silence & submission."[55] John remarried a year or two later.

Other prominent citizens who died during this period were Robert Bates and his wife, the brothers Daniel and Richard Scofield, Francis Holmes, William Newman, Richard Webb, Jonas Weed, the second John Pettit, and Caleb Knap. Among the women were Unica Knap, who had been married three times, and Francis Bell's daughter, Rebecca Tuttle. Jonathan Bell's wife also died, and he remarried a year later. One man, who perhaps fortunately remains unidentified, died in 1679. John Bishop described the circumstance. "... a notorious drunkard who (in the pursuance of that lust & seeking more drink, but being denyed as having too much before) went forth in the night & was found in the morning drownd dead in the mill river."[56]

Chapter Five: 1680-1689

In 1680 the Privy Council in England sent a questionnaire to its various colonies in America. Connecticut, upon receiving it, set to work to answer in as much detail as she was able to discover. The answers to the twenty-seven questions shed some light on how the inhabitants viewed their way of life and their resources at this time. They represented themselves as "poor people in this wilderness" who made their meager living by laboring "in tilling the soil."[1] Of course, it could be claimed that the use of the term "wilderness" was primarily adopted from the Bible, as it was apt; John Bishop also used it in a letter. "The Lord is proceeding stil to humble his poor wildernes people...."[2] The results of their labor had been disappointing as there were "blastings and mildews" in the grain crops and worms in the peas. The land itself is described as "mountainous, full of rocks, swamps, hills and vales" with almost all arable land already taken up. One wonders where the Connecticut mountains really were, especially as northwestern Connecticut was not settled until the 1730s. Certainly, though, in Stamford men did struggle with rocky terrain and swamps.

In spite of this rather dreary picture, one does note a counterbalancing pride of achievement in that Hartford said there were twenty-six small towns, one with two churches, and then presented a full list of the produce used for trade. These were: wheat, peas, rye, barley, Indian corn, pork, beef, wool, hemp, flax, cider, perry (a pear juice), tar, deal boards, pipe staves, and horses. The deal boards were of pine or oak; these woods plus spruce were also used for masts.

Some of these commodities were ones that the Stamford men were engaged in producing. That very year the townsmen rated the produce to be gathered for the benefit of Mr. Bishop as 1/3 summer wheat at four shillings sixpence, 1/3 pork at three and a quarter shillings per pound, and 1/3 either of Indian corn at two shillings sixpence per bushel or wheat at three shillings per bushel.[3] These, therefore, were Stamford's main commodities. Hartford stated that what was exported went mainly to Boston to trade for clothing, which was very expensive. There was some trade also with New York. The questionnaire fails to point out, though, that recently trade with both Boston and New York had been seriously interrupted (in 1678) because of smallpox in both towns; Connecticut had been obliged, therefore, to forbid entrance of ships from those places without special license.[4] Some ships did carry produce to Barbados and Jamaica in return for sugar, cotton, wool, rum, "and some money." Also ships went occasionally to Madeira and Fayal in the Azores for wine. No longer did they have to go to Virginia for tobacco, for enough was now grown locally. All of this suggests a certain well-established economy, though Hartford does point out that no foreign vessels had appeared in her eleven ports. "Standford" is referred to as having a good tidal harbor where vessels of thirty or forty tons might enter. She also had one pink of eighty tons and a sloop of ten tons. One would presume that both of these belonged to the Selleck brothers, and one was probably the *Brothers Adventure* listed as theirs on a trip to Barbados in 1679.[5]

Most of the remaining information in the answers to the questionnaire dealt with the people themselves and with the military provisions. In 1679 for the whole of Connecticut there were 1507 men; this figure included all those aged sixteen to sixty. It was noted that there were about twenty merchants and the rest were considered planters. There were only about thirty servants and slaves - three or four Blacks from Barbados being brought in per year and sold for about twenty-two pounds each. During this period there were some slaves in Stamford. Robert Bates mentioned his two, Thomas and Meriam, in his will, in which he freed them.[6] John Jagger had a young slave named Harry who was to be freed when John's son Jonathan was twenty-three.[7] Sarah Selleck also freed Jack, a faithful slave of her husband, who, regardless, continued as a servant within the family.[8] As far as Indians were concerned, Hartford stated that there were about 500 fighting-aged Indians in Connecticut, but little trade was engaged in with the Indians as they no longer had an abundance of furs.

The last part of Hartford's response answered the request for information on the position of religion in the Connecticut towns. Ministers preached twice on Sundays and sometimes on Lecture days, and the masters of families took care to conduct religious exercises also. The inhabitants were mostly Congregational, either strict ones or "large" (others being Presbyterians, Seventh Dayers, and Quakers).

It was during this same year of 1680 that several men saw opportunity for gaining good fertile lands in the very north of Stamford in what was called the Hop Grounds. Stamford encouraged the use of these lands, and as a result a deed was drawn up. The Indians under Catonah readily signed over the land in return for "twelve coats, six blankets, two yards of red broadcloth, six yards of cotton and a quantity of wampum."[9] Twenty-two men, most of them in their twenties or early thirties, became the proprietors of what was recognized by Hartford in 1682 as a new settlement called Bedford.[10] The men involved were:

Richard Ambler,# and his son, Abraham Ambler
Richard Ayres
William Clark, son of Samuel who had gone to
Long Island in the very early days
John Cross and his brother, Nathaniel
John Green
John Holmes
Daniel Jones,# a newcomer
Jonathan Kilborn, nephew of Mrs. Law
John Miller
Thomas Penoyer#
Jonathan Pettit
Jonas Seely#
Eleazer Slawson
Benjamin Stephens, and his brother, Joseph#
Joseph Theale
David Waterbury#
Nicolas Webster#
Daniel Weed,# and his brother, Samuel
John Westcott,# the brother of Sergeant Daniel

# denotes men who returned to Stamford

Richard Ambler and John Green, who were about seventy, probably were the leaders of the group of new settlers.

Stamford failed to recognize that by granting neighborliness to those in Bedford in the form of any disputed lands, she was later to lose the large northern section of her bounds. In 1683 Bedford and land known later as the "Oblong" were turned over to New York by Connecticut in return for clear claim to Greenwich and Stamford.[11] Bedford inhabitants were unhappy over this, and thirteen families did move away, nine returning to Stamford. Rye, too, was turned over to New York, and though Captain Jonathan Selleck and his men marched to Rye in 1697 to try to regain it, they failed.[12]

Within Stamford expansion progressed rapidly during the 1680s. To the west of Mill River about fifteen house lots had now been laid out. The Clasons, the two Crosses, Peter June and Henry Rich, who were two newcomers to Stamford, Mr. Holly, and Jonathan Selleck each had lots there. Peter Ferris bought Eliphalet Jones' lot, and the Webb sons began living across the river near enough to the mill but away from it. Daniel Weed's ordinary over there must have been appreciated, as was the foot bridge, the fastest way into town and carefully maintained.

The northern extension of North Street also saw more break-up of the common land with Richard Ayres, Samuel and Abraham Finch, Abraham Ambler, John Scofield, Jeremiah Jagger, Ephraim Stevens and others settling there; in all a total of about twelve lots were given out.

The east end along East Street to the Noroton River saw a plethora of development. With the opening up of lands as far as the Norwalk line (with the fields as Noroton Neck, Long Neck, and Runkenkeag) the Country Road became increasingly traversed. The presence of four rivers, Stony Brook (later called Goodwives), Tokeneke, Pine, and Five Mile River with their mouths opening on Long Island Sound offered great future prospects. So far, however, the Noroton River served as a bound for Stamford's house lots. The major owners in this area were Stephen and Joseph Bishop near the Eastfield Gate, and the young Stevens and Greens and Abraham Ambler. John Crissy, William Turney, William Clark, Jonathan Kilborn, and Nicolas Webster also had house lots along towards Noroton Hill.

Several people with an eye to the future and an eagerness to advance their own interests offered new facilities. Chief among these was Joshua Hait. Not only was he involved in establishing the sawmill at Five Mile River but also he was running his cider mill in town for which he requested more land; he then requested the town's permission to build a dam at Toilsome Brook outside the North Field to service a fulling mill as well as an oatmeal mill. The town accepted.[13] A fulling mill[+] was particularly needed as before there was no mill to handle the making of cloth. Joshua's suggestion of having a mill totally devoted to oats was seen as a boon also. Specialization was beginning to be evident. The following year Joshua requested the right to build a windmill on the rock between his yard and the field. Was this for his cider business?[14]

+ A fulling mill functioned rather like a grist mill except that the water power drove great pounding blocks onto the loose woven cloth. The cloth was soaked in vats of water and solvent to shrink and clean it. The whole process was noisy, messy, and smelly.

Richard Webb, who died in 1676, had left the grist mill on Mill River to his oldest son, Joseph. Eight years later, Joseph died, leaving his wife with a young son and four younger daughters. Richard's second son, Joshua, had been devised land in Huntington, Long Island, but he seemingly did not wish to settle there.[15] Instead he applied to the town in 1681 to build and run a sawmill and lumber yard on Stony Brook.[16] This venture, however, proved to be a failure, for there was insufficient timber in the area. The following year the town agreed that Joshua could build a mill on the Noroton River instead.[17]

Richard's two other sons, Caleb and Samuel, may have been trying to help their brother Joseph's widow, but in the late 1680s the grist mill on Mill River was not functioning efficiently. The town was dissatisfied.

In 1688 Peter Ferris and Lt. Jonathan Bell studied the enterprise with the widow Hannah and Daniel Westcott, the overseer. It was decided that the mill should be appraised and then sold. Jonas Weed and a man from Greenwich, John Marshall (who signed with his mark only), made the appraisal and set the value at seventeen pounds.[18] Therefore, the following December Hannah, now John Finch's wife, and Daniel Westcott sold the mill to the town for twenty pounds.[19]

It was recognized that there was potential for another mill on Mill River - at its mouth. The sawmill at Five Mile River was a long way off and the Noroton one was in its infancy; so it was decided in 1686 to build a tidal mill below the Oxpasture Gate on the west side of the river. John Selleck evidently sponsored it, but a committee was to check on the town's willingness to support such a venture.[20]

Another man who was interested in mills and in building was David Waterbury, who gained lands in the Noroton Cove area. He and John Selleck, in order to gain more meadows, decided to build a dam there, a dam which could take ten years in the building.[21] One wonders where it was placed. Was it built along the east and west sides of the Cove to prevent flooding, or was it built at the northern end? David was busily becoming established in that area generally. He was given the right to mow the field areas on the Noroton Islands, but in 1685 he was released from paying rent for the privilege as they were not productive.[22] David had his eye on other Cove lands as well. Once the Horsepasture had been divided up to private ownership in 1677, there was no longer a use for the pound at the end of Noroton Cove (another pound for horses was now to be built in the woods).[23] As a consequence, people who owned land in the Cove area began accruing more. In 1686 Stephen Bishop, for example, requested a small cove at the mouth of the Pound, a cove still known as Bishop's Cove.[24] Before long David Waterbury gained the island on the west side of the Cove known for years as Waterbury's Island. It is now the little promontory called Weed Circle.[25]

A new venture began developing at the juncture of Noroton River and Noroton Cove - a shipbuilding business. In 1687 "Mr. Mills, carpenter," requested a house lot on the east side of Noroton River "above the building place."[26] He had become well known to the town as he had been involved in building the new meeting house.[27] House lots east of the river began to be laid out thereafter.

A ship builder, George Phillips, from Middletown was to be welcomed with his family if he wished to settle in Stamford.[28] He built "the good briggandine called the 'Friends Adventure'...now riding in Norrowton River."[29] It was a two-masted vessel of seventy-six tons and was sold by Phillips in 1688 to Daniel Weed for Ŀ 326.[30] The "friends" with Daniel Weed were Lt. Jonathan Bell, Abraham Ambler, Joshua Hoyt, Samuel Webb, Richard Scofield, plus the two Arnold brothers, John the blacksmith and Joseph, called mariner, of Boston. The Arnolds had very recently (1685 and 1687) been accepted as inhabitants, presumably to engage in the shipbuilding enterprise. The six highly respected men of Stamford had an unexpected adventure with their new acquisition. There was a bitter falling-out with the Arnolds. In the Town Meeting book it is stated that work on the rigging by Joseph Arnold and others on the rigging.[31] Joseph, believing himself master of the ship, had bought the rigging on his own. Affairs reached such a state that the Arnolds sold out their 4/13s interest in the "hull with all her masts, yards, pumps and blocks except the iron works" to Daniel Weed, who turned it over to the Sellecks.[32] John Arnold returned to Boston; Joseph went off to sea and never returned. The Court at Hartford endeavored to settle the accounts in February of 1690 as to who owed whom, all to be paid in wheat and Indian corn at the going rate.[33] However, John Arnold appealed to the Superior Court, which demanded the presence of four of the owners at the hearing. The Stamford men seem to have vindicated themselves, though final settlement of the case is not recorded.

To turn our attention once again to Stamford's principal concerns in the town meetings, concerns about the public buildings, use of land, and livestock, one notes that there were major changes being made in the 1680s to the three town buildings.

The new meetinghouse had proved successful, but the ever-changing population required new seating of the inhabitants in December of 1679. This was carried out by trustworthy and upstanding churchmen: Captain Jonathan Selleck, Lt. Francis Bell and his son, Lt. Jonathan, Joseph Theale, and Joseph Garnsey. They seated the members once again by dignity, age, and estate.[34] A sign of how much the population was changing is to be seen in the fact that again in 1689 a new seating had to be made. Also, space was at a premium. It was decided that more room could be gained by moving the pulpit to the north with the seats arranged to face it.[35] Outside, the fortification around the meetinghouse was removed, the wood being turned over to Mr. Bishop whose home was close by.[36] However, the ammunition held always in readiness by the town was now to be stored in the meetinghouse, Francis Bell being in charge of seeing it done.[37] Undoubtedly the ammunition previously had been placed in some part of the fortifications - now deemed unnecessary. Stephen Bishop, who was released from "keeping school," agreed to sweep the meetinghouse.[38] Mr. Bishop's oldest son was proving useful to the community!

Construction of the townhouse seems to have been moving along very slowly or else a new one was being built in 1681. Joseph Garnsey and Daniel Weed were to finish the work there.[39] In 1683 the building was ready for the stone chimneys, and a committee was set up to call out men to do this.[40] Four years later John Arnold made a bid to hire the townhouse, and the town initially offered to sell it plus agreeing to make it habitable. However, a month later both parties nulled the idea, and the town declared that the townhouse should be turned over to the church in perpetuity.[41] Interestingly, though, it was eventually bought by Ebenezer Bishop in 1694.[42]

The schoolhouse also received some attention, for in 1685 it was agreed that a stone chimney should be constructed and the building made comfortable.[43] Surely the children must have been grateful for that! Was Stephen Bishop their teacher for awhile? In 1687 a tantalizing reference is made to the schoolmaster - it was agreed that he should be paid upon hiring, but unfortunately no name is given.[44] Clearly it was being recognized that the new generation was growing up isolated from the rich culture brought from England. John Bishop, as he wrote in 1687 and again in 1688, was concerned: "... we have cause to fear the worst, for our unworthy walking, & that contempt of the Gospel and Gospel-libertys so long continued to us....Oh what will become of N. E. (New England) shortly? The rising graon (generation) the ungodly posterity of godly parents, pious and precious ones, in any such I mean, whose offspring are greatly degenerate."[45]

Since new lands were coming under cultivation and fields and meadows and swamps laid out to individuals, it stands to

reason that livestock was becoming increasingly evident and important. The biggest development was in the number of sheep. In 1681 it was ruled that the sheep were to be brought to the town lot or common at the meetinghouse where Ensign Brown and Jonas Weed as sheepmasters that year were to be in attendance every sixth day at sunset to let those gathered out into pasture land. The rams for the time being were to be kept in the town lot.[46]

Cattle and horses were also subject to new regulations. Each year it was stated that a cowkeeper should be employed "if one can be found," to care for all cows over two years old. The bulls to be used by the town were those of Peter Ferris, Daniel Westcott, and Nicolas Webster.[47] In 1682 Lt. Jonathan Bell was made horse brander, and he and Richard Hardy were given authority to sell "jades" or unclaimed horses on a certain afternoon in the pound.[48] Now that the Horsepasture and the pound at Noroton Cave were to be abandoned and a new pound made in the woods, a real effort was made to round up the jades.

Both cattle and swine were proving troublesome in the winter wheat fields and were made poundable. However, it was decided that swine could still roam at large, not subject to ringing or yoking.[49]

What can one learn about the people themselves in the 1680s? Certain references in the various records do allow for some knowledge of individuals. An event of considerable excitement and rejoicing for the village took place in 1684. This was the marriage of Mr. Bishop's daughter Rebecca. The bridegroom was the Reverend Joseph Whiting of Long Island, a man twenty-one years her senior whose first wife had died. Very recently, in 1984, John Bishop IV of Boston found a sermon of John Bishop that had been printed in Boston in 1687. It is truly exciting to learn of this work! It allows us to see John Bishop in the full light of his life's work where he exhibits both his learning and his warm concern for people. This sermon was preached at the marriage ceremony and was evidently so acclaimed that arrangements were made to have it published. John Bishop modestly stated that "none can readily entertain meaner thoughts of it than himself." The sermon was entitled "A Good Wife" and likened such a one to "a Fruitful Vine."[50] Interestingly, on the title page, Stamford even at this date appears as "Stanford" as it does so often in the early records. For us the sermon does not make for enjoyable reading, larded as it is with Biblical references and some Hebrew and Latin. The theme is that a wife of a godly man is like a vine; she smells sweet in her way of life, offers shade or comfort, and gives fruit or is a productive person. She must also be tended as a vine by being nurtured and sheltered from harm by her sturdy husband. Surely this sermon reflects Bishop's long and rich union with his wife, Rebecca, and also the few years with his second wife, who had died a year or so before. One little personal reference suggests Bishop's own way of life: "When the Good-man comes in weary from his work, Sweating, melted out of the field; or comes down out of his Study almost 'exanimated'; having his spirits exhausted and drunk up," how a good wife can refresh him.[51]

Most of all, this sermon exhibits the wealth of learning and care for Christian culture that John Bishop stood for. He perceived all too clearly that ties to both church and scholarly achievement were being sadly neglected by Stamford's rising population, but his own steadfast nature was an example to all.

In spite of the fact that all of the Fairfield Court records have been lost (records which, as in the case of Plymouth, can allow one to discover many personal details about individuals), one can piece together a few interesting bits of information about some of Stamford's inhabitants from the town and probate records.

Let us look first at what we can learn of the Bell family in the 1680s. This was to prove a catastrophic decade for that family because of the deaths that took place. It has already been noted that Francis' daughter, Rebecca Tuttle, and Jonathan's wife died in the 1670s. Then in 1684 Francis' wife, Rebecca, died. A list was made of all her linens and clothing, not, as has been suggested, because of Francis' desire to show the community how rich she was but because her personal effects were to be divided between her daughter, Mary Hait, and her deceased daughter's family.[52] The list is given below:

Inventory of Rebecca Bell

Her Clothes as Apprised by Goodwife Slason & Mrs. Holly

Item	Ł s p
A red broad cloth petticoat and a red tamy petticoat	3-10-0
A fine cloth westcot a gray serge petticoat	3-0-0
A serge gown a red serge wescot	3-0-0
A gray serge strait bodied gown a short loose coat	3-6-0

A mohair petticoat a homespun gown almost new	3-0-0
A serge green apron tamy green apron	1-0-0
A blue apron 3 pieces of old silk	0-7-0
A caster hat an old caster hat	1-4-0
Dresings 3 caps and seven neckhandkerchers	3-2-0
3 single hankerchers & nine caps	1-9-0
1 white cap 14 coifs 4 headbands	0-12-0
2 old neckcloths a pair of fore sleeves & a coyle	0-2-0
5 long linen neckcloths 2 black caps	0-4-6
1 fine homespun shift 1 hollon apron 1 linen apron	1-8-0
1 linen shift 1 linen shift	0-18-0
1 cotton shift 1 cotton shift	0-18-0
1 hollon shift 1 linen shift	1-6-0
1 new cotton shift	0-16-0
1 pair of fine sheets	2-0-0
1 pair of fine sheets to Rebecca Tuttle on ye island	2-0-0

by order of my father entered as it was prised as above said & by the same persons divided this June 11 1684

Jonathan Bell, recorder

In summary, Rebecca had 4 petticoats, 3 gowns, 2 waist-coats, 1 coat, 6 aprons, 2 hats, 15 caps, 15 neckcloths, 4 headbands, 15 coifs, 3 handkerchiefs, 8 shifts, and 4 fine sheets. She does seem to have been plentifully supplied. Some words that might not be familiar today are "tamy" or tammy, a kind of woolen cloth that was often glazed, "castor" which was either heavy broadcloth or beaver, and "hollon" or holland, a fine quality of linen.

Francis Bell survived his wife by only five years and presumably during those years he was well cared for by his son Jonathan, whose home was on the same lot and who had an ever-growing family of three children by his first wife and five living children by his second wife. Francis' inventory is not exceptional as he had probably given away many of his belongings. It amounted to £317. One does note that he owned leather and kid - a suggestion of his grandson's later tanning and shoemaking business. He also owned seven books, three of them Bibles.[53]

Jonathan's own family was experiencing considerable sorrow also with the deaths of three babies, and little Rebecca, whom Francis said he had brought up, dying in 1689 at age twelve.

In 1681 Mr. John Holly died at age sixty-three. Stamford was stunned to lose their long-serving town treasurer. For almost forty years he had served his community well in a great variety of positions, from marshal and collector of excise tax to townsman, delegate, and commissioner. His family proved to be a strong and flourishing one. Holly provided his sons Samuel, John, Increase, and Elisha with homes and lands of their own, John and Jonathan receiving their parents' home lot on South Street with Samuel's place adjoining on the south.[54] Five sons and four married daughters survived him, as did his wife Mary.

The third of Stamford's leading triumvirate, Richard Law, died in 1687 or 1688 though there is no record of this death. He did sign a deed giving his effects over to the Selleck sons-in-law in return for care in his old age. The Sellecks agreed that they "shall keep and maintain him" with all things necessary "condusing to the comfort of his natural life so long as he shall live."[55] His wife, Margaret Kilbourne, had died a few years previously. His son, Jonathan, who had disappointed him by moving to Milford, Connecticut, was well established there. Richard was accompanied in his old age, therefore, by his two daughters and their husbands, the Selleck brothers, plus nine grandchildren. The whole family was soon to face a real worry, a worry that was to last through long years. John Selleck, the sea captain, went forth in 1689, was captured by the French, and never was heard from again.[56] All the family affairs and all the business affairs the two brothers had shared were now entirely Jonathan's responsibility. He had a heavy burden, for both men had previously held much land in common as well as their wide business interests. Evidently, if one accepts the Earl of Bellomont's indictment, Selleck's mercantile enterprises had a shady side to them. The Earl wrote to the English Lords of Trade in 1700:

> One Major Selleck...has a ware house close to the sea that runs between the mainland and Nassau (Long Island). That man does us great mischief with his ware house, for he receives abundance of goods from our vessels, and the merchants afterwards take their opportunity of running them into this town (New York). Major Selleck received at least Ł10,000 worth of treasure and East India goods, brought by one Clarke of this town from Kid's sloop, and lodged with Selleck."[57]

Virtually all the older generation had left the scene by 1690 and the second generation had taken control. The men of Stamford, in addition to the three above, who died during the 1680s were:

Francis Brown 1685	Obadiah Seely 1680
Jonathan Clason 1685	(John Selleck 1689?)
William Crissy 1684	Henry Smith 1687
Joseph Garnsey 1688	John Waterbury 1688
Richard Hardy 1683	Joseph Webb 1684
John Jagger 1684	Nicolas Webster 1687
John Ogden 1682	John Weed 1689
William Potter 1685	

With the deaths of Francis Bell, Henry Smith, and Richard Law, not one of the first settlers of Stamford remained, and the only man left of the old guard from the 1641-1642 period was George Slason; he died in 1695 at the age of seventy-nine.

If one studies the inventories of these men, one notices that most of them contain practically the same basic possessions as those of John Whitmore's, for example. However, in the case of John Jagger, who died when he was in his early forties and whose wife had presumably predeceased him, there is a very full inventory.[58] His household effects included several beds (for his five children), some chairs, five chests, and a cupboard; no tables are mentioned though there must have been some. A few luxury items are listed, such as a flower jug, a quart glass bottle, a razor, a brass candlestick, a pair of scissors, a chamber pot, and a silver cup. Jagger's cooper's tools appear on the list. As to livestock, he had the usual spread from oxen to swine plus sixteen sheep.

The really noteworthy change in these later inventories is in the listing of real estate. Since, as we have seen, fields had been laid out continuously over the past twenty years, men accrued small lots scattered all over Stamford. John Jagger had eighteen pieces valued at Ł337. These were located in "Shiphand," the North Field, the South Field, the Cove, the Oxpasture, the great pasture, "Runcanhage," the Horsepasture, and the "casie" (causeway - probably Rocky Neck).

It has already been noted that details about the lives of Stamford's early inhabitants are meager at best. (There are a few unimportant references during the 1680s to several young men's being fined for drunkenness and disorderly conduct - Joseph Turney, John Austin, Thomas Matthews, and John Lockwood; Samuel Hardy was fined for entertaining people.) So, too, when one turns to the colonial records of the Court in Hartford for any references to individuals from Stamford, aside from notations of the deputies to the Court, there is little else. Stamford, it seems, was far from the scene of action in the eyes of the central government of the colony. The principal deputies from Stamford for the 1680s should be noted, though there are no surprises: these were Mr. Abraham Ambler, Ensign John Bates, Lieutenant Jonathan Bell, Captain Jonathan Selleck, and Joshua Hoyt.[+] The commissioners were Richard Law through 1686(?), Lieutenant Jonathan Bell, and Captain Jonathan Selleck.

In the mid-1680s the Colony of Connecticut became increasingly aware of Sir Edmund Andros' efforts to enforce his authority over the colonies of New England. It was decided, therefore, by the Court at Hartford to issue patents to the proprietors of the individual plantations within its jurisdiction in order to formalize land ownership. Accordingly, on May 26, 1685 a patent was issued to ten men in Stamford who were the principal landowners and leaders. The list is, for the most part, an obvious one in light of this study. The proprietors were: the Reverend John Bishop, Richard Law, Captain Jonathan Selleck, Captain John Selleck, Lieutenant Francis Bell, Lieutenant Jonathan Bell, Ensign John Bates, Abraham Ambler, Peter Ferris, and Joshua Hoyt.[59]

In 1686 Andros became governor of the Dominion of New England. He took up residence in Boston and systematically tried to force the individual colonial governments into his jurisdiction. In 1688 no meetings of the Hartford legislature were recorded as

----

+ About this time several of the Hoyt family were being called Hait. For convenience I am using Hoyt throughout.

Andros' central control had superseded it. The only reflection of this situation in the Stamford town records is a statement in 1689: the corn that had been stored at Samuel Hoyt's by order of Sir Edmund Andros would now be distributed to the inhabitants who had gathered it; Hoyt was to receive payment for his "damages."[60]

Very fortuitously the so-called Glorious Revolution in England took place at the end of 1688 with the abdication of James II. William of Orange and his wife Mary (daughter of James II) came to the throne. Immediately, New England acted; James' righthand man, the "tyrant" Andros, was seized in Boston and cast into prison. Following a short stay, he was returned to England.

Thereafter each colony was quick to restore its individual government. Hartford must have been particularly relieved as the legislators there had refused to give up their charter when Andros traveled from Boston to take it. (It was hidden, as was later told, in the famous Charter Oak.) All of the Connecticut towns must have rejoiced to have had the lowering clouds of suspicion and disfavor removed.

Chapter Six: 1690-1700

Soon after the accession of William and Mary to the throne of England, William gathered a formidable group of European allies in an effort to combat the growing power of France. The resulting war lasted from 1689 to 1697 and inevitably spread to America, where it was known as King William's War. The Colony of Connecticut, finding herself very open to attack by the French and Indian forces on her northwest, hastily began preparations for war. Real fear developed in 1690 when Schenectady was subjected to a devastating massacre.[1] Stamford, too, called out her men to rebuild the fortifications and prepare her citizens.

However, as the years passed, the course of the war moved farther and farther to the north, no longer a menace to Stamford. In 1695 the fort was dismantled and the wood was sold to Stephen Clason for seventeen shillings and sixpence. "The gates, wheels of the great guns, and woodwork for the guns" were sold to Nathaniel Cross (the gunsmith who was, of course, interested in acquiring them) and Jonathan Holly for five shillings and sixpence.[2]

It is strange to think that Stamford became involved in the witchcraft furor of 1692. But Stamford, unlike Salem, retained its sanity over it. There is no hint of the matter in the Stamford town records, and in the Hartford records there is only a reference to three Stamford men who served on the juries for the trial of Elizabeth Clason; these were Peter Ferris, Jonas Weed, and Eleazer Slason.[3] It was the Fairfield Court that was the center of action. Again, since all those records were lost, we might never have known of the case. However, thanks to the diligent research of Mr. Ronald Marcus and to the Wyllys papers, which contained a bundle marked "Trials for Witchcraft," we gain a full account.[4]

Sergeant Daniel Westcott happened to have a maid called Katherine Branch, who was subject to epileptic fits; these admittedly do give rise to feelings of awe and fear in those who witness them. She, finding herself the center of some attraction, began blaming her predicament on Elizabeth Clason, wife of Stephen and a woman in her sixties. The Westcotts and the Clasons lived near each other west of the Mill River.

Abigail Westcott and Elizabeth Clason had had a falling out over the weight of some flax and had kept up the quarrel. It was natural, accordingly, for Abigail's maid to point her finger at Mrs. Clason. Katherine's fabricated tale of cats and weird women and her shrieks and fits finally prompted Daniel Westcott to take action. First, he called in Sarah Bates, the estimable Ensign John's wife. She, a midwife, served as a doctor, there being none at all in Stamford till the 1700s.[5] Katherine, not responding to treatment, began enlarging the number of witches, though both Abigail and Sarah doubted her tales. In fact, Lydia Penoyer stated later in court that her aunt Abigail said that Katherine couldn't be believed at all and that none of those named could be witches.

One can imagine the excitement in Stamford. Here they had a case like those that were going on in Salem! In May Elizabeth was examined for witch's marks on her body but none was found on her although another accused woman of Fairfield (Mercy Disborough) did have suspicious marks. Both women were imprisoned in Fairfield. Captain Jonathan Selleck, who had become Stamford's leading spokesman, in the wake of his father-in-law, undertook to examine Katherine Branch more closely. She was brought to his home where the very elderly John Bishop and the minister from Norwalk joined in the questioning. The case was considered serious, for not only did the church condemn witches but also the Connecticut Book of Laws stated, "If any man or woman bee a Witch, that is, hath or consulteth with a familliar spirritt, they shall bee put to death."[6] The examiners tended to believe the maid and endeavored to have her reveal other witches. Very naturally she played up the situation. On leaving with Selleck's Indian maid, she fell into another fit so that Jonathan's son, John, and his nephew, David, had to carry her back.

One wonders how Elizabeth Clason survived her summer ordeal in Fairfield. In June she had submitted to the water test and with hands and feet cross-bound had "boyed up like a corck."[7] This was deemed by many to prove that she was guilty. In September the Fairfield Court was convened and issued an indictment: "Elizabeth Clauson...thou deserveth to die" as having had "familiarity with Satan."[8]

In court Abraham Finch, Jr., David Selleck, and Ebenezer Bishop testified that strange witch-like happenings had occurred at Daniel Westcott's house. However, Eleazer Slawson and Clement Burton had the courage to pronounce Elizabeth Clason a woman of peace.

Stephen, her husband, encouraged by their many friends in Stamford, presented a most unusual document signed by seventy-six inhabitants. It supported the view that Elizabeth was an upstanding woman in their eyes. The upshot was that the jury, after much deliberation, was unable to reach a verdict. So both women were returned to jail.

On October 28 a special court was convened at Fairfield. No doubt the horrifying scandal of the Massachusetts trials had sobered people. Connecticut wished to be careful. New personal examinations of the two women were carried out. Mercy Disborough was pronounced guilty by the new jury but was thereafter reprieved. Elizabeth, thanks probably to the support of so many in Stamford, was declared innocent. One can imagine her homecoming, her welcome as she set foot in Stamford once again and entered her home to rejoice with her husband and children and grandchildren. One can't help wondering what eventually happened to the unfortunate Katherine Branch and how the Clasons and the Westcotts faced each other thereafter.

We should pause for a look at the famous document involved in this story. How many of Stamford's inhabitants are represented? Are there any significant omissions? At least two-thirds of the householders are represented. The major omissions are five or so of the Holly family, David and Jonathan Waterbury, the Reverend John Bishop, and his son Joseph, Captain Jonathan Selleck, and Nathaniel Cross. One has to allow, of course, for sickness or for being away from Stamford at the time. Certainly it was quite clear to everyone that the witch trial of Elizabeth Clason was unpopular in Stamford.

This must have been the last important public issue addressed by Reverend John Bishop. The fact that he was present at Jonathan Selleck's house for the questioning of the wild, epileptic maid shows his concern. He was still deeply aware of his responsibility as a religious leader. It was this same year of 1692 that he was seen giving in to old age. The town appointed the usual leaders, Captain Selleck and Lieutenant Jonathan Bell, to find an "able, faithful, orthodox minister"[9] - in other words, one as like Mr. Bishop as could be found. A wise choice was made: Mr. John Davenport of New Haven. He was the third John Davenport of that town, had had a Harvard education, and was twenty-three. Presumably he considered the situation in Stamford carefully. There were several assets for him. It wasn't too far from New Haven, he had friends and acquaintances there, and the people were quite loyal to their church, which was still expanding. (In fact, in 1691 a new effort had been made to enlarge the seating area in the meetinghouse, though it was stipulated that there should be no breach in the walls.)[10] Lastly, he would be stepping into the shoes of a predecessor renowned for his good sense, moral sturdiness, and learning--a real challenge to a young man of like attributes.

The following year saw Stamford busily working to provide for the coming of Mr. Davenport. Ebenezer Bishop had evidently inherited the house and land of William Potter. Potter had lived just to the north of the Bishops and had left his home to the three Bishop sons when he died in 1684.[11] It is to be noted that in Mr. Bishop's will of 1694 he gave his own house to his son Benjamin and Potter's house to Ebenezer.[12] Since Ebenezer was not married at this time and was probably still living with the family, he was prevailed upon to give up that property with "house and barn and frame" in exchange for the town house that had been built over near Mill River.[13] It was desirable, of course, to locate the minister's house near the meetinghouse. A committee of nine was set up to handle the matters of the house, digging a good well, planting an orchard, and erecting a fence around the parsonage lands.[14] If Mr. Davenport came before Mr. Bishop died, he was to receive a hundred pounds; otherwise he was to get ten pounds plus the sixty given him for moving expenses. He did, in the end, receive forty pounds and Mr. Bishop fifty for that year.[15] In 1695 in order to settle Mr. Bishop's estate, Stephen and Joseph were made responsible for collecting an additional thirty-five pounds from the inhabitants.[16]

One matter that was of concern year after year was collecting firewood, a year's supply, for the minister. Each inhabitant, from age sixteen on, had to provide one ox-load of good wood (no longer than six feet) by the end of November. All were to gather with the teams on a certain day and expected to devote one or two days to the job. Those who failed to participate were fined.[17]

Mr. Davenport wasted little time in settling in. Only a year later he married the widow of John Selleck, who was Captain Jonathan's ill-fated son. The young Selleck had graduated from Harvard in 1690 not having distinguished himself there.[18] He married Martha Gold, daughter of the prominent Nathan Gold of Fairfield, and he died shortly thereafter. Perhaps John Davenport had known them both earlier. Martha and John Davenport settled down together in 1695; seven children followed. For thirty-six years Mr. Davenport tended to the needs of his parishioners in Stamford. At the time of his death in 1731 the Reverend Samuel Cooke gave a most laudatory funeral sermon in which he said, "A Person of such Distinction as we now have lost, was seated so near to the Western Limits of New-England, as a Bulwark against any Irruptions of corrupt Doctrines and Manners."[19] John Davenport did indeed follow the path laid out by Mr. Bishop and in some ways even surpassed his able predecessor.

In focusing attention on the demise of Mr. Bishop and the arrival of his successor, Mr. Davenport, we have moved well into the last decade of the seventeenth century, a decade that marked the passing of the early, quite tight community and the men and women who had set it firmly into position. Stamford now was looking ahead to the third generation to guide its welfare in the new century. Close ties to England and to Boston were gone, for the new group of inhabitants were born in Connecticut and felt ties to their town and their colony only.

The two institutions of the Church and the town government had withstood the years of uncertainty and were well established now. The position of the Church, as we have seen, changed remarkably little. The church in Stamford was of prime importance in the affairs of the town. The people were loyal to it and to their ministers, willing to give both of their time and of their money to support all needs that arose. The system of government, soundly based on open town meetings and elected officials, functioned well. The support of the Fairfield Court for solving difficult cases and the Connecticut Colony's protective power added to the local stability.

The older, second-generation leaders of Stamford were still largely in control during this decade, but they were leaving the scene. Joshua Hoyt died in 1690 as did Jeremiah Jagger. Thomas Lawrence died in 1691 and Edmund Lockwood in 1692. George Slason died in 1695, as did Daniel Newman, and Daniel Weed died in 1697. George Slason's will is amusing in that he left his widow, his second wife, the right to remain in the house until she could remove her clothes. He also gave her a half barrel of pork, "for she has been a loving wife to me."[20] At the end of the century both Abraham Ambler and Jonathan Bell, Stamford's first child, were at rest after their years of toil for the town they knew and loved. They were life-long friends, dying when they were about fifty-eight. They did die at a relatively early age when one notes that Richard, Abraham's father, died shortly thereafter in his late eighties. However, in those days a man who lived into his fifties was considered to have had a normal life-span.

As the town grew, more specialization of jobs is to be noted. At first the early farmer had to be jack-of-all-trades: he had to be farmer, builder, blacksmith, cooper, shoemaker, home doctor, and clothes maker for his own family, and then with the whole community of settlers he had to learn road building, dam building, the arts of war, etc. Gradually, certain men who were adept at certain trades or small crafts were emerging. The men who were

millers have already been mentioned--the Webbs and Joshua Hoyt, in particular. There were several carpenters, such as Henry Ackerley, John Austin, and the special builders, John Ogden and his brother, Richard. Two shipbuilders were John Mills and young John Holly. Two known coopers were John Jagger and a second John Holly. Samuel Blatchley, Benjamin Hoyt, and Samuel Hoyt were blacksmiths. In 1693 Samuel Hoyt (out of three possible Samuel Haits/Hoyts) was given permission to have a shop on the common between his own land and that of David Waterbury. Was this the man known often in the records as Samuel Hait Smith? That designation can be confusing at times, but it does serve to distinguish him from Deacon Samuel and his son Samuel. The same is true in the case of the Jonas Weeds. Since there were three of them, too, one is called Jonas Weed, shoemaker. It is difficult for a novice, when reading the town records, to know, for instance, that John Holly Cooper is really a member of the Holly family.

Other trades and crafts that developed in Stamford were concerned with clothes making. Joseph Turney, like Thomas Stedwell before him, was a hatter; John Austin, Jr. and Richard Higginbotham were tailors;[21] John Slason was a weaver, and the Bells and the Newmans made shoes. These local industries lessened the dependence upon the importation of goods from Boston and England.

An interesting development occurred in 1697 in relation to the town's grist mill. This property was turned back to the Webb family, to Joseph and Samuel Webb "according to the will of Richard Webb, deceased."[22] Joseph Webb was the son of Richard's son, Joseph, who had been left the mill. He was now twenty-four and evidently deemed capable of the job along with his uncle Samuel, who undoubtedly had been training him.

Still another sawmill was to be built. This time (1691) it was to be on the Mianus River. Ensign Bates, Samuel Webb, and Nathaniel Cross were granted permission with the understanding that timber was to be cut for the use of the town.[23] One wonders where this mill was situated as the lower part of the Mianus River was in Greenwich. It must have been just above the Sequest Line.

Daniel Weed and Sergeant David Waterbury requested the right to run an ordinary in 1696.[24] Since Daniel Weed had already been in the business with Daniel Westcott, this was no really new venture for him. One wonders how many ordinaries there actually were in Stamford at this time.

At the Cove a ship built by John Mills was a pink called *The Blossom*. It was a vessel of seventy tons. In 1691 he turned it over to Major Jonathan Selleck, Jonathan Selleck, Jr., John

Belden, Daniel Westcott, and Lieutenant David Waterbury.[25] Interestingly, these men were all new owners in the shipping enterprise except for Major Jonathan Selleck. One notation in the town records gives rise to perplexity. In 1693 a John Leeds complained about the lack of iron work being done by Mr. Courtland of New York on Leed's vessel. Stephen and Abraham Finch acted as witnesses. He also complained that no proper provisions had been provided and the meat that had been received was "stinking meat."[26] Jonathan Slason and Eleazer Slason, Jr., plus one other, were witnesses to that. Was this vessel being built at the Cove shipyard? Probably.

A further sign of the growth of the town at this time was the recognized need for a new schoolhouse. In 1699 the town sold by public outcry the old building to Stephen Bishop for twenty shillings and sixpence. He must have had fond memories of teaching there. However, he was not given the floor boards nor the door hinges; these were evidently deemed to be worthy of further use.[27] It wouldn't be long before one central school for all the children would be insufficient as Stamford's population moved west and east and north.

Two buildings that were built in the 1690s must be singled out as worth our special attention, for they are both still standing. One was Nathaniel Pond's house on the Post Road, then called the Country Road. It is just to the east of the Noroton River and is a fine old house, restored to its former simplicity of line. It is of saltbox construction with full facade of two windows on each side of the door and five above. Nathaniel bought the two-acre lot in 1696 and soon married Jonathan Slason's sister. The Slasons were the children, incidentally, of the murdered Rebecca Tuttle Slason. They formed part of the little community involved in the shipyard. Nathaniel himself was a blacksmith.[28]

The other house that is still standing is also outside the center of the early Stamford village. Samuel Hoyt (smith), the son of Joshua, received his piece of land from his father's estate.[29] Since Samuel was married in 1700 to Susannah Slason, he must have built his house shortly before. This house lot was on the extension of North Street not far from Toilsome Brook and near a rock formation. The house was carefully restored recently under the direction of Mrs. Virginia Davis and belongs to the Stamford Historical Society. Such features as the cellar door and one window on the back, wide-board floors, and vertical wainscoting, the kitchen fireplace, and a section of the early exterior of the house are particularly noteworthy. The stone wall along the street had a special hole built in it to allow free passage for the pigs.

The Colonial Records of Connecticut's government give evidence of the increasing recognition of Stamford. In 1695 the legislature voted to have Captain Jonathan Selleck's rank raised to sergeant major. He was thereafter known as Major Jonathan Selleck, Esquire. He also was reelected Assistant+ to the government.[30] Probably the promotions in military rank were the result of the war with the French, for shortly thereafter Lieutenant Jonathan Bell became a captain, Sergeant David Waterbury a lieutenant, and Samuel Hoyt and Increase Holly were made ensigns.[31]

The three men who served as justices of the peace for Fairfield during the 1690s were Captain and Major Jonathan Selleck, Lieutenant and Captain Jonathan Bell, who often was commissioner, and Mr. Abraham Ambler. These men plus Samuel Hoyt, Daniel Weed, and Daniel Westcott also served many times as deputies as well as commissioners.

Within Stamford itself, town government was changing with an increase in specialized official positions. In addition to the townsmen (or selectmen) who were five of the leading citizens, there were the positions of constable, constantly increasing numbers of fence viewers, surveyors, listers, pounders, and collectors, the sealer of weights and measures, the town clerk, and the warner. New positions were designated in 1699. Abraham Ambler (who died that year) was to be registrar and treasurer; Lieutenant David Waterbury took his place. Jonathan Bell was to be brander; Samuel Holly was to be recorder and town clerk. Horse hunters and makers of pounds, cowkeepers, shepherds or sheepmasters also appear increasingly in the town records.[32]

1700. A new century. Fifty-nine years of hard work and true pride have gone into establishing Stamford, once a precarious venture in the far-off wilderness of southwest Connecticut. What was the physical appearance of Stamford really like by 1700? It is very hard to shift one's view from the metropolis of massed tall buildings and streaming cars on congested highways to the little village of the seventeenth century. Two rather unflattering views emerge from travel accounts at this time. One, recorded by Huntington is written in a journal by Roger Gill, a Quaker: "Came yt Evneing to a town Caled Stamford in Conacktecok Colony--it being a prity larg but a very dark town." Of course it would have been dark at night. Roger Gill and his fellow Quaker went to an inn where they discussed with the woman there the possibility of call-

---

+ Similar to a Senator of today.

ing a Quaker meeting. They also took the precaution of announcing their intention to the justice, "an independent" (Captain Jonathan Bell?) who treated them kindly but stated that the town forbade Quakers to preach. However, he implied "as he would wink at ye meeting." The constable (was it Jonathan Bell, Jr. or Samuel Webb?) went to the meeting and did his duty by forcing the men out. Roger Gill then went roaming through the streets crying "Woe, woe," etc., and "so alarmed ye peopel yt houl [whole] body of the town hard [heard]." The two men then moved on to Fairfield where some ministers were meeting. There Mr. Davenport treated them with respect and listened to their arguments.[33]

This does give us a little picture of Stamford and its people. There were, quite evidently, some Quaker inhabitants, but they were living quietly beside their Congregational neighbors. It is to be noted that a disturbance in the village would call forth the inhabitants. It is also to be noted that law and order prevailed but that there was at the same time a spirit of tolerance.

The other picture is that given by the famous Mrs. Knight. She travelled through Stamford just a few years later, in 1704. She was not impressed by Stamford: she wrote "...and descending the mountainous passage that almost broke my back, before we came to Stamford, a well compact town but miserable meeting-house which we passed and through many great difficulties, as bridges which were exceeding high, and very tottering, and of vast length, steep and rocky hills and precipices..." on to Norwalk.[34] We wonder why she considered the meetinghouse "miserable." Was it merely that it was small, compared to others she had seen?

Mrs. Knight does call Stamford "a well compact town." She merely saw the central area, of course, as she travelled along the Country Road. Most of the homes were by this time built close to each other from well beyond Noroton Corners on the east to the borders of Greenwich on the west. There were somewhere between 500 to 600 people living in Stamford by 1700, and their real estate holdings were extensive.[+] It wasn't unusual for men to own twelve (even twenty) pieces of land all over Stamford. The time was coming when even the acres to the north were to be divided up into the so-called Long Lots and taken over by the proprietors. And soon, too, countless land buyings and sellings would take place as owners tried to consolidate their holdings.

Today, three hundred and fifty years since the founding of Stamford, it has become a metropolis, a flourishing corporate

---

+ See tax list of 1701 in Appendix.

headquarters in which the first hardy founders are practically forgotten. How astonished these early people would be if they could experience Stamford with its present population of 106,120 (1987) and its maze of high block buildings. An acre and a half, a houselot, in the center of Stamford today could cost as much as three million dollars.[35] Where, the early settlers would cry, are our homes, our gardens, our trees, our boggy pathways, our peaceful pastures of animals, our open spaces with children at play, our grist mill, and our meetinghouse on the common?

APPENDIX

Landowners in 1650

Henry Ackerley
Richard Ambler
Robert Bassett
Robert Bates
Elias Bayley
Francis Bell
John Bishop
Clement Buxton
John Chapman
John Coe
Richard Crab
Samuel Dean
John Eliot
Jeffrey Ferris
John Finch
William Graves
Richard Hardy
John Holly
Thomas Hunt
Robert Husted
Thomas Hyatt
Henry Jackson
Jeremiah Jagger
Edward Jessup
Nicolas Knap
James Lareson
Richard Law
Edmund Lockwood
Thomas Lyon
David Mitchell
Joseph Mead
Thomas Morehouse
Thomas Newman
William Newman
Henry Olinson
William Potter
John Reynolds
Robert Rugg
Daniel Scofield
Obadiah Seely
Vincent Simkins
George Slason
Henry Smith
Thomas Stevens
James Steward
George Stuckey
Henry Sweede
Nicholas Theale
Robert Usher
John Waterbury
Jonas Weed
wd. Whitmore
Simon Hoyt
John Rockwell?

1701 Tax List

	Ł	s	p
John Ambler	92	10	0
Jeremiah Andrews	96	18	0
John Austin	34	4	0
John Bates, Sr.	135	0	0
John Bates, Jr.	90	0	0
Mrs. Bell	105	0	0
Jonathan Bell	55	5	0
Benjamin Bishop	38	0	0
Joseph Bishop	55	12	6
Stephen Bishop	143	10	0
Samuel Blachley	37	7	6
Joseph Brown	78	10	0
Clement Buxton	112	0	0
Simon Chapman	26	0	0
Joseph Clark	21	0	0
Daniel Clason	64	5	0
Samuel Clason	55	12	6
William Clemence	27	12	6
John Crissy	40	16	3
Jonathan Crissy	18	0	0
Nathaniel Cross	54	0	0
Francis Dan	27	0	0
Mr. John Davenport	100	0	0
John Dean	30	0	0
Matthew Dean	18	0	0
Samuel Dean	14	13	3
Zachariah Dibble	26	5	0
Joseph Ferris	72	2	6
Peter Ferris, Sr.	118	12	6
Peter Ferris, Jr.	39	0	0
Abraham Finch, Sr.	37	2	6
Abraham Finch, Jr.	31	0	0
Isaac Finch, Sr.	27	10	0
Isaac Finch, Jr.	22	0	0
John Finch	22	0	0
Joseph Finch	42	2	6
Samuel Finch	46	2	6
Joseph Garnsey	46	10	0
John Gold	88	2	6
Benjamin Green	55	9	0
John Green	28	17	6
Joseph Green	81	1	0

Samuel Hardy	47	0	0
Benjamin Hoyt, Sr.	112	0	0
Benjamin Hoyt, Jr.	52	5	0
John Hoyt	19	0	0
Joshua Hoyt	31	12	6
Samuel Hoyt, Sr.	94	10	0
Samuel Hoyt, Jr.	24	02	6
Samuel Hoyt (smith)	36	12	6
Mr. Higgenbotham	30	0	0
Elisha Holly	61	16	3
Increase Holly	63	0	0
John Holly, Sr.	71	10	0
John Holly, Jr.	30	0	0
John Holly, Jr.	20	10	0
Jonathan Holly	58	10	0
Joseph Holly	25	0	0
Samuel Holly, Sr.	52	0	0
Samuel Holly, Jr.	20	0	0
John Holmes	31	0	0
Samuel Holmes	18	0	0
Stephen Holmes	83	5	0
Jonathan Jagger	39	5	0
Orp. Jones	4	10	0
Peter June	75	15	0
Caleb Knap	34	17	6
John Knap	111	5	0
Moses Knap	45	5	0
Daniel Lockwood	38	2	6
Edmond Lockwood	28	10	0
Joseph Lockwood	28	10	0
John Mills	18	0	0
William Mills	21	0	0
Thomas Newman	83	0	0
Thomas Penoyer	72	5	0
John Pettit	56	7	6
Nathaniel Pond	36	0	0
Daniel Scofield, Sr.	115	5	0
Daniel Scofield, Jr.	55	10	0
John Scofield	27	3	9
Richard Scofield	56	2	0
Wid. Scofield	66	5	0
Jonas Seely, Sr.	116	17	6
Jonas Seely, Jr.	18	0	0

1701 Tax List (continued)

Obadiah Seely	26	0	0
Major Selleck	91	15	0
Captain Selleck	123	10	6
Nathaniel Selleck	57	8	0
Wd. Selleck	106	5	0
Eleazer Slason	18	0	0
James Slason	43	2	0
John Slason, Sr.	101	5	0
John Slason, Jr.	57	15	0
Jonathan Slason	53	0	0
Daniel Smith	148	0	0
John Smith	107	2	6
Joseph Stevens	46	17	6
Obadiah Stevens	79	7	0
Thomas Stevens	18	0	0
John Stone	22	0	0
Edward Trahern	41	10	0
Joseph Turney	63	5	0
David Waterbury	136	10	0
Jonathan Waterbury	100	0	0
Joseph Webb	61	8	9
Samuel Webb	56	10	0
David Webster	30	0	0
John Webster	41	0	0
Daniel Weed	26	7	6
Jonas Weed, Sr.	154	10	0
Joseph Weed	55	6	3
Samuel Weed	22	15	0
Wd. Weed	96	10	0
Mr. Wood	119	10	0
John Youngs	46	10	0

Note: There probably was a mistake in the original copying of this list because there is no Jonas Seely, Jr. in the records at this time except for the Jonas born 1692. Also, Jonas Weed, Jr. (1667-1706) is missing from this list. There are a number of errors in Huntington's list on pages 174-176.

NOTES

Chapter One

1 Charles J. Hoadly, ed., *Records of the Colony and Plantation of New Haven* (Hartford, Ct., 1857), I, p. 45. (RCPNH hereafter)

2 Estelle F. Feinstein, *Stamford from Puritan to Patriot 1641 to 1774* (Stamford, Ct., 1976), p. 13.

3 *Stamford Town Meeting Records*, (1886 copy), p. 6. (STMR hereafter)

4 Capt. David DeVries, logbook of 1641, quoted by George Orr Pershing in *The Stamford Shopper and Weekly Mail*, January 15, 1958.

5 STMR, p. 12.

6 STMR, p. 13.

7 H. Stanley Finch, miscellaneous paper (property of the Stamford Historical Society).

8 Elijah B. Huntington, *History of Stamford, Connecticut* (Stamford, Ct., 1868, and reprint Harrison, N.Y.: Harbor Hill Books, 1979), p. 272.

9 STMR, p. 8.

10 STMR, p. 7.

11 Records of Newtown (Cambridge), Massachusetts, as related by Miss Elizabeth Sumner of Carmel, California, a direct descendant.

12 Feinstein, *op. cit.*, p. 13.

13 Huntington, *op cit.*, pp. 102-103.

14 RCPNH, I, p. 106.

15 RCPNH, I, p. 127, and Spencer P. Mead, *Ye Historie of Ye Town of Greenwich* (N.Y.: Knickerbocker Press, 1921), p. 16.

16 RCPNH, I, p. 85.

17 RCPNH, I, p. 130.

18 RCPNH, I, p. 118 and p. 128.

19 "Journal of New Netherland" in The Hague, Holland found in H. Stanley Finch miscellaneous papers, *op. cit.*

20 Huntington, *op. cit.*, p. 73.

21 *Ibid.*, p. 119.

22 RCPNH, I, p. 135 and p. 146; *Winthrop Papers*, II, p. 188.

23 Huntington, *op. cit.*, p. 37; and Fairfield, Ct., *Probate Court Records*, Vol. II, p. 13.

24 STMR, p. 13.

25 STMR, p. 57.

26 Huntington, *op. cit.*, p. 95; and *Stamford Land Records*, Bk. B, p. 33.

27 STMR, p. 199.

28 STMR, p. 200.

29 *Ibid.*

30 STMR, pp. 200-201.

31 STMR, p. 18.

32 STMR, p. 17.

33 STMR, p. 198.

34 STMR, p. 204.

35 Feinstein, *op. cit.*, p. 54 from *Acts, United Colonies*, I, p. 141.

36 RCPNH, I, p. 482 and p. 458 ff.

37 STMR, pp. 70-72.

38 Letters of Thomas and Martha Lyon, 1647-1649, *Lyon Memorial Book* (Lyon(s) Families Association of America, 1976), Vol. 4, pp. 135-149.

39 STMR, p. 18.

40 Eugene Aubrey Stratton, *Plymouth Colony Its History & People 1620-1691* (Salt Lake City: Ancestry Publishing, 1986), p. 176.

41 STMR, p. 205.

42 STMR, pp. 205-206.

43 STMR, p. 206.

Chapter Two

1 STMR, pp. 27-47, *passim*.

2 David M. Ellis, James A. Frost, Harold C. Syrett, Harry J. Carman, *A Short History of New York State* (N.Y.: Cornell University Press, 1957), p. 25.

3 James Riker, Jr., *The Annals of Newtown in Queens County, New York* (Lambertville, N.J.: Hunterdon House, 1982), p. 31.

4 *Ibid.*, p. 27.

5 RCPNH, II, p. 16.

6 *Ibid.*, p. 48.

7 Riker, *op. cit.*, p. 31.

8 RCPNH, II, pp. 61-65.

9 *Ibid.*, pp. 48-49.

10 *Ibid.*, p. 61.

11 *Ibid.*, p. 65.

12 *Ibid.*, p. 162.

13 *Ibid.*, p. 165 ff.

14 *Ibid.*, p. 167.

15 *Ibid.*, p. 168.

16 *Ibid.*, p. 216.

17 *Ibid.*, p. 144.

18 *Ibid.*, p. 216.

19 *Ibid.*, pp. 122-123.

20 *Ibid.*, p. 223.

21 *Ibid.*, p. 325.

22 *Ibid.*, p. 319.

23 *Ibid.*

24 *Ibid.*, p. 326.

25 Huntington, *op. cit.*, p. 97.

26 RCPNH, II, p. 301.

27 Leon Manley, *Long Island Discovery* (Garden City, N.Y.: Doubleday & Co., Inc., 1966), pp. 164-165.

28 Richard N. Powdrell, ed., *Long Island* (Port Washington, L.I.: Kennikat Press, 1963), p. 81.

29 RCPNH, II, pp. 242-247.

30 *Ibid.*, p. 244.

31 *Ibid.*, pp. 245-246.

32 *Ibid.*, p. 303 and p. 313.

33 Edward E. Atwater, *History of the Colony of New Haven to Its Absorption into Connecticut* (Meriden, Ct.: The Journal Publishing Co., 1902), pp. 368-369.

34 STMR, pp. 23, 24, 72-76, 93-94, 98, 104-108.

35 STMR, pp. 108, 79 and 98, 74, 93.

36 Huntington, *op. cit.*, p. 35.

37 Franklin Bowditch Dexter, ed. *Ancient Town Records, New Haven Town Records 1662-1684* (New Haven, 1919), II, pp. 441-442.

38 *Ibid.*, p. 30.

39 *Ibid.*, p. 114.

40 RCPNH, II, p. 135 and p. 141.

41 STMR, pp. 93-94

42 RCPNH, II, p. 229.

43 Letters of John Bishop, *The Mather Papers* (Boston: the

Massachusetts Historical Society, 1868), VIII, p. 305.

44 RCPNH, II, p. 583.

45 *Ibid.*, p. 325.

46 Robert Bolton, *History of the County of Westchester from Its Settlement to the Present Time* (New York: Alexander S. Gould, 1848) II, pp. 163-164.

47 Riker, *op. cit.*, p. 50.

Chapter Three

1 Feinstein, *op. cit.*, p. 69.

2 *Ibid.*, p. 72.

3 J. H. Trumbull, ed., *The Public Records of the Colony of Connecticut* (Hartford, 1850-1890), I, pp. 391 and 412. (PRCC hereafter)

4 RCPNH, II, p. 318.

5 *Ibid.*, pp. 380-383.

6 *Ibid.*, p. 452.

7 PRCC, I, p. 389.

8 *Ibid.*, p. 525.

9 *Ibid.*, p. 467.

10 *Ibid.*, p. 14.

11 PRCC, II, p. 10.

12 *Ibid.*, p. 61 and p. 119; RCPNH, II, pp. 217 and 219, 593, 594, 597.

13 STMR, pp. 213-215 and p. 217.

14 STMR, p. 214.

15 STMR, pp. 217, 219, 221.

16 STMR, p. 227.

17 STMR, p. 233.

18 STMR, p. 230.

19 *Ibid.*

20 STMR, p. 226. Deed in case--Stamford Town Hall.

21 STMR, p. 233.

22 STMR, pp. 232 and 235.

23 *Stamford Land Records*, Bk. A, p. 245. (SLR hereafter)

24 STMR, p. 234; pp. 227-228.

25 STMR, p. 232.

26 PRCC, II, p. 68.

27 STMR, p. 235.

28 PRCC, II, p. 66.

29 *Ibid.*, p. 109.

30 *Ibid.*, p. 110.

31 STMR, p. 215.

32 *Ibid.*, p. 216.
33 *Ibid.*, p. 217 and p. 219.
34 *Ibid.*, pp. 220-221.
35 *Ibid.*, p. 224.

Chapter Four

1 STMR, pp. 236, 237, 238, 242.
2 STMR, p. 241.
3 STMR, p. 239.
4 STMR, p. 245.
5 STMR, p. 263, p. 272, p. 273.
6 STMR, p. 262.
7 STMR, p. 264.
8 STMR, p. 271.
9 PRCC, II, p. 175.
10 STMR, p. 239.
11 STMR, p. 241.
12 STMR, p. 244 and p. 236.
13 PRCC, II, p. 174, pp. 202-203, p. 176. 14 *Ibid.*, p. 203.
15 *Ibid.*, p. 561.
16 *Ibid.*, p. 203, p. 207, p. 219.
17 STMR, p. 253.
18 PRCC, II, p. 222.
19 *Ibid.*, p. 242.
20 *Ibid.*, p. 189.
21 *Ibid.*, p. 197; STMR, p. 275.
22 STMR, p. 251.
23 PRCC, II, p. 244 and p. 224.
24 *Ibid.*, p. 224 and p. 241.
25 *Ibid.*, p. 242.
26 *Ibid.*, p. 190, and *Records of the Court of Assistants of Connecticut 1665-1701* (Hartford: The Connecticut State Library) p. 184.
27 STMR, pp. 247, 248, 250-251.
28 PRCC, II, p. 241.
29 *Ibid.*, p. 261.
30 Letters of John Bishop, *op. cit.*, p. 302 and p. 305. 31 PRCC, II, pp. 281-282.
32 *Ibid.*, pp. 257, 268-269, 271.
33 *Ibid.*, p. 271.
34 *Ibid.*, p. 261 and p. 279.
35 STMR, p. 259 and p. 260.
36 STMR, p. 257 and p. 258.

37 STMR, p. 251 and p. 252.
38 STMR, p. 259; PRCC, II, p. 253.
39 Letters of John Bishop, *op. cit.*, p. 300.
40 STMR, p. 263.
41 STMR, p. 262.
42 STMR, p. 265.
43 STMR, p. 272.
44 STMR, p. 271.
45 STMR, pp. 264, 270, 268, 277.
46 STMR, pp. 267, 269.
47 STMR, p. 269.
48 PRCC, II, p. 294.
49 STMR, p. 49.
50 Letters of John Bishop, *op. cit.*, p. 306.
51 *Ibid.*, p. 299.
52 *Records of the Court of Assistants of Connecticut 1665-1701*, *op. cit.*, pp. 68-69.
53 *Ibid.*, p. 34.
54 Letters of John Bishop, *op. cit.*, p. 299.
55*Ibid.*, p. 307.
56*Ibid.*, p. 309.

Chapter Five

1 PRCC, III, pp. 294-298.
2 Letters of John Bishop, *op. cit.*, p. 298.
3 STMR, p. 279.
4 PRCC, III, p. 264.
5 Louise H. McLean, "The Sellecks of Early Stamford," *Darien Historical Annual*, March 1961, p. 5.
6 Will of Robert Bates, *Fairfield, Ct. Probate Court Records*, II, pp. 83-84.
7 Will of John Jagger, *Fairfield, Ct. Probate Court Records*, IV, p. 26.
8 Inventory of John Selleck, *Fairfield, Ct. Probate Court Records*, V, pp. 15a, b, c, 23, 133; inventory of John Selleck, Jr., V, p. 96; SLR, B, p. 18.
9 STMR, p. 282; "Frontispiece," *Town of Bedford, Bedford Historical Records*, 1978, IX.
10 Title page, Town of Bedford, *op. cit.*
11 Feinstein, *op. cit.*, pp. 93-94.
12 *Ibid.*, p. 94.
13 STMR, p. 290 and p. 292.
14 STMR, p. 296.

15 Will of Richard Webb, *Fairfield, Ct, Probate Court Records*, pp. 3-4.

16 STMR, p. 281.

17 STMR, p. 284.

18 STMR, p. 293 and p. 317.

19 STMR, p. 318.

20 STMR, p. 301.

21 STMR, p. 294.

22 STMR, p. 297 and p. 299.

23 STMR, p. 292.

24 STMR, p. 306.

25 STMR, p. 315.

26 STMR, p. 305 and p. 308.

27 Louise H. McLean, "The Noroton River Settlement," *The Darien Historical Society Annual*, 1980, p. 5.

28 STMR, p. 316.

29 SLR, A, p. 194.

30 *Ibid.*

31 STMR, p. 319.

32 *Connecticut Archives: Private Controversies* (Hartford: Connecticut State Library), IV, pp. 70a, 71, 72, 74, 75a.

33 *Records of the Court of Assistants, op. cit.*, p. 163 and p. 167.

34 STMR, p. 279.

35 STMR, p. 321.

36 STMR, p. 282.

37 *Ibid.*

38 STMR, p. 286.

39 STMR, p. 279.

40 STMR, p. 288.

41 STMR, p. 303 and p. 309.

42 SLR, A, p. 249.

43 STMR, p. 298.

44 STMR, p. 310.

45 Letters of John Bishop, *op. cit.*, p. 314 and p. 316.

46 STMR, p. 281 and p. 285.

47 STMR, p. 303.

48 STMR, p. 284 and p. 280.

49 STMR, p. 298 and p. 301.

50 John Bishop, IV, "A Good Wife by John Bishop. Is This Stamford's First Book?" *Connecticut Ancestry* (Stamford Genealogical Society, September, 1987), pp. 21-44.

51 *Ibid.*, p. 36.

52 STMR, pp. 16-17.

53 Inventory of Francis Bell, *Fairfield, Ct. Probate Court*

Records, III, p. 301.

54 SLR, A, p. 75; *Fairfield, Ct. Probate Court Records*, pp. 61-62.

55 SLR, C, p. 415.

56 McLean, "The Sellecks of Early Stamford", *op. cit.*; Huntington, *op. cit.*, p. 192.

57 Huntington, *op. cit.*, p. 176.

58 Inventory of John Jagger, *Fairfield, Ct. Probate Court Records*, IV, p. 26.

59 SLR, F, p. 418.

60 STMR, p. 321.

Chapter Six

1 STMR, p. 321.

2 STMR, p. 338.

3 PRCC, IV, p. 76.

4 Ronald Marcus, *"Elizabeth Clauson...Thou Deseruest to Dye"* (Stamford Historical Society, 1976).

5 Huntington, *op. cit.*, p. 361.

6 *The Code of 1650* (Hartford: Judd, Loomis & Co., 1836) p. 28.

7 Marcus, *op. cit.*, p. 9.

8 *Ibid.*, p. 8.

9 STMR, p. 328.

10 STMR, p. 324.

11 Will of William Potter, *Fairfield, Ct. Probate Court Records*, III, pp. 165-167.

12 Will of John Bishop, *Fairfield, Ct. Probate Court Records*, IV, pp. 118a and b.

13 STMR, p. 334 and SLR, A, p. 249.

14 STMR, p. 331.

15 STMR, pp. 328, 333, 334.

16 STMR, p. 335.

17 STMR, p. 333 and p. 344.

18 McLean, "The Sellecks of Early Stamford," *op. cit.*, p. 8.

19 Rev. Samuel Cooke, Sermon, 1731, New Haven Historical Society.

20 STMR, pp. 188-189.

21 STMR, p. 280 and p. 340; Huntington, *op. cit.*, p. 185.

22 STMR, p. 342.

23 STMR, p. 327.

24 STMR, p. 340.

25 McLean, "The Noroton River Settlement," *op. cit.*, p. 7. 26

STMR, p. 210.

27 STMR, p. 352.

28 McLean, "The Noroton River Settlement," *op. cit.*, pp. 8-9.

29 Estate of Joshua Hait, *Fairfield, Ct. Probate Court Records*, IV, p. 25 and p. 224.

30 PRCC, IV, p. 168.

31 *Ibid.*, p. 253 and p. 300.

32 STMR, pp. 351-352.

33 Huntington, *op. cit.*, pp. 132-134.

34 *Ibid.*, pp. 169-170.

35 Carol Majdalany Williams from the Stamford Chamber of Commerce, Census of 1987.

Bibliography

Banks, Charles Edward, *The Planters of the Commonwealth*, Baltimore: Genealogical Publishing Co., 1979.

Bishop, John, IV, "A Good Wife by John Bishop," *Connecticut Ancestry*, September 1987.

Bolton, Robert, *History of the County of Westchester from Its First Settlement to the Present Time*, New York: Alexander S. Gould, 1848, Vol. II.

Bond, Henry, *Bond's Genealogies and History of Watertown*, Boston, 1860.

Bradford, William, *Of Plimouth Plantation*, Boston: Wright & Potter Printing Co., 1899.

Bushman, Richard L., *From Puritan to Yankee*, Cambridge, Mass.: Harvard University Press, 1967.

Calder, Isabel MacBeath, *Letters of John Davenport*, New Haven: Yale University Press, 1937.

The Code of 1650, Hartford: Judd, Loomis & Co., 1836.

Connecticut Archives: Private Controversies, Hartford: Connecticut State Library.

Cooke, Rev. Samuel, "Sermon preached at the funeral of John Davenport, 1731," New Haven Historical Society.

Deloss, William, *The Colonial History of Hartford*, Centennial Hill Press, 1974.

Demos, John, *A Little Commonwealth*, N.Y.: N.Y. University Press.

Dexter, Franklin Bowditch, ed., *Ancient Town Records: New Haven Town Records*, New Haven, 1919.

Earle, Alice Morse, *Home Life in Colonial Days*, Stockbridge: The Berkshire Traveller Press, 1974 (written in 1898).

Ellis, David M.; Frost, James A.; Syrett, Harold C.; Carman, Harry J., *A Short History of New York State*, N.Y.: Cornell University Press, 1957.

Fairfield, CT, Probate Court Records.

Feinstein, Estelle F., *Stamford from Puritan to Patriot*, Stamford, 1976.

Finch, H. Stanley, miscellaneous papers, Stamford Historical Society.

Fuller, Hon. Clement A., *The History of the Southern Commons or Sequest Land in Stamford, Connecticut.*

Grant, Charles S., *Democracy in the Connecticut Town of Kent*, N.Y.: W. W. Norton & Co., Inc., 1972.

Hall, David, *Medieval Fields, Shire Archaeology*, Princes Risborough: Cromwell House, 1982.

Hibbert, Christopher, *The English: A Social History*, 10661945, N.Y.: W. W. Norton & Co., 1987.

Hill, Douglas, *The English to New England*, N.Y.: Clarkson N. Potter, Inc., 1975.

A History of the Town of Hempstead, 1644-1969, Hempstead, N.Y.

Hoadly, Charles J., ed., *Records of the Colony of the Jurisdiction of New Haven*, Hartford: Case, Lockwood & Co., 1858.

Hodges, Maude deLeigh, *Crossroads on the Charles, A History of Watertown, Massachusetts*, Canaan, NH: Phoenix Publishing Co., 1980.

Huntington, E. B., *History of Stamford 1641-1868*, Harrison, N.Y.: Harrison Hill Books, 1979.

Innes, Stephen C.; Melvoin, Richard I.; Thomas, Peter A., *Early Settlement in the Connecticut Valley*, Historic Deerfield, Inc. & Institute for Massachusetts Studies, Westfield State College, 1984.

Jacobus, Donald Lines, *Families of Old Fairfield, Fairfield*, CT: DAR, 1930.

Jacobus, Donald Lines, *List of the Officials of the Connecticut Colony and New Haven Colonies*, New Haven: Roland Mather Hooker, 1935.

Jameson, J. Franklin, ed., *Johnson's Wonder-Working Providence 1628-1651*, New York: Barnes and Noble, 1910.

Kelly, J. Frederick, *Early Domestic Architecture of Connecticut*, New York: Dover Publications, Inc., 1963.

"Letters of John Bishop," *The Mather Papers*, Massachusetts Collections, Massachusetts Historical Society, 4th series, Vol. VIII.

"Letters of Thomas Lyon," *Lyon Memorial Book IV*, Lyon(s) Families Association of America, 1976.

Lockridge, Kenneth A. *A New England Town the First Hundred Years*, New York: W. W. Norton & Co., Inc., 1970.

Main, Jackson Turner, *Connecticut Society in the Era of the American Revolution*, (Series XXI), American Revolution Bicentennial Commission of Hartford, 1977.

Manley, Leon, *Long Island Discovery*, Garden City, N. Y.: Doubleday & Co., Inc., 1966.

Marcus, Ronald, *"Elizabeth Clawson...Thou Diseruest to Dye,"* Stamford, CT: The Stamford Historical Society, 1976.

McCrum, Robert; Cran, William; MacNeil, Robert, *The Story of English*, New York: Elisabeth Sifton Books, Viking, 1986.

McLean, Louise H., "The Noroton River Settlement," *The Darien Historical Society Annual*, 1980.

McLean, Louise H., "The Sellecks of Early Stamford," *The Darien Historical Society Annual*, 1961.

Mead, Spencer P., *Ye Historie of ye Town of Greenwich*, New York: Knickerbocher Press, 1921.

Miller, John C., *The First Frontier: Life in Colonial America*, New York: Dell Publishing Co., 1966.

Miller, Perry, ed., *The American Puritans: Their Prose and Poetry*, Garden City, N.Y.: Doubleday & Co., Inc., 1956.

Richard Mills of Westchester, White Plains Historical Society papers, Valhalla, New York.

The Minor Diaries, John A. Minor (publisher), 1976.

Morgan, Edmund S., *The Puritan Family*, New York: Harper & Row, 1944.

Muir, Richard, *The English Village*, Great Britain: Thames and Hudson, Ltd., 1980.

Pershing, George Orr, newspaper articles in the *Stamford Shopper and Weekly Mail*, 1958-1959.

Riker, James, Jr., *The Annals of Newtown in Queens County, New York*, Lambertville, N.J.: Hunterdon Press, 1982.

Roberts, Brian K., *Village Plans, Shire Archaeology*, Aylesbury, Bucks.: Shire Publications, Ltd., 1982.

Robinson, G. Frederick, and Wheeler, Ruth Robinson, *Great Little Watertown*, Watertown Historical Society, 1930.

Stamford Land Records, (1886 edition), Stamford, CT Town Hall.

Stamford Town Meeting Records, (1886 edition), Stamford, CT Town Hall.

Schultz, Bernice, *Colonial Hempstead*, Lynbrook, N.Y.: The Review Star Press, 1937.

Seymour, Malcolm, *Puritan Migration to Connecticut*, Canaan, NH: Phoenix Co.

Stiles, Henry R., *The History of Ancient Wethersfield*, New York: The Grafton Press, 1904.

Stratton, Eugene Aubrey, *Plymouth Colony Its History & People 1620-1691*, Salt Lake City, Utah: Ancestry Publishing, 1986.

Town of Bedford: Bedford Historical Records, Town of Bedford, N.Y., Vol. IX, 1978.

Trumbull, Benjamin, *History of Connecticut*, New London: H.D. Utley, 1898.

Van Dusen, Albert E., *Connecticut*, New York: Random House, 1961.

Willison, George F., *Saints and Strangers*, New York: Reynal and Hitchcock, 1945.

The Winthrop Papers, Vols. II, III and IV, Boston: The Massachusetts Historical Society.

Stamford Families of the Seventeenth Century

Introduction

In the course of writing a history of a particular place and its inhabitants over a period of a century, family genealogies play a vital role; however, one accrues considerable information that cannot be part of one's study. It is true, though, that what one learns about family relations is important, particularly to present-day descendants. Consequently, I finally decided to include this separate section devoted to the members of the principal families of Stamford during the seventeenth century, giving their relationships and dates as accurately as possible.

Mrs. Edith M. Wicks, the president of the Stamford Genealogical Society, very graciously agreed to help me with this project. She has given unstintingly both of her time and of her very extensive records and has thereby strengthened my own research, especially as I have not made the detailed study of the many family genealogies that she has. Much of the material about where the settlers originated in England and where they first settled before moving to Stamford she has provided. The particular sources she has used are to be found at the end of the family write-ups.

It is perhaps needless to say that there are serious difficulties in trying to give authentic genealogical material for this early period in Stamford's history. First, one can only be as accurate as the records are, and they can be both wrong and woefully incomplete. Many females are omitted entirely. Even accounts and genealogies written by descendants are not necessarily accurate. For example, there are several Holly genealogies, and they differ considerably about the birth dates of John Holly's children. Secondly, the universal custom of using time-honored names in a family for generation after generation leads to confusion, especially in cases where the men died at an early age. Such names as Jonas Weed, John Pettit, and John Waterbury are examples. Then too, since women's maiden names were often omitted in the records, and there were innumerable Marys, Sarahs, Hannahs and Abigails, one cannot determine which is which in certain cases.

Sometimes one is tempted to make an educated guess but must not do so. Sarah Rockwell, for example, married a Webb, and in looking over the Webb genealogy, one finds that Caleb married a Sarah. The dates are suitable, but one cannot without detailed study determine that Caleb married Sarah Rockwell. A third problem results from the custom at that time of calling step-relationships "in law." Thus a man's mother-in-law could be either his wife's mother or his father's second or third wife. Sometimes a further problem develops, for wives often did remarry once and even twice, and when a daughter had the same first name, it is hard to determine in certain cases whether it was the mother or the daughter that was being married.

Genealogists normally place a double date such as 1647/48 to show that an event occurred during the period in which there is a discrepancy between the old calendar, the Gregorian, and the present-day Julian calendar for the first three months of each year. I have not, although I realize that for strict accuracy one should. Instead I used only the modern date when the problem arose.

The families included in this genealogical section are those that stayed in Stamford for a reasonable period of time. Therefore, those families who stayed for only two or three years before moving on to Long Island have been omitted except for the Reverend Richard Denton who played a vital role in the original move from Wethersfield to Stamford. I also have omitted families like the Lounsburys, the Reeds, and the Youngs. They came very late in the 1600s and therefore had little impact during the seventeenth century. John Underhill, a man of considerable importance in Stamford's history, has been omitted because in the course of his military career he moved about considerably and made his final home on Long Island. The Stamford settlers who moved to the nearby settlements of Greenwich and Bedford I have included when appropriate but have not pursued their families thereafter unless there were later marriages to Stamford residents.

My cut-off date was 1700. However, I did include the children born in a family that already had children before that date; their ensuing history was not included except for cases in which they married persons born before 1700.

Both Mrs. Wicks and I have done our utmost to be as accurate as possible, but many errors will undoubtedly be brought to our attention. We apologize for them.

The principal general sources that I have used are:

The Stamford Town Meeting Records.
The Stamford Land Records.
The Fairfield, Connecticut, Probate Court Records.
E. B. Huntington, *History of Stamford.*
H. Stanley Finch's genealogies of the early families (in manuscript).
Donald Lines Jacobus, *Families of Old Fairfield,* Vols. I and II.
The vertical files at the Ferguson Library, Stamford.
Connecticut Vital Records - Stamford 1641-1852, Barbour Collection.
The Town of Bedford, *Bedford Historical Records,* Vol. IX.
Spencer P. Mead, *Ye Historie of Ye Town of Greenwich,* and *History and Genealogy of the Mead Family.*
The New Haven Colony Records.
Henry R. Stiles, *The History of Ancient Wethersfield.*
The Watertown, Massachusetts, Town Records.
Henry Bond, *Genealogies and History of Watertown.*
Mary Louise Marshall Hutton, *Seventeenth Century Colonial Ancestors.*
Charles Edward Banks, *The Planters of the Commonwealth.*
The Order of the Founders and Patriots of America Register, Third Supplement.

Additional general sources used by Edith M. Wicks (Others are cited in the individual family genealogies):

American Historical Society, *The Encyclopedia of Connecticut Ancestry.*
W. S. Appleton, *Boston Births and Baptisms: 1630-1699.*
E. E. Atwater, *History of the Colony of New Haven to Its Absorption into Connecticut.*
John Valentine Hecker, *New York Genealogical and Biographical Record.*
David Lines Jacobus (ed.), *The American Genealogist.*
The New England Historical and Genealogical Society Register.
James Savage, *Dictionary of the Settlers of New England.*
Benjamin Trumbull, *The Complete History of Connecticut and Ecclesiastical Societies.*

Genealogies

ACCORLEY, ACKERLEY, AKERLY, Henry - d1658, mc1606 Ann ____ (bc1587, d aft 1662).

Henry Accorley possibly came from Yorkshire. He was in New Haven in 1640 where he built a cellar and sold it without permission. He moved to Stamford by December of 1641 and was a farmer and a carpenter. He lived on the north side of East Street. In 1653 he sold his house and moved to Greenwich. His will speaks of an adopted daughter, Mary Dickason, who was living in his home. His wife received a house on West Street in 1656 from Edmund Lockwood. Descendants:

A. Mary - m1 Vincent Simkins, m2 aft 1653 William Oliver.

References: Donald Lines Jacobus, *The American Genealogist*, Vol. 10, p. 112; E. E. Atwater, *History of the Colony of New Haven to Its Absorption into Connecticut*, 1902.

AMBLER, Richard - bc1611, d1700, m1 Sarah ____ (dc1649), m2 Elizabeth ____ (d1685).

Richard Ambler was possibly from Lincolnshire, the son of Richard. He was in Watertown, MA in 1639 and in Stamford by 1648. He held many positions over the years and was a townsman in 1666. In 1680 he went with the group to settle Bedford and was known there as the "Patriarch of Bedford." However, he returned to Stamford before his death. He lived on North Street where the Ferguson Library is today.

His son Abraham was born in Watertown and was known to be well educated and of a gentle, generous nature. He served Stamford with distinction over the years, even gaining the title of "Mr." He was recorder from 1670 to 1686, nine times a deputy, and a justice for Fairfield County the year he died. In 1680 he went to Bedford and was town clerk there until he returned to Stamford in about 1688.

Descendants of AMBLER, Richard:

A. Sarah - b1639.
B. Abraham - b&d 1641.
C. Abraham - b1642, d1699, m1 1662 Mary Bates (bc1642, d/o Robert), m2 Hannah ____.
   1. Mary - b1664, d by 1699, m John Brown?
   2. Abraham - b1666, d by 1694, m1692 Hannah Gold (d/o John), she m2 1697 Jeremiah Andreas.
      a. Abraham - b1693, m1717 Abigail Clason (d/o Samuel).
   3. John - b1667, d1711, m Martha Wildman (dc1735, d/o Thomas), she m2 1712 Edward Bach or Beach.
      a. John - b1695, m1721 Elizabeth Morehouse (d/o Thomas).
      b. Stephen - b1698, m1724 Deborah Hoyt (b1698, d1768, d/o Benjamin).
      c. Martha - b1700.
   4. Joshua - b1670, d by 1699?
   5. Sarah - b1672, m John Brown?
   6. Mehitabel - bc1677, d1737, m1702 James Slason.

References: *Conklin Manuscript*, Connecticut State Library.

ANDREAS, ANDRUS, ANDREWS, Jeremiah - d1713, m1697 Hannah Ambler (d/o John Gold, wd/o Abraham Ambler).

Jeremiah Andreas was born in Fairfield, the son of Francis, formerly of Hartford. He moved from Stamford, where he had a house in 1682 on the extension of North Street, to Bedford in 1697. He served as deputy there. Descendants:

A. Dea John - b1700, d1742.
B. Anne - b1702, d1706.
C. Robert - of Pound Ridge, NY.
D. Jeremiah - b1705, d1715.
E. Samuel -.

References: *The New England Historical and Genealogical Society Register*, Vol. 12, p. 315.

AUSTEN, AUSTIN, ASTIN, John - d1657, m1 Constance Robinson (wd/o William), m2 Katharine ____ (dc1683), she m2 William Hubbard.

John Austin came from England on the *Hercules* with his first wife. He was in New London, CT in 1647. By 1651 he was in Greenwich and was a carpenter. His son John was a tailor and returned to Stamford. He had a house on the west side of West Street.

Descendants of AUSTEN, AUSTIN, ASTIN, John:

A. Samuel - d1657.
B. Elizabeth - m1 1670 Joseph Finch, m2 1714 Jonathan Newman.
C. John - d1699, m by 1682 Hannah Hardy (d1710, d/o Richard).
D. Thomas -.

A Rebecca Austin married Thomas Skelding in 1701, and Jonathan Austin (1685-1769) married Hannah Ferris.

References: Duane Hamilton Hurd, *History of New London*, p. 364.

AYRES, Richard - bc1640, m Mary ____.

Richard Ayres was in Stamford in 1670 when he received a house lot on the extension of North Street. He sold it in 1681 when he moved to Bedford where he helped with lay-outs and was also a fence viewer. He and his son Richard later returned to Stamford but probably later returned to Bedford as there is no Ayres on the 1701 tax list. Descendants:

A. Richard - bc1676, d1719, m1712 Abigail Buxton (b1689, d aft 1735, d/o Clement), she m2 1721 John Mott.
B. dau - bc1679, m Samuel Wood.
C. Lawrence - bc1681, d1717.
D. Philip - bc1683.
E. prob Hannah - m William Clark.
F. prob Elizabeth - d1715, m1698 Joseph Lockwood.

BASSETT, John - d1653, m Margery ____ (d1656).

John and his wife were hired in England to be servants of Mr. Stephen Goodyear, Deputy Governor of New Haven. John, a master carpenter, signed the Oath of Fidelity in 1644 in New Haven. He was in Stamford in 1651, perhaps to be with his son Robert, a carpenter too, and a shoemaker. Robert had a house lot on the east side of West Street in 1650. John Bassett died in New Haven in 1653, but his wife died in Stamford in 1656. Robert moved to Hempstead, L.I. about 1658. Descendants:

A. Robert - d1670, m Mary ____. Hempstead, L.I.
   1. Mary - b1650.
   2. dau -.
   3. Sarah -.
   4. John -.
   5. Robert -.

Descendants of BASSETT, John (continued):

B. dau - m John Emery.
C. dau - m John Webb.
D. Sarah -.
E. Elizabeth - m1658 Isaac Finch.

References: Paul W. Prindle, *Gillespie Genealogy*.

BATES, Robert - d1675, m1 ____, m2 aft 1655, Margaret Weeche Cross (wd/o William of Fairfield), m3 aft 1657 Susanna Smith Hoyt (d1674, wd/o Simon).

Robert Bates came from England in 1630 with Sir Richard Saltonstall. He was in Watertown, MA until 1636 or 1638 when he went to Wethersfield, MA. He was one of the original settlers in Stamford in 1641, and his home was on the north side of North Street. In his will he requested that his negro slaves be freed at the age of forty.

His son Ensign John lived on the northeast corner of North Street and "River Street", but no deed exists in the records for that house lot. Descendants:

A. Ens John - b1641, d1714, m1663 Sarah Cross (d1712, d/o William).
    1. John - bc1663, d bef 1752, m1 1694 Elizabeth Lockwood (d1702, d/o Gershom), m2 1702 Sarah Smith (d1727, d/o Daniel), m3 1728 Mrs. Hannah Mead.
        a. John - b1694, d bef 1754, m1722 Mary Webb (d/o Samuel).
        b. Nathaniel - b1697, d1754.
        c. Elizabeth - b1699.
        d. David - b1702.
        e. Nehemiah - b1704.
        f. Hannah - b1705.
        g. Mary - d1700 or 1702, m1693 John Pettit.
        h. Samuel - bc1667, d1754, m1704 Sarah Scofield (bc1658, d1718, d/o Daniel).
        i. Jonathan - bc1670, d1753, m1705, Joanna Selleck (b1686, d/o John).

B. Mary - bc1644, m1662 Abraham Ambler.

References: Harry S. Gorham, *Bates, Selleck and Allied Families*.

BELL, Lt Francis - d1689, m Rebecca ____ (d1684).

Francis Bell was in Wethersfield, MA where he was a lieutenant but not a freeman. He was one of the original settlers of

Stamford and in 1641 was a deputy with Andrew Ward. He was a lieutenant in Stamford in 1643. His house was on the corner of East Street and South Street, his son later owning the southern portion of his land. Cotton Mather referred to Francis as "a firm Puritan in form and principles." For more than forty years he was prominent as a leader in Stamford affairs.

He and his son Jonathan seem to have carried on a tanning business. His grandson Jonathan was a shoemaker.

Francis' Bible is owned by the Stamford Historical Society. An Abraham Bell married Hepzibah Clason. Descendants:

A. Lt & Capt Jonathan - b1641, d1699, m1 1662 Mercy Crane (d1671, d/o Jasper), m2 1672 Susanna Pierson (d1707, d/o Abraham).

1. Jonathan - b1664, d1745, m1 1693 Grace Kitchell (d1694), m2 1702 Deborah Ferris (d1724, d/o Peter), m3 1734 wd Mary Brush.

a. Jonathan - b1694, d aft 1770, m1717 Eunice Reed (b1698, d/o Thomas).

b. Francis - b1702, d1787.

c. Hannah - b1706, d1745.

d. Rebecca - b 1708.

e. James - b1710, d1775.

f. Deborah - b&d1713.

g. Abigail - b1717.

h. Hannah - b1665, m by 1689 John Betts.

i. Rebecca - b1667 or 1669, d1689.

j. Mercy - d1671.

k. Abigail - b&d1674.

l. Abraham - b1675, d1744, m1 1704 Hannah Hoyt (b1681, d1711, d/o Joshua), m2 1714 Mary Leeds (Lewis?, d1714), m3 c1719 Hepzibah Clason (d/o David).

m. Mercy - b1678, m1 1702 John Holmes, m2 1704 Dea Samuel Hoyt, m3 1716 Peter Ferris, m4 Dr Richard Barnum.

n. John - b1681, d1732, m1 Sarah _____ (d1701), m2 1711 Sarah Slason (d1713, d/o John), m3 1714 Hannah Whiting (d bef 1732).

o. James or a dau - b&d1683.

p. Susanna - b1686, d1756, m1 1706 Abraham Weed, m2 1715 Thomas Talmadge.

q. Mary - b1689, m1713 Lt Ebenezer Weed.

2. Rebecca - b1643, m by 1664 Jonathan Tuttle.

3. Mary - b1646, m1 1663 Joshua Hoyt, m2 1691 Joseph Turney.

BELL, Francis (continued):

References: John Valentine Hecker, *New York Genealogial and Biographical Record,* Vol. 28, pp. 153-154 and 201-207.

BISHOP, Rev John - bc1610, d1695, m1 Rebecca Goodyear (b1626, d1679, d/o Stephan), m2 Joanna Prudden (b1602, d1683, d/o Rev John Boyse, wd/o of Peter Prudden, wd/o Thomas Willett).

Although it is fairly certain that John Bishop was educated at Oxford University, his background is still uncertain because there happened to be two John Bishops there at the same time. John Bishop IV is endeavoring to solve this problem.

John Bishop lived next to the meeting-house common on the north side of the Country Road (probably West Street originally). He was buried in the old town cemetery "between his two wives" as he requested. His remains were removed to St. Andrew's Cemetery, and a stone was erected to his memory by his descendants.

His son Joseph was referred to once as "worshipful esquire." Descendants:

A. Stephen - bc1648, d1723, m1683 Mercy ____.
  1. John bc1683, dc1757, m1 1704 Mary Talmadge (b1683, d1725, d/o Enos), m2 1726 Sarah Lewis (b1689, d1729, d/o Capt John Osborn, wd/o Nathan), m3 Abigail ____.
  2. Abraham - b1684, d1711.
  3. Stephen - b1684, d1731, m1713 Waitstill Waterbury (b1685, d1730, d/o Joseph Green, wd/o David).
  4. Theophilus - b1687, d1710.
  5. Isaac - b1689, d1759?, m1718 Susanna Finch (b1694, d1748, d/o Samuel).
  6. Rebecca - b1692, d1757, m1717 Elisha Holly.
  7. Abigail - b1696, d1757, m1720 John Seely.

B. Capt Joseph - d1733, m1691 Elizabeth Knowles (b1669, d1754, d/o John).
  1. Joseph b1692, m1 1723 Hannah Holly (b1694, d/o John), m2 aft 1743 Hannah Newman (d/o John Jagger, wd/o Thomas Newman).
  2. Alexander - b1694, d1706.
  3. Charles - b1695.
  4. Andrew - b1696, d1753, m1 1734 Mary Crissey, m2 1748 Hannah Thorp (d/o Nathan Ferris, wd/o ____ Thorp).
  5. Hannah - b1698.
  6. Nathan - b1699, d young.

Descendants of BISHOP, Rev. John (continued):

7. Elizabeth - b1700, d1706.
8. Sarah - b1701.
9. Rebecca - b1703.
10. Elizabeth - b&d1705.
11. Helena - b1705, d1721.
12. Elizabeth - b1706, d1777.
13. Mary - b1708, d1766.
14. Martha - b1709.
15. Alexander - b1711.

C. Mary - b&dc1658.

Note: John and Rebecca had four other sons who had d by 1678.

D. Rebecca - b1663, d1726, m1684 Rev Joseph Whiting.
E. Ebenezer - bc1666, d1710 m1700, Sarah Slason (b1667, d1744, d/o John).
F. Benjamin - b1670, d1728), m1696 Susanna Pierson (d1748, d/o Rev Abraham).

1. Abigail - b1697.
2. Susanna - b1699.
3. Benjamin - b1701.
4. James - b1704.
5. Ruth - b1706.
6. David - b1708.

References: Paul W. Prindle, *Genealogy of Elizabeth Barrett Gillespie.*

BLATCHLEY, BLACHLEY, Samuel - b1672, d1756, m1 1699 Abigail Finch (d/o Abraham), m2 by 1710 Sarah ____.

Samuel Blatchley was born in New Haven, the son of Aaron Blatchley. He was a blacksmith who rose to a position of some prominence in Stamford. He first received land in 1695; he lived on the north side of East Street. Descendants:

A. Samuel - b1700, m1727 Hannah Bates.
B. Sarah - b1702.
C. Abigail - b1705.
D. Mary - b1710.
E. dau - b1712.
F. Martha - b1717.

References: Shirley Hathaway Stebbing, "Blatchley Physicians and Pioneers," *New England Historical and Genealogical Society Register*, Vol. 58, p. 357.

BROWN, Francis - bc 1628 - d1708, mc 1654 Adrea Corlet (b ___, d1655), m2 1657 Martha Chapman (d1680, wd/o Thomas Lawrence, wd/o John), m3 c1682 Judith Ogden (d/o Lt John Budd, wd/o John).

As there was also a Francis Brown in New Haven, the two are subject to confusion. According to Winthrop, the Stamford Francis had a daughter Mary, who at age twelve in 1667 was living in Hartford with Nathaniel Ruscoe as his adopted daughter. In Ruscoe's will of 1673 she is called "kinswoman." Francis was a servant of Henry Wolcott of Windsor, CT. He was freed from service in 1649 and by 1657 he was in Stamford and lived in his deceased father-in-law's house on the east side of South Street. In 1670 he had a house on the north side of East Street. By 1683 he moved on to Rye, NY. Descendants:

A. Mary - bc1655, m Thomas Hurlbut.
B. Joseph - bc1658, d1738, m Mary ____ (d1744).
   1. Francis - b1686, d1754, m1 1713 Mercy Webb (b1693, d/o Samuel), m2 Hannah ____.
   2. Joseph - b1689, d1730, m1 1720 Elizabeth Buxton (b1696, d1725, d/o Clement), m2 1726 Mary Hoyt (d1728, wd/o Benjamin of Windsor), m3 1729 Ruth Scofield (wd/o Ebenezer, she m3 Benjamin Close).
   3. Hannah - b1692, d young.
   4. Sarah - b1694, m 1714 Josiah Blackman.
   5. Nathaniel - b1696, m1725 Anna Brush (d/o Jacob).
   6. Nathan - b1697, d1747, m1726 Ruth Brush (d/o Jacob).
   7. Jonathan - b1701, d1747.
   8. David - b1704, d1711.
   9. Mary - b1705.
C. Rebecca - bc1662, d1743, m by 1682 Benjamin Galpin. Woodbury, CT.
D. Sarah - m Jonathan Scudder. Huntington, L.I.
E. Mercy -.

Note: The two oldest sons of Joseph may be reversed as to birth dates.

References: Rye, New York, *Town Records*.

BROWN, Peter - bc1610, d1658, m1 Elizabeth ____ (d1657), m2 1658 Unice\Unica Buxton (wd/o Clement, she m2 1659 Nicolas Knap).

Peter Brown was of Concord, MA in 1632 and of New Haven in 1639 where he was a baker. In 1647 he was in Stamford. He probably was a brother of Francis. He lived on the west side of "River Street."

Descendants of BROWN, Peter:

A. Thomas - bc1638 or 1642, d1694. Rye, NY.
B. Hachaliah - bc1640 or 1644, dc1720, m Mary Hoyt (d/o John). Rye, NY.
C. Mercy - bp1645.
D. Elizabeth - bp1647, m John Purdy of Fairfield.
E. Ebenezer - bc1653, dc1658.
F. Deliverance - bc1656, dc1727, m by 1678 Mary Purdy (d/o Francis). Rye, NY.

References: Grenville McKensie, *Families of Old Philipsburg.*

BUXTON, Clement - d1657, m Unice (Unica) ____ (d1670, she m2 1658 Peter Brown, she m3 1659 Nicolas Knap).

Where Clement came from is not known. He may have been previously married as his first daughter was considerably older than the next child, Clement. Clement lived on the east side of West Street. Descendants:

A. Elizabeth - m1655 Robert Husted.
B. Clement - b1647, d1724, m1676 Judith Prence (d1723).
  1. Unica - b1678, m1 1704 Samuel Scofield, m2 1709 Joseph Scofield.
  2. Clement - b1683, d by 1750, m1711 Elizabeth Ferre.
  3. Moses - b1686, d bef 1766, m1712 Mary Miller (d aft 1766, d/o John).
  4. Sarah - b1689, m1717 Jonathan Holly.
  5. Abigail - b1689, m1 1712 Richard Ayres, m2 John Mott.
  6. Mercy - b1692, d by 1720, m1718 Joseph Ferris.
  7. Elizabeth - b1696, d1725, m1720 Joseph Brown.
  8. Samuel - b1699, d1761, m1727 Hannah Bell (b1706, d1745, d/o Jonathan)
C. Sarah - m1680 Joseph Stevens.
D. Unica (Unice) - m Jonathan Waterbury?

References: Robert W. Spiers, *Descendants of Clement Buxton.*

CHAPMAN, John - d1655, m Martha Lawrence (wd/o Thomas of Milford, she m2 1657 Francis Brown).

John Chapman was an original settler of New Haven; he was in Fairfield, CT in 1647 and then moved to Stamford.

His wife Martha brought her two children, Martha and Thomas Lawrence, to Stamford.

They lived on the east side of South Street; they also had had a house and lot on the east side of North Street in 1648. Descendants:

A. Mary - m by 1665 Eleazer Slawson.
B. Elizabeth - m1674 John Judson.

CLASON, CLAUSON, CLOYSON, Stephen - dc1700, m1655 Elizabeth Periment (b1631, d1714).

Stephen Clason was married in Stamford in 1654, but who Elizabeth Periment was remains a mystery. Eardeley suggests that her name was Penoyer. Stephen's son Stephen moved to Bedford. His two grandchildren, children of the late Jonathan, lived with him, according to his will. The witch trial of his wife took place in the early 1690s.

The Clasons lived on the east side of West Street from 1654 to the late 1670's when they moved west of Mill River north of the road. Descendants:

A. Jonathan - b1656, d1685, m1681 Sarah Roberts (b1661, d1684, d/o Thomas).
  1. Stephen - b1682, d1746, m1709 Abigail Green (d/o John).
  2. Sarah - b1683.
B. Stephen - b1658, m1 1692 Rebecca Jones (wd/o Samuel Drake, wd/o Joseph), m2 ____ Rogers. Bedford, N.Y.
C. Rebecca - b1660.
D. David - b1662, d1721, m1688 Mary Hardy (b1659, d1716, d/o Richard).
  1. Mary - b1689, d1745, m1705 Peter June.
  2. Deborah - b1695, m Abraham Wanser.
  3. Hepzibah - b1698, m1720 Abraham Bell.
  4. Martha - b1699, m John Miller.
E. Samuel - d1723, m1693 Hannah Dunham (d1721).
  1. Abigail - m1717 Abraham Ambler.
  2. Sgt Jonathan - b1697, dc1746, m1719 Elizabeth James (she m2 1746 ____).
  3. Sarah -.
  4. Waitstill -.
  5. Hannah -.
  6. Mercy -.
  7. Rebecca -.
  8. Jemima -.
  9. Kezia -.
  (continued next page)

Descendants of CLASON, Stephen (continued):
F. Elizabeth - bc1665, m1685 Francis Dan.
G. Abigail? - mc1713 Stephen Holmes (she div & m1717 Daniel Holly).
H. Daniel - bp1675.

References: William B. Lapham, *Genealogical History of the Clason Family*.

CLEMENTS, CLEMENCE, William - d1702, m Elizabeth (d1728, wd/o ____).

William Clemence, called a joiner, was in Stamford by 1667. He was the teacher after Mr. Rider left. He had a home lot but no house at the east end of town in 1670, north of the road. Later he moved west of Mill River. In 1659, a William Clemence of Cambridge petitioned the General Court of Boston for a divorce, saying his wife had made him lead a kind of death for fifteen years (Mass. Historical Society). This may have been the Stamford William's father. Descendants:

A. Hannah - m1694 Caleb Knap.
B. Mary - m1694 John Butler.
C. Elizabeth - m1694 John Bolt or Buell.
D. Hester - d1712, m1696 Benjamin Green.
E. Sarah - d1747, m1 1698 Zachariah Dibble, m2 by 1719 John Youngs.
F. Charity - m1702 Daniel Lockwood.

References: Harriet Hodges, *The Lockwood Genealogy*; Alfred Averill Knapp, *The Nicolas Knapp Genealogy*.

CRAB, Richard - dc1680, m Alice Wright (sis/o Anthony).

Richard Crab was a deputy to the Hartford General Assembly in 1639-1640. He was an original settler in Stamford in 1641 with the Wethersfield group. He was given land in the Greenwich area. After his troubles as a Quaker, he moved in 1660 to Oyster Bay, L.I. Descendants:

A. Jeremiah -.
B. Richard -.

References: Pelletreau, *Poughkeepsie Documents*.

CRISSY, CRESSEY, William - bc1636, d1684, m Sarah ____.

William Crissy came to America in 1649 with his brother

Michael. he was employed by Capt. Thomas Lothrop of Beverly, MA. In 1661 he was with the family of Mordeca Larcon. He was in Stamford by 1662. He lived on the south side of East Street. Descendants:

A. Mary? - d1658.
B. Nathaniel - b1663.
C. John - b1665, m1 1692 Abigail Knap (d1706, d/o Moses), m2 1708 Rebecca Morehouse (d/o John Knowles; wd/o Jonathan).
   1. Sarah - b1693, d by 1723, m1717 John Green.
   2. Abigail - b1695.
   3. John - b1696.
   4. Deborah - b1698, m1720 Joseph Ferris.
   5. Nathaniel - b1700, m1726 Hannah Hoyt.
D. Moses -.
E. Elizabeth - m1698 Moses Knap.
F. Jonathan - m1 by 1701 _____, m2 1705 Ann Powell (d1715), m3 1716 Rebecca Weed (d/o Richard Higgenbotham, wd/o Joseph).
G. Mary - m1697 John Holly.

In William's estate proceedings, two sons and four daughters are recorded.

References: Ernest W. Cressey, *The Cressey Family*.

CROSS

The six Cross children, who were the children of Margaret and William, moved to Stamford when Margaret married Robert Bates after the death of William in 1655. William Cross had lived in Windsor, CT, then in Wethersfield in 1644, and lastly in Fairfield, CT. The three daughters may have been older than the sons. Nathaniel went to Bedford, NY for a year in 1680, and John, who also moved there, stayed until 1685 or 1686, when he went to Windsor, CT. Nathaniel was a gunsmith. While in Stamford, they lived west of Mill River, north of the road. Descendants:

A. Nathaniel - bc1646, d1714, m1 Abigail Holly (b1646, d/o John), m2 1696 Hannah Knap (b1671, d/o Moses), she m2 1715 Samuel Palmer.
   1. Hannah - b1687, d1756, m1710 Sgt John Waterbury.
   2. Abigail - b1694, d1710.
   3. Deborah - b1702, d1735, m1723 John Knap.
   4. Nathaniel - b1703, d1714.

CROSS (continued):

5. Sarah - b1705, m1725 Israel Holly.
6. John - b1707.
7. Mary - b170-.

B. Samuel - m Elizabeth Chapman (d/o ______ Fox, wd/o Edward).

C. John - bc1648, m1 1686 Mary Grant (d/o Josias Hull, wd/o John), m2 c1720 Mary ____.

1. Hannah - b1694, d1696.

D. Sarah - d1712, m John Bates.

E. Mary - d1687, m1 1673 John Pickett, Jr., m2 1698 Joshua Hoyt.

F. Hannah - d by 1682, m John Jagger.

References: *The Lester Card Manuscript*

DAN, DANN, Francis - d1724, m1685 Elizabeth Clason (d aft 1749, d/o Stephen).

Francis Dan went from Barbados to Stamford about 1684. He lived west of Mill River north of the road. Later in the northern part of Stamford there was an area known as Dantown. Descendants:

A. Elizabeth - b1686, mc 1712 John Jones.

B. John - b1691, m1719 Deborah Green (b1701, d/o Benjamin).

C. David - bc1693, m1724 Hannah Lockwood (b1701, d/o Joseph).

D. Abigail - b1700.

E. Francis - bc1704, d1706.

F. Rebecca - b1706.

G. Jonathan - b1709.

References: Harvey M. Dann, *Dan and Montgomery Chronicles*; William B. Lapham, *The Clason Memorial*.

DAVENPORT, Rev John - b1669, d1731, m1 1695 Martha Selleck (bc1668, d1712, d/o Maj Nathan Gold, wd/o John), m2 Elizabeth Maltby (d1758, d/o John Morris, wd/o _______ Maltby).

John Davenport was born in Boston, the son of John Davenport, son of John who founded New Haven. He went to Harvard and then in 1692-1693 accepted the offer to be minister in Stamford. His home was on the south corner of North Street where it turns towards Mill River.

Descendants of DAVENPORT, John:

A. Abigail - b1696, m Rev Stephen Williams.
B. John - b1698, d1742, m1721 Sarah Bishop (b1701, d/o Capt Joseph).
C. Martha - b1700.
D. Sarah - b1702.
E. Theodora - b1703, d1712.
F. Dea Deodate - b1706.
G. Elizabeth - b1708.
H. Abraham - b1715, d1789.
I. Rev James - b1716, d1755.

References: "The History and Genealogy of the Davenport Family," *The New England Historical and Genealogical Society Register*, Vol. 1, pp. 518-519.

DEAN, Samuel - bc1630, d1703, m Ann Holmes (bc1634, d1707, d/o Francis).

Samuel Dean was in Stamford by 1650. He lived on the east side of North Street. A part of northern Stamford was later called Deantown. There was also a poor man called Robert Dean, who had to be cared for by the town. He was given a house on the west side of West Street in 1684 and was designated as coming from Hempstead, L.I. Descendants:

A. John - b1659, d1706, m Abigail ____.
   1. John - d1740, m1724 Ann Bishop.
   2. Elizabeth -.
   3. Mercy - m1719 Ebenezer Seely.
B. Joseph - b1661.
C. Matthew -.

DENTON, Rev Richard - b1586, d1662, m1 ____, m2 ____.

The Reverend Richard Denton came from Owram, Yorkshire and was on the *James* with Matthew Mitchell, arriving in Watertown, MA by 1634. He was in Wethersfield, CT in 1635 and was the leader of the first group of settlers in Stamford in 1641. His house was later that of John Bishop. He also led the group that went to Long Island in 1644, and then returned to England in 1659. Cotton Mather wrote a glowing account of him (cf. Huntington). Descendants:

A. John - b1618.
B. Daniel -.
C. Timothy - bc1627.

Descendants of DENTON, Richard (continued):

D. Nathaniel - bc1628, d1730 m Sarah ____.
E. Richard - d1658, m1657 Ruth Tileston.
F. Samuel - d1714, m Mary Smith.

References: Edythe Whitley, *Some of the Descendants of Rev. Richard Denton*; Frances Isabel Denton Womack, *The Denton Genealogy*.

DIBBLE, John - d1646, m Sarah ____ (d1656, she m2 1647 William Graves).

John Dibble's son Samuel may have been born in Springfield, MA in 1644. John never appears as a landowner in the Stamford records. His son Zachariah's wife divorced him on the grounds of "desertion and infidelity." Descendants:

A. Samuel - b1644?
B. Zachariah - m1666 Sarah Waterbury (bc1643, d1712, d/o John, div in 1672 & she m2 Nicolas Webster, she m3 Edward Trehern).
   1. Zachariah - b1667, d1712, m1698 Sara Clements (d1747, d/o William, she m2 1718 John Youngs).
      a. Zachariah - b1699.
      b. John - b1701.
      c. David - b1704.
      d. Rev Ebenezer - b1706, d1799.
      e. Reuben - b1708.
      f. Benjamin - b1710.
      g. Jonathan - b1711, d1760.

References: Van Beuren Lamb, *The Ancestry of the Dibbles*.

FERRIS, Jeffrey - bc1610, d1666, m1 ____ Freeman (d1658), m2 1659 Susannah Lockwood (d1660, prob d/o Richard Norman, wd/o Robert), m3 1662 Judith Palmer (d/o James Feake, wd/o Lt. William). She m3 John Bowers.

Jeffrey Ferris, possibly of Leicestershire, came to America in 1634. He was first in Watertown and was made freeman in 1635. He was in Wethersfield by 1640 and signed the original deed with the Dutch in 1640 in Greenwich. He and his sons seem to have lived in both the Greenwich area and in Stamford, where by 1650 he had a houselot on the north side of North Street. For many years he ran the town grist mill. He brought up the four Palmer sons of his third wife.

Descendants of FERRIS, Jeffrey:

A. Peter - bc1634, d1706, m1 1654 Elizabeth Reynolds (b1634, d1703, d/o John), m Ruth Weed (wd/o Daniel).
  1. Joseph - b1657, d1733, m1 Mary Hoyt (b1664, d/o Joshua), m2 Mary (d/o Joseph Turney).
    a. Joseph - b1688, m1 1718 Mercy Buxton (b1692, d1718, d/o Clement), m2 1720 Deborah Crissy (b1698, d1748, d/o John).
    b. Mary - b1690, m Jonathan Weed.
    c. Nathan - b1694.
    d. Samuel - b1696, m Experience Crissy.
    e. Elizabeth - b1699, m1723 Joseph Pardee.
    f. Abigail - b1702, d1737, m1725 John Penoyer.
    g. Hannah - b1704.
    h. Deborah - b1706.
    i. Jonathan - bc1714.
  2. Jeffrey - b&d1658.
  3. Elizabeth - b&d1659.
  4. Peter - b1660, d1737, m1 1706 Sarah Hoyt (b1674, d1715, d/o Joshua), m2 1716 Mercy Hoyt (b1678, d1748, d/o Capt Jonathan, wd/o John Holmes, wd/o Samuel, she m4 Dr Richard Barnum).
  5. Mary - b1662, m? Jeremiah Jagger.
  6. Elizabeth - b1664, m? Jeremiah Jagger.
  7. Hannah - b1666, d1724, m1692 Capt John Knapp.
  8. Deborah - d1724, m1702 Jonathan Bell.

B. Joseph - bc1638, d1699, m1657 Ruth Knap (b1641, d/o Nicolas, she m2 John Clapp). Greenwich.
  1. Peter - b1660, d1690, m Mary ____?
  2. John - m1695 Abigail Hait of Norwalk.
  3. James - mc1705 Rachel Mead (wd/o Nathaniel).
  4. Ruth - d1745, m1685 Samuel Peck.
  5. Moses - d1748, m Eunice ____.
  6. Benjamin - bc1668, d1709, m Sarah Waterbury (b1675, d/o Daniel Weed, wd/o Lt David Waterbury, she m3 1711 Nathaniel Pond).
  7. Caleb - b1679, m Elizabeth ____.
  8. Joseph - d1735, m Abigail ____.
  9. Joshua - b1683, d1746, unm.
  10. Hannah -b1687, d1711, m Jonathan Austin.

C. Mary - bc1637, d1708, m1 Lt Jonathan Lockwood, m2 1696 Thomas Merritt.

D. John - bc1640, d1715, m1 Mary Jackson, m2 Grace Pauling (d1716). Westchester, NY.

E. James - bc1643, d1726, m Mary ____.
  1. James -.

FERRIS, Jeffrey (continued):

References: Captain James Ferris, *The Ferris Genealogy*; and *Harriet Scofield notes*

FINCH, Daniel - bc1585, d1667. Fairfield, CT.

FINCH, John - bc1590, d1657, m1 _____, m2 Martha Betts. She m1658 John Green.

Daniel and John Finch came to America in 1630 on the *Arbella* with Abraham and Abraham, Jr. They may have come from Yorkshire. While they were in Watertown, MA, the Finch house and belongings were destroyed in a fire. Daniel was the first constable in Wethersfield in 1636. He was among the first settlers in Stamford in 1641 and lived on the north side of North Street, where the Ferguson Library is today. John Finch lived next to him by 1650 but three years later moved to the north side of East Street where his son John continued to live. Daniel moved to Fairfield about 1649. His will mentions his young son Nathaniel and gives bequests to four men who may have been sons-in-law. An earlier son, Abraham, was killed by an Indian in Wethersfield in 1637. John's son, John, called a mariner, died in Huntington, L.I. Descendants of John:

A. John - bc1630, d1658, m1652 Hannah Fuller (d/o ____ Marsh, wd/o Lancelot). Huntington, L.I.
B. Isaac - bc1635, d1702, m1 1658 Elizabeth Bassett (d/o John), m2 by 1688 Ann _____ (d1703).
    1. John - b1659, d1703, m1 Sarah Pettit (b1666), m2 aft 1684 Hannah Webb (d/o Richard Scofield, wd/o of Joseph).
        a. Abraham -.
    2. Isaac - b1662, m1704 Mary Rundle. Greenwich & Goshen, NY.
    3. Abraham - b1665, d1708, m Martha Couch (d/o Simon).
        a. Isaac - b1696, d1749, of Goshen, NY.
        b. Elizabeth - b1698.
        c. Solomon -.
    4. Elizabeth - b1669, dc1692, mc1691 Jonathan Pettit.
    5. Martha - b1672.
    6. Rebecca - b1683.
    7. Sarah - b1687.
    8. Jacob - b1691, d1702.
    9. Benjamin - b1695, m1717 Elizabeth Palmer (bc1697, d/o James). North Castle, NY.
C. Martha -.
D. Samuel - bc1638, d1698, m Sarah Hoyt (b1639, d1713, d/o Simon).

Descendants of FINCH, John (continued):

1. Sarah - b1662, d1751, m1686 Jonathan Holly.
2. Sgt Samuel - bc1666, d1751, m Sarah Gold (d/o John).
   a. Mary - b1693, m1714 Nathan Hoyt.
   b. Susanna - b1694, d1748, m1718 Isaac Bishop.
   c. Sarah - b1695, d1715, unm.
   d. Abigail - b1697, d1715, unm.
   e. Hannah - b1701, d1762, m1 1728 Joseph Hoyt, m2 by 1732 Thomas Waterbury.
   f. Martha - b1703.
3. Joseph - d1752, m1703 Abigail Seely (prob d/o Obadiah).
4. Martha - b1665, prob m Jonathan Mead.
5. Susannah - d1710, m1692 Obadiah Seely.
6. Rachel - m a Finch?

E. Joseph - b1647, d1714, m1670 Elizabeth Austin (d/o John, she m2 1714 Jonathan Newman). Greenwich.

F. Abraham - bc1648, m ____.

1. Abigail - m1699 Samuel Blatchley.
2. Comfort - m1700 John How.

References: Col. Clause D. Thummel, *Finch Family*, DAR Library; *The Finch Family Bulletin*; *Finch manuscript*, The Ferguson Library, Stamford.

GARNSEY, GUERNSEY, Joseph - d1688, m1659 Rose Waterbury (bc1618, d by 1688, wd/o John).

Joseph Garnsey was in New Haven in 1646 where a record states he was to be punished for disobeying his master's commands. He took the Oath of Fidelity there in 1647 and was in Stamford in 1651. In 1667 he bought a house on the west side of South Street. Descendants:

A. Joseph - b1662, d1709, m1693 Mary Lockwood (b166-, d/o Edmund).

1. Mary - b1693.
2. Joseph - b1695.
3. John - b1697.
4. Rose - b1699.
5. Jonathan - b1701.
6. Hannah - b1702.
7. Deborah (Debro) - b1704.
8. Susanna -.

References: Eva G. Card and Howard Abram Garnsey, *The Garnsey Genealogy*, 1967.

GOLD, Sgt John - d1712 m by 1660 Hannah Slason (bc1640, d1730, d/o George, she m2 1714 Dea Samuel Hoyt).

John Gold was in Stamford by 1669 when he received land. In 1707 he is referred to as a shoemaker. He lived on the west side of South Street in 1680, a house he received from his father-in-law. Descendants:

A. Sarah - m1692 Samuel Finch.
B. Hannah - m1 1692 Abraham Ambler, m2 1697 Jeremiah Andreas.
C. Mary - m1699 Eliphalet Lockwood.
D. John - d1720, m1707 Hannah Higginbotham (d/o Richard). She m2 1724 John Seymour.
E. Ann - m1707 John Pettit.
F. Sgt Jonathan - d1730.

GREEN, John - bc1610, d1693, m1 Mercy (or Mary) Jarvis (d1657), m2 1658 Martha (Brett?) Finch (wd/o John).

John Green's background is uncertain because there were several John Greens who came to America in the early 1630s. He was in New Haven before 1650 and in Stamford by 1654 where he lived on the north side of East Street. He was a shepherd in 1669 and was a constable and a deputy several times. He moved to Bedford, NY in 1680 and died there. His sons Joseph and Benjamin returned to Stamford about 1685. They lived at the east end of town north of the road.

Note: The two Sarahs (dau. of John and dau. of Benjamin) may be wrong re. their husbands. Descendants:

A. John - b1651, d young.
B. Joseph - b1656, d1710, mc1680 Elizabeth ____ (d1721).
  1. Mary - b1681, d1714 m1707 John Perry.
  2. Elizabeth - b1683, d1716, m1 Ebenezer Darling, m2 Dr John Drew.
  3. Waitstill - b1685, d1730, m1 1707 David Waterbury, m2 1713 Stephen Bishop.
  4. Joseph - b1687, m1712 Sarah Brown.
  5. John - b1691, d1728, m1717 Sarah Crissy (b1693, d/o John).
  6. Mercy - b1694, m1723 Benjamin Bunnell.
  7. Nathaniel - b1697, m1722 Elizabeth Frost.
C. John - b1660, d1728, m1683 Abigail ____.
  1. Abigail - b1685, m1709 Stephen Clason.
  2. Sarah - b1688, d1713, m1710 Stephen Holmes.
  3. Deborah - b1690, m1712 Cornelius Delevan.
  4. Martha - b1692, m1716 Nehemiah Churcher (or Churchill).

Descendants of GREEN, John (continued):

5. Samuel - b1694.
6. David - b1700.
7. Jonathan - b1702.
8. John - b1704.

D. Mary - mc1680 Thomas Stevens.

E. Benjamin - b1662, d1727, m1 1683 Susan Roberts (b1663, d1694, d/o Thomas), m2 1696 Hester Clements (d1712, d/o William), m3 1713 Mary Holmes (d aft 1717, d/o John Hobby, wd/o Stephen).

1. Benjamin? - bc1684, d young.
2. Sarah - b1684, m1727 Joseph Lockwood.
3. Phebe - b1686, m1 c1708 John Smith, m2 by 1727 ____ Lockwood.
4. Benjamin? - bc1687, d1690.
5. Lucretia - b1690, d bef 1720, m1719 John Dow?
6. Benjamin - b1693, m1730 Rebecca Weed (d/o Joseph).
7. Hester - b1696, m Nathan Smith.
8. Deborah (Debro) - b1701, m1719 John Dann.
9. Joanna - b1703.
10. Ebenezer - b1705.
11. Nathan - b1706.
12. Reuben - b1709.
13. Charles - 1710.

References: *Paul W. Prindle records.*

HARDY, Richard - d1683, m1653 Ann Husted (bc1623, d1707, d/o Robert).

Richard Hardy was in Concord in 1639 probably. He was in Stamford by 1650 and lived on the north side of East Street. A place west of Mill River was named Hardy's Hole after him. He served as a deputy to the Connecticut Assembly three times. Descendants:

A. Sarah - m1669 Thomas Close.

B. Susannah - m Edmund Sherman.

C. Hannah - m by 1682 John Austin.

D. Samuel - b1656, m1 1686 Rebecca Hobby (bc1669, d/o John), m2 1693 or 1698 Rebecca Firbush.

1. Rebecca - b1687.
2. Hannah - b1693.
3. Samuel - b1699.
4. Daniel - b1701.
5. Phinehas - 1704.

Descendants of HARDY, Richard (continued):

E. Elizabeth - m _____ Pearson or Parsons.
F. Ruth - m1681 John Mead.
G. Mary - b1659, d1716, m1688 David Clason.
H. Ann -.
I. Abigail -.

HIGGINBOTHAM, HIGGINBOTTOM, Richard - d1731, m1 Elizabeth Cooper (d1706, d/o Thomas Munson, wd/o Timothy), m2 1707 Eunice Waterbury (d1710, wd/o Jonathan), m3 1711 Nedemiah _____.

Richard Higginbotham was in New Haven and then in Elizabethtown before moving to Stamford about 1696. He was a tailor. In the 1701 tax list he is called Mr. He later moved to Greenwich. Descendants:

A. Rebecca - b1682, m1 1701 Joseph Weed, m2 1716 Jonathan Crissy.
B. Hannah - m1 1707 John Gold, m2 c1724 John Seymour.
C. Richard - m Mary Tuttle.

HOLLY, John - b1618, d1681, m Mary (Waitstill?) (d aft 1692).

John Holly was in Cambridge, MA in 1645. He and his father Samuel, who died in 1641, had a mill there. John was in Stamford by 1647 and rose to positions of prominence in the community. The dates of his children's births are uncertain. One account says that he had ten children, one of them Martha. John and his sons Samuel, John, and Jonathan lived on the west side of South Street. Descendants:

A. Samuel - b1641 or bc1644, d1709, m1668 Mary Close (b1650, d1714).
  1. John - b1670, d1719, m1697 Mary Crissy (d/o William).
     a. Abigail - b1697.
     b. Ebenezer - b1699.
     c. Noah - b1701.
     d. Joseph - b1702, d1706.
     e. Hannah - b1702.
     f. Samuel - b1704.
     g. Bezaleel - b1706.
  2. Samuel - b1672, d young.
  3. Hannah - b1676, d1700.
  4. Joseph - b1678, d1706.
  5. Mary - b1680, d1740, m1703 John Scofield.
  6. Benjamin - b1684, d1733.

Descendants of HOLLY, John (continued):

7. Daniel (Samuel?) - b1687, m1 Susanna (d1710), m2 1717 Abigail Holmes (d/o Stephen Clason, div from Stephen Holmes). Bedford, NY.

B. Elizabeth - m Robert Turney.

C. Capt Increase - bc1643 or 1646, d1727, m1679 Elizabeth Newman (b1654, d1713, d/o William).

1. John - b1680, d1718, m1704 Susanna Selleck (b1682, d1745, d/o John).
2. Jonathan - b1684, d1751.
3. Joseph - b1687, m1713 Waitstill Webb (b1691, d/o Samuel).
4. Nathan - b1692, m1718 Sarah Webb.
5. Increase - d1732.

D. Abigail - b1646, d aft 1707, m Nathaniel Cross.

E. John - b1649, d1716, m1679 Hannah Newman (b1657, d1712 or 1714, d/o William).

1. Samuel - b&d1680.
2. Abigail - b1682, d1707, m1706 David Webster.
3. Benjamin - b1684.
4. John - b1685, d1724, m1708 Abigail Hoyt (b1685, d/o Joshua).
5. Nathaniel - b1687, m Mary ____ (d1730).
6. Josiah - b1690, d1715.
7. Hannah - b1694, d1745, m1723 Joseph Bishop.
8. Elizabeth - b1698, d1742, m1722 Nathaniel Seely.
9. Sarah - b1701, d1785.

F. Hannah - b1651, d1710, m1671 Dea Samuel Hoyt.

G. Bethia - b1652 or 1655, d1713, m1676 Jonas Weed.

H. Elisha - b1659, d1719, m1686 Martha Holmes (bc1667, d1724, d/o Stephen).

1. Elisha - b1687, d1752, m1717 Rebecca Bishop (b1692, d1757, d/o Stephen).
2. Eliphalet - b1690, d1744, m1714 Mercy Penoyer (b1693, d1734?, d/o Thomas).
3. Martha - b1691, m1713 Cary Leeds.
4. Elizabeth - b1694, d by 1719, m1716 Thomas Waterbury.
5. Elnathan - b1696, m1728 Hannah Jagger.
6. Israel - b1698, m1725 Sarah Cross (bc1750, d/o Nathaniel).
7. Abigail - b1700.
8. John - b&d1702.
9. Mary - b&d1705.
10. Sarah - b1705, d1764.

I. Jonathan - b1662, d1712, m1686 Sarah Finch (b1662, d1751, d/o Samuel).

Descendants of HOLLY, John (continued):

1. Jonathan - b1687, d1769, m1717 Sarah Buxton.
2. Sarah - b1690, d1733.
3. Charles - b1694, m1718 Elizabeth Bradley (d/o John).
4. David - b1696, d1751, m1 1722 Margery Webb (d1742), m2 1743 wid Sarah Little.
5. Bethia - b1698, d1699.
6. Jabez - b1699, m1727 Waitstill Clason.
7. John -b&d1703.
8. Increase - b1703.
9. Deborah - b1706.
10. Nathaniel - b1708.

References: Charles Moses Holly, *The Holly Family*, 1861, The Stamford Historical Society; Charles Arthur Hoppen, *Washington Ancestry and Other Colonial Families*

HOLMES, HOMES, Francis - bc1600, d1675, m1 _____, m2 aft 1658 Ann Stevens (d1675, wd/o Thomas).

Francis Holmes was probably from Yorkshire and came to America about 1635. He was in Stamford by 1648; his home was on the south side of East Street. His son John moved to Bedford, NY and held important positions there as did his son John. Francis' son Richard moved to Norwalk.

Francis had a servant named Cornelius Hunt.

Francis' grandson John (son of Stephen) was killed by the meetinghouse bell. Descendants:

A. Stephen - bc1632, m Martha _____ (d1728).
   1. Martha - bc1667, d1721, m1686 Elisha Holly.
   2. John - bc1675, d1703, m1702 Mercy Bell (b1678, d/o Capt Jonathan, she m2 1704 Dea Samuel Hoyt, she m3 1716 Peter Ferris, she m4 Dr Richard Barnum).
      a. John (first named Jonathan) - b1703.
   3. Stephen - bc1677, m1 1704 Margaret Gibbs (d/o John), m2 1710 Sarah Green (d1713, d/o John), m3 Abigail Clason (she div him and m1717 Daniel Holly).
   4. Rebecca - d1749 m1700 Jonathan Jagger.
   5. Abigail - m1710 Dea John Hoyt.
   6. Mary - m1692 John Slason.
   7. Sarah - d1709, m1707 Sgt John Waterbury.
   8. Samuel - d1734, m1725? Anne Orry.

B. Ann - bc1634, m Samuel Dean.

C. Richard - bc1637, d1704, m Sarah Warner (or Varnum?) (d by 1704, d/o Robert), no issue, of Norwalk.

Descendants of HOLMES, Francis (continued):

D. John - bc1638, d bef 1715, m1659 Rachel Waterbury (bc1639, d/o John). Bedford, NY.

1. John - b&d1600.
2. Mary - b1662 m John Miller
3. Stephen - b1664, d1710, m1686 Mary Hobby (bc1670, d/o John), she m2 1713 Benjamin Green. Greenwich.
   a. Jonathan -.
   b. Benjamin -.
4. Richard - bc1665, d bef 1710, mc1693 Mary Miller (b1671). Bedford, NY.
5. Sarah - bc1667, m1691 Jonathan Miller.
6. Rachel - b1669, m Richard Westcott. Bedford, NY.
7. John - b1670, d1729, m Sarah Clark (bc1674, d/o William). Bedford, NY.
8. Jonas - b1672, m1692 Sarah (Appleton?).
9. Capt Jonathan - b1674 m Dorothy Roberts (d/o Zachariah).
10. Rose - b1678, m1702 John Westcott.
11. David - b1680, m Ruth ____.
12. Joseph - b1683 m Joanna ____.

HOYT, Simon - b1590, d1657, m1 1612 Deborah Stowers (b1593, d/o Walter), m2 at Scituate Susannah Smith (d1674, she m2 Robert Bates).

Simon Hoyt was probably born in Upway, Dorchester, the son of John. He came to America on the *Abigail* in 1628. He was in Charlestown in 1628, Salem 1629, Dorchester 1630, Scituate 1635, Windsor, CT 1639, Fairfield, CT 1649, and in Stamford shortly thereafter. He lived on the north side of East Street. His many children established families in several towns so that there are many branches of his family in many places.

There is a reference to a Jonas Hoyt marrying a Jemima in 1716. Descendants:

A. John - b1614, d1684. Fairfield CT & Rye NY.
B. Walter - b1616, d1696, m Rhoda Taylor. Norwalk.
C. Thomas - b1618, d1656.
D. Deborah - b1620, d1628.
E. Nicholas - b1622, d1655. Windsor.
F. Ruth - b1625, d1628.
G. Mary - b1635, m aft 1665 Thomas Lyon.
H. Moses - b1637, d1712.
I. Sarah - b1639, d1713, m1665 Samuel Finch.
J. Joshua - bc1640, d1690, mc1663 Mary Bell (b1646, d/o Francis, she m2 1691 Joseph Turney).

Descendants of HOYT, Simon (continued):

1. Mary - b1664, m Joseph Ferris.
2. Rebecca - b1667.
3. Joshua - b1671, d1745, m1 by 1695 _____ Turney (d/o Joseph), m2 1698 Mary Pickett (d1732, d/o John & niece of John Cross), m3 Hannah Coley (d/o Simon Couch, wd/o Peter).
   a. Jerusha - b1698, m1719 David Stevens.
   b. Joshua - b1700.
   c. Mary - b1702.
   c. Job - b1703, d1754.
   d. Sarah - b1706.
   e. Charles - b1710.
   f. Rebecca - b1712.
4. Sarah - b1674, d1715, m1706 Peter Ferris.
5. Samuel - b1678, d1738, m1 1700 Susannah Slason (d1707, d/o Eleazer), m2 1707 Mary Weed (d/o Daniel Scofield, wd/o Jonas).
6. Hannah - b1681, d1711, m1701 Daniel Scofield.
7. Moses - b1683, d1731.
8. Abigail - b1685, m1708 John Holly.

K. Miriam - m1662 Samuel Firman.

L. Dea Samuel - bc1643, d1720, m1 1671 Hannah Holly (b1651, d1710, d/o John), m2 Rebecca Gold (d1713), m3 1714 Hannah Gold (bc1640, d1730, d/o John Slason, wd/o John).

1. Dea Samuel - bc1673, d1712, m1704 Mercy Holmes (b1678, d/o Jonathan Bell, wd/o of John), she m2 1716 Peter Ferris, and she m3 Dr Richard Barnum.
2. Dea John - b1675, d1732, m1702 Abigail Holmes (d/o Stephen).
3. Hannah - b1680, d by 1730.
4. Jonathan - b&d1682.
5. Capt & Dea Jonathan - b1683, d1769, m1710 Millicent Penoyer (b1691, d/o Thomas).
6. Benjamin - b1684, d bef 1720, m by 1718 Mary _____ (of Danbury).
7. Joseph - b1686, d1730, m1728 Hannah Finch (b1701, d1762, d/o Samuel), she m2 by 1732 Thomas Waterbury.
8. Ebenezer - b1689, d young.
9. Nathan - b1691, d1772, m1714 Mary Finch (b1692, d/o Samuel).
10. Nathaniel - b1694, dc1712.

M. Benjamin - b1645, d1736, m1 1670 Hannah Weed (bc1650, d1711, d/o Jonas), m2 1730 Abigail _____ (d1730).

Descendants of HOYT, Simon (continued):

1. Benjamin - b1671, d1747, m1697 Elizabeth Jagger (d/o Jeremiah).
   a. Deborah - b1698, d1768, m1724 Stephen Ambler.
   b. Benjamin - b1700.
   c. David - b1702.
   d. Hannah - b1703.
   e. Abraham - b1704.
   f. John - b1705.
   g. Samuel - d1706.
   h. Elizabeth - b&d1710.
   i. Ebenezer - b1712.
   j. Jagger - b1714.
   k. Hannah - b1716.
   l. Benjamin - b1718.
   m. Jonas - b1720.
2. Mary - b1673, d1750, m1698 Joseph Webb.
3. Hannah - b1676, 1710, m1704 Abraham Bell.
4. Simon - b1678, d young?
5. Capt Samuel - bc1680, dc1767, m1 1705 Mary Jagger (bc1683, d aft 1744, d/o Jeremiah), m2 aft 1746 Elizabeth Clason (d/o _____ James, wd/o Jonathan).
6. Jonas - bc1682, d1711, m1705 Sarah Smith (d1637), she m2 1714 Thomas June.

References: David W. Hoyt, *A Genealogical History of the Hoyt, Haight and Hight Families.*

HUSTED, HEUSTED, HUSTIS, Robert - bc1595, d1652, m Elizabeth Miller (d1654).

Robert Husted sailed from Weymouth, England in 1636. He was in Braintree and Boston in 1638 and in Stamford soon thereafter. His home was west of Mill River near the Oxpasture. He left his lands in Greenwich to his son Angel and those in Stamford to his son Robert. Descendants:

A. Angel - bc1620, d1706, m Rebecca Sherwood. Greenwich.
1. Rebecca - m by 1656 Jonathan Reynolds.
2. Jonathan - bc1647, d1705, m by 1681 Mary Lockwood (d/o Robert, she m2 Joseph Knap).
3. David - bc1649, d bef 1706.
4. Joseph - bc1652.
5. Angel - bc1654, dc1728.
6. Elizabeth - b1656 m _____ Baldwin.
7. Moses - bc1659.

Descendants of HUSTED/HUSTIS, Robert (continued):

8. John - bc1662, m Mary ____.
9. Samuel - bc1665, d1741, m Sarah Knap (b1674, d1717, d/o Caleb).

B. Ann - bc1623, d1707, m Richard Hardy.
C. Robert - bc1626, d1704, m1655 Elizabeth Buxton (d/o Clement). Westchester, NY.

HYATT, HIOUTE, Thomas - d1656, m Elizabeth Russell? (she m2 1657 Cornelius Jones.)

Thomas Hyatt was in Stamford in 1641. He had brothers-in-law in Dorchester, MA named John and Henry Russell. The two names of Hoyt and Hyatt can often be confused and may once have been the same. He lived on the west side of South Street. Descendants:

A. Caleb - b1646, of Rye, NY by 1678.
B. Ruth - b1647, m John Westcott.
C. Deborah - b1649, m1672 Moses Jackson.
D. John - b1651, of Rye, NY c1681 and Yonkers, NY bef 1689.
E. Rebecca - b1654, m1678 Thomas Hine, Jr (she is recorded at Milford, CT).
F. Thomas - b1656?, m1677 Mary Saint John.

References: Grenville McKenzie, *The Jones Family of Mile Square, Yonkers, New York.*

JAGGER, GAGER, Jeremiah - bc1606, d1658, m Elizabeth ____ (she m2 1659 Robert Usher).

Jeremiah came with the Winthrop fleet on the *Arabella* and was in Watertown in 1630. He was in Wethersfield and was a soldier in the Pequot War in 1637. He was one of the first group of settlers in Stamford in 1641, and later was master of a trading vessel to the West Indies; he died on one of his trips. He lived on the south side of North Street towards Mill River. Descendants:

A. John - bc1634, d1684, m Hannah Cross (d by 1682, d/o William).

1. Elizabeth - b1665, d1690.
2. Hannah - bc1668, d1729, m by 1690 Samuel Webb.
3. Sarah - b1670.
4. Mary - b1673.
5. Jonathan - b1675, d1752, m1700 Rebecca Holmes (d1749, d/o Stephen).

B. Stephen - bc1647.

Descendants of JAGGER, Jeremiah (continued):

C. Jeremiah - b bef 1647, d1690, m Mary or Elizabeth Ferris (b1662 or 1664, d bef 1706, d/o Peter).
   1. Sarah - b1677, d1760, m1 1702 John Webster, m2 aft 1717 James Slason.
   2. Elizabeth - b1679, d1713?, m1697 Benjamin Hoyt.
   3. Mary - b1683, d aft 1744, m1705 Capt Samuel Hoyt.
   4. Jeremiah - bc1684, 1706.

D. Elizabeth - b1657, d1678.

References: The Ferris records of Harriet Scofield; *Lester Card Manuscript.*

JESSUP, JESSOP.

The three Jessups were the children of John Jessup, who left Weymouth, England, about 1636. He was in Hartford in 1637 and Wethersfield a year later where he died. His wife Joanna then married John Whitmore. The Whitmores and the Jessup children came to Stamford with the first group of settlers in 1641. John moved to Southampton, L.I. about 1653. Edward and his mother moved to Newtown, L.I. in 1652, and he later moved to West Farms in Westchester County, N.Y.

Edward had a house on the east side of South Street in 1650. Was this the Whitmores' house previously?

Note: Jacobus states that Joanna was a daughter of Edward. Descendants:

A. John - b bef 1638.

B. Edward -b bef 1638, d1666, m Elizabeth (Bridges?), she m2 1668, Robert Beacham. Fairfield & Long Island.

C. Joanna? - b bef 1638, m John Burroughs?

References: Rev. Henry Griswold Jessup, *Edward Jessup.*

JONES, Cornelius - d1690, m1 _____, m2 1657 Elizabeth Hyatt (d/o _____ Russell?, wd/o Thomas).

Cornelius Jones was in Stamford by 1657. He married Thomas Hyatt's widow and moved into the Hyatt home on the west side of South Street. He must have had quite a houseful of children. Descendants:

A. Ebenezer - b1646, m Mary _____. Yonkers, NY.

B. Mary - b1648, m John Hyatt?

C. Cornelius - b1650, d1676.

D. Joseph - b1652, dc1690, m by 1677 Rebecca Drake (wd/o Samuel, she m2 c1692 Stephen Clason).

Descendants of JONES, Cornelius (continued):

1. Mary - b1677, m Cornelius Seely.
2. Hannah - b1680, m David Miller.
3. Joseph - b1682.
4. Samuel - b1685, d by 1707.
5. Cornelius - b1688, m aft 1703 Hannah Bradley (d/o Thomas Sherwood, wd/o John)

References: Grenville McKensie, *The Jones Family of Miles Square, Yonkers, New York.*

JUNE, JUIN, Peter - d1707, m Sarah ____ (she m2 Henry Rich?).

Peter June was in Stamford by 1677. In 1681 he bought a houselot west of Mill River on the south side of the road. His family settled chiefly in the northwest section of Stamford near the Mianus River. Descendants:

A. Sarah - b1680.
B. Peter - b1683, d1744, m1705 Mary Clason (b1689, d1745, d/o David).
C. James - b1687, m1 Ruth ____, m2 1729 Ruth Smith (d1740, d/o Daniel).
D. Thomas - b1690, d1768, m1 1714 Sarah Hoyt (d1737, d/o ____ Smith, wd/o Jonas), m2 c1738 Tamar ____.
D. Mercy - b1692, d1735, m1719 Richard Chester or Chesser or Chichester. She had a child Mindwell by Edward Beach/Bach. She m2 1728 Hugh Norton.
E. Mary - b1699, d1715.

KNAP, KNAPP, Nicholas - bc1600, d1670, m1 c1630 Elinor (prob Lockwood) (d1658, sis/o Robert and Edmund), m2 1659 Unica Brown (d by 1670, wd/o Clement Buxton. wd/o Peter).

Nicolas Knap, his wife Elinor, and seven children came to America on the *Arbella* in 1630. They came from Burys St. Mary in Suffolk, probably. In 1631 Nicolas was fined in Watertown, MA for selling water for scurvy at too high a price. He was in Stamford by 1649, having been previously in Rye, NY, and Greenwich. After the death of his wife, he married Unica Brown, the recent widow of Clement Buxton, and moved into the Buxton home on the east side of West Street.

His grandson Moses was a blacksmith in the 1680s.

Descendants of KNAP, Nicolas:

A. Jonathan - b&d1631.

B. Timothy - b1632, d by 1685, mc1665 Bethia Brundage (d/o John). Rye, NY.

C. Joshua - b1634, d1684, m1657 Hannah Close (bc1632, d1696, she m2 John Bowers). Greenwich.

D. Caleb - b1637, dc1674, mc1660 Hannah Smith (d1685?, d/o Henry, she m2 167- Thomas Lawrence.

- 1. Caleb - b1661, d bef 1717, m1694 Hannah Clements (d/o William), of Norwalk and Goshen, CT.
  - a. Caleb - b1695, d1761.
  - b. William - b1697, d1770.
  - c. Sarah - b1700.
  - d. Abigail - b1702.
  - e. Joshua - b1704.
  - f. Joseph - b1706.
  - g. Hannah - b1710.
  - h. Jonathan - b1713.
  - i. Benjamin - b1717.
  - j. Reuben - b1717.
- 2. Capt John - b1664, d1749, m1 1692 Hannah Ferris (b1666, d1724, d/o Peter), m2 1727 Mrs Martha Weed.
  - a. Lt Samuel - b1695, d1751, m1 1720 Martha Slason (b1699, d1747, d/o John Jr), m2 1749 Mrs Marcy Bouton.
  - b. Lt John - b1697, d1763, m1 1723 Deborah Cross (b1702, d/o Nathaniel), m2 1736 Abigail Hoyt (d/o Samuel).
  - c. Hannah - b1699, d1724, m1 1716 Isaac Quintard, m2 _____ Jessup.
  - d. Peter - b1701.
  - e. Charles - b1703, d1773.
  - f. Deborah - b1705.
  - g. Moses - b1709, d1787.
- 3. Moses - b1666, d1753, m1688 Elizabeth Crissy (d/o William). Reading, CT.
  - a. Elizabeth - b1690.
- 4. Samuel - b1668, d1739, mc1696 Hannah Bushnell. Greenwich and Danbury, CT.
- 5. Sarah - b1670, m1691 Ebenezer Mead.
- 6. Hannah - b1672.

E. Sarah - b1639, d1681, m1 John Disbrow, m2 1657 Peter Disbrow.

F. Ruth - b1641, m1 1657 Joseph Ferris, m2 1708 John Clapp.

G. Hannah - b1643, d1674, m1673 Zarubbabel Hoyt.

Descendants of KNAP, Nicolas (continued):

H. Moses - b1646, d aft 1713, m1669 Abigail Westcott (bc 1642, d aft 1713, d/o Richard).
  1. Lydia - bc1670, d1710, m1685 Thomas Penoyer.
  2. Abigail - b1672, d1706, m1692 John Crissy.
  3. Sarah - b1674, d1717, m Samuel Husted.
  4. Hannah - bc1676, m1 1696 Nathaniel Cross, m2 1715 Samuel Palmer.

I. Lydia - b1648, d1716, m Richard Mills.

J. Josiah? -.

References: Alfred Averill Knapp, *The Nicolas Knapp Genealogy*.

LAW, Richard - b1610, dc1687, mc1635 Margaret Kilbourne (b1612, d by 1684, d/o Thomas).

Richard Law was an attorney in England before coming to America. He married Margaret in Wethersfield. While there, he and George Hubbard were the only men entrusted with trading with the Indians for beaver. He was with the earliest group of settlers in Stamford and lived on the central road (where the Webb Tavern later stood). He was very much the leader in Stamford affairs for more than forty years. Descendants:

A. Jonathan - bc1636, d1712, m1664 Sarah Clark (b1644, dc1705, d/o Dea George). Milford, CT.

B. Abigail - b1637, d1711, m1663 or 1665 Jonathan Selleck.

C. Sarah - d1732, m1669 John Selleck.

LAWRENCE, LARRENCE

Thomas Lawrence, Sr. lived in Milford, CT. After his death in 1648, his wife Martha married John Chapman, and in 1657 she married Francis Brown. Thomas, Jr. lived on the corner of West Street and the road to the mill. A section to the northwest of Stamford was known as Lawrence's Farm. When he died in 1691, he left bequests to his step-sisters Mary Chapman Slason, Sarah Brown Scudder, Rebecca Brown Galpin, and to his sister Martha Lawrence Jones. He also included his step-nephew Joseph Jones and his wife's children, particularly John Knap. Descendants:

A. Martha - b1646, m Rev Eliphalet Jones.

B. Thomas - b1648, d1691, mc1674 Hannah Knap (dc1685, d/o Henry Smith, wd/o Caleb).

LEEDS, John - d1695.

The Leeds family was a prominent one in England, connected with the city of Leeds. There is little in the Stamford records about them except that a John Leeds died in 1695; a John Leeds and Mary had the children here listed, and that a Mrs. Mary Leeds married Abraham Bell in 1714. In 1692 John Leeds lodged a complaint against Mr. Johannes Courtland of New York concerning the iron work on a vessel Leeds was building. There are no Leeds on the 1701 tax list.

There was a John Leeds in New London, CT in 1685. Descendants:

A. John - prob s/o above, m Mary ____.
   1. Jonathan - b1693.
   2. John - b1694.
   3. Sarah - b1696.
   4. Samuel - b1697.
   5. Ebenezer - b1700.
   6. Mary - b1702.

References: *The Scovill Genealogy.*

LOCKWOOD

Two Lockwood brothers from Combes, Suffolk, sons of Edward, came to America on the *Arbella* in 1630. Edmund, thirty-six, came with his wife and child; Robert was thirty. They settled first in Cambridge, MA and then to Watertown, MA where Edmund died in 1634.

Robert's family moved to Norwalk, CT sometime after 1645. For a brief time he owned the Rev. Denton's home in Stamford between 1644 and 1650 when it was turned over to John Bishop. After he died in 1658, his wife married Jeffrey Ferris. Robert's oldest son, Jonathan, had a home on "River Street" by 1660; he sold it to his cousin Edmund in 1665 and moved to Greenwich.

There is some confusion over a possible sister Rose to the two brothers Edmund and Robert.

Descendants of Edmund:

A. Edmund - b1624, d1692, m1656 Hannah Scott (d1706, d/o Thomas).
   1. John - bc1657, d1692.
   2. Mary - bc1664, m1693 Joseph Garnsey.

Descendants of LOCKWOOD, Edmund (continued):

3. Joseph - bc1666, d1759, m1 1698 Elizabeth Ayres (d1715, d/o Richard), m2 1716 Margery Webb (b1683, d1737, d/o Joseph), m3 Susannah ____.
    a. Joseph - b1699.
    b. Hannah - b1701, m1724 David Dan.
    c. John - b1703.
    d. Nathaniel - b1706, d1715.
    e. Elizabeth - b1708.
    f. Israel - b1710.
4. Edmund - bc1668, d1740, unm.
5. Daniel - bc1670, d1744, m1702 Charity Clements (d/o William).
6. Abigail - m Joseph Clark.
7. Sarah - bc1679, d1749, m1707 Michael Lounsbury.

Descendants of LOCKWOOD, Robert:

A. Jonathan - B1634, 1689, m Mary Ferris (d1708, d/o Jeffrey Ferris, she m2 1696 Thomas Merritt), of Rye, NY.
B. Gershom - of Greenwich.
C. Robert - of Greenwich.
D. daughters.

References: Harriet Woodbury Hodge, *Some Descendants of Edmond Lockwood of Cambridge, Massachusetts.*

LYON, Thomas - bc1621, d1690, m1 Martha Winthrop (bc1630, dc1654, d/o of Henry), m2 aft 1665 Mary Hoyt (d/o Simon). Fairfield & Greenwich.

Thomas Lyon was married first in Groton, Suffolk to the granddaughter of Governor Winthrop of Boston. He was in Stamford in the late 1640s and owned a home on the corner of East and North Streets by 1650. He later moved to Fairfield and to Greenwich. Descendants:

A. infant - d young.
B. Mary - b1649, d by 1713, m John Wilson.
C. Abigail - b1655, d by 1713, m1672 John Banks.
D. John - m Rebecca Hull (d/o Cornelius).
E. Thomas - m Abigail Ogden.
F. Samuel - d1713.
G. Joseph -.
H. Elizabeth - m John Marshall.
I. Sarah - m ____ Merritt.
J. Deborah - m ____ Cove.

LYON, Thomas (continued)

References: *The Lyon Memorial Book.*

MEAD, William - b1600, d1663, mc1629 Philippa ____ (d1657).

William Mead was born in Kent. He came with his brother on the *Elizabeth* in 1635. He was one of the earliest group of Stamford settlers from Wethersfield in 1641. In 1659 he went to Greenwich. While in Stamford, he lived on the west side of West Street and gave that home to his son Joseph. Joseph moved to Long Island; he was married in Ridgefield. He sold his house in 1663 and was in Greenwich by 1669. John sold his house on the west side of West Street in 1659, went to Long Island, and later settled in Greenwich. Descendants:

A. Joseph - b1630, d1690, m1654 Mary Brown (d1708).
  1. Zachariah - d by 1703.
  2. Joseph - bc1657, d1714, m Sarah Reynolds b1665, (d/o Jonathan?).
  3. Daniel - b1659, m Hannah ____.
  4. Elisha - b1661, d1727.
  5. Richard - b1664, d by 1703.
  6. Mary or Mercy -.

B. Martha - bc1632, m1 John Richardson, m2 1695 Thomas Williams.

C. John - bc1634, d1697 or 1699, mc1657 Hannah Potter (b1635, d/o William).
  1. John - bc1658, d1693, m1681 Ruth Hardy (d/o Richard).
  2. Joseph - bc1660, d1714, m Mary ____.
  3. Hannah - m1677 John Scofield.
  4. Ebenezer, b1663, d1728, m1691 Sarah Knap (b1670, d/o Caleb).
  5. Jonathan - bc1665, d1712, mc1688 Martha Finch b1665, prob d/o Samuel).
  6. David - b1665, d1727.
  7. Benjamin - b1666, d1746, m1700 Sarah Waterbury (b1667, d/o Jonathan).
  8. Nathaniel - bc1668, d1703.
  9. Samuel - b1673, d1713, m Hannah ____.
  10. Abigail - bc1675.
  11. Mary - bc1678, m Jonathan Reynolds.

D. son - d1658.

References: Spencer P. Mead, *The History and Genealogy of the Mead Family.*

MILLER, John - bc1609, d1642, m Mary Angell (b1625, sis-in-law of Robert Husted?), she m2 Obadiah Seely.

John Miller was in Wethersfield, came to Stamford in 1642, and died soon after. His home, built by Obadiah Seely, was on the east side of South Street; it became the home of the Miller sons and the Seelys when John's wife married Obadiah. The oldest son John bought Richard Mills' house on the south side of North Street in the early 1670s. He went to Bedford in 1680 and held prominent positions before he died there. His children continued to live in Bedford. Descendants:

A. John - b1635 or 1638, dc1702, m ____. Bedford, NY.
- 1. Sarah - b1662.
- 2. John - b1665, d aft 1726, m Mary Holmes (b1662, d/o John).
  - a. Mary - b1693, d aft 1766, m1712 Moses Buxton.
  - b. Martha - b1697, m1711 Zachariah Mills.
  - c. John - b1698, m Sarah Theale (d/o Ebenezer).
  - d. Abigail - bc1702.
  - e. Abner - bc1702.
  - f. Daniel - b1711, d young).
- 3. Capt Jonathan - b1667, m1691 Sarah Holmes (b1667, d/o John). Bedford, NY.
- 4. Mary - b1670, m Richard Holmes.
- 5. David - b1676, m1701 Hannah Jones (b1680, d/o Joseph).

B. Jonathan - b1640, d1697, m1685 wd Mary Teed.

C. Joseph - b1642.

MILLS, Richard - bc1595, d1668, m ____ Constable (d/o Francis Nichols, wd/o William)?

Richard Mills was in Wethersfield and later in New Haven where a son was born in 1636. He was in Stratford, CT and then in Stamford by 1654. His home was on the south side of North Street. He was the schoolteacher in the late 1650s and early 1660s when he moved to Newtown, L.I. to be schoolteacher there. Later he moved to Westchester, NY, and later still to Virginia.

It is presumed that John was his son. He was a ship carpenter by 1687 and owned a pink called *The Blossom* which he sold in 1691. He sold his holdings to the Sellecks in 1695. Descendants:

A. Richard - bc1630, m Lydia Knap (d/o Roger). Greenwich.

B. Samuel - bc1632, d1685, m Mary? ____. Long Island.

C. John - b1636, d1706, m Mary ____ (d1732?).
- 1. John - d1723, m1702 Mary Fountain (d/o Aaron). Fairfield.

Descendants of MILLS, Richard (continued):
2. William - d1710.
3. Robert -.
D. some daughters?

MITCHELL, Matthew - b1590, d1646, m1616 Susan Butterfield (d/o Thomas Butterfield).

Matthew Mitchell was born in South Owram, Yorkshire. He traveled to America on the *James* with his wife and Jonathan, his son, in 1635. Possibly his other children were with him as well. He was first in Charlestown, MA and then in Concord where his house burned. Later he was in Springfield with his friend Walter Pyncheon. He was in Saybrook, CT where he suffered losses from the Indians. In about 1637 he went to Wethersfield where he met with opposition from the Connecticut Assembly and was made to pay a fine. In 1641 he removed with the Rev. Denton, whom he had known in England and on the *James*, to settle Stamford. He served as one of the leaders in Stamford and was by far the richest. For awhile he went to Long Island but returned to die "of the stone" in Stamford at the age of 56. His house in Stamford burned also, but he left the home lot in the north side of the central road to his son David. Descendants:

A. Abigail - b1618, m Rev Abraham Pierson.
B. David - bc1619, d1684, m Elizabeth ____. Stratford.
C. Sarah - b1621, mc1640 Samuel Sherman.
D. Martha - b&d1623.
E. Rev Jonathan - b1624, d1668, m1650 Margaret Shepard (wd/o Rev Thomas)
F. Susanna - b1627, m Rev Abraham Pierson.
G. Matthew - b&d1629.
H. Hannah - b1631, d1703, m1 Robert Coe. Stratford. m2 1667 Nicolas Estey. New Haven.

MOREHOUSE, MORRIS, Thomas - d1658, m1 ____, m2 Isabel ____.

Thomas Morehouse was probably from London. He came with the first group of settlers from Wethersfield in 1641. His home was on the east side of South Street. In 1653 he moved to Fairfield, where he ran a grist mill. Descendants:

A. Hannah -.
B. Samuel - b1637 or c1642, d1687, m Rebecca Odell (b1642, d/o William).

Descendants of MOREHOUSE, Thomas (continued):

C. Thomas - dc1706, m1 ____ Keeler (d/o Ralph), m2 Martha Hobby (bc1666, d/o John), she m2 Abraham Adams.
D. Mary - m Joseph Patchen?
D. Ens John - d1701. Southampton, L.I.
E. Jonathan - d by 1708, m1 Mary Wilson (d/o Edward), m2 1690 Rebecca Knowles (d1727, d/o John), she m2 1708 John Crissy.

NEWMAN, Thomas - bc1584, d1659, m1 Mary Moorton, m2 1655 Mary Carles (b1637, d/o Joseph).

In 1633 Thomas and Mary and their son John came over to America on the *Mary and John*. He was the son of William and probably his own son William came with him or a little later. They were first in Ipswich, Mass. William came to Stamford in 1642. His home was first on the west side of South Street and then by 1650 on the south side of East Street. William is once called Wildman in the Stamford records--an error. Thomas, the father, lived on the corner of west side of West Street and the road to the mill. He moved to East Town in New Netherland.

William was a shoemaker and held a number of important positions in Stamford. Descendants:

A. William - bc1610, d1673?, m Elizabeth ____ (b1610, d1676).
  1. Thomas - b1643, d1714, m Mary ____.
    a. Elizabeth - bc1686, m1704 Daniel Briggs.
    b. John - bc 1690 m1 1708 Abigail Waterbury (b1688, d1729, d/o Jonathan), m2 1730 Elizabeth Finch.
    c. Nathaniel - b1692?, d1773?, m Sarah ____.
    d. Jonathan - b1694, dc1730, m1714 Elizabeth Finch (d/o John Austin, wd/o Joseph).
    e. Thomas - bc1697, d1743, m1723 Hannah Jagger (d/o Jonathan, she m2 Joseph Bishop).
  2. Mary - d1659.
  3. Daniel - bc1650, d1695, m Sarah ____.
  4. Sarah - mc1680 Lt David Waterbury.
  5. Elizabeth - b1654, d1713, m1679 Increase Holly.
  6. Hannah - b1657, d1712 or 1714, m1679 John Holly.
  7. John or Jonathan - b1661, d by 1676.

OLIVER, William - mc1657 Mary Simkins (d/o Henry Ackerly, wd/o Vincent). Greenwich. Descendants:

A. ____ - b1657.
B. son - b1659.
C. Samuel - b1662.

ΟΥΕR, PENNOYER, PENOIR, Robert - b1614, ... Mary ____, m2 1671 Elizabeth Scofield (wd/o Rich-

Robert Penoyer was the son of Thomas Butler of Dorston, ...ord, a weaver. He left from Bristol, England, and changed ... name because he had been a witness to a murder. He came on the *Hopewell* with his brother Thomas, aged 10, in 1635. He was in Stamford by 1648 when he was cited for drunkenness. He had a house on the corner of the west side of West Street and the road to the mill in 1659. In 1677 he moved to Mamaroneck, NY.

Thomas, his son, went to settle Bedford, NY in 1680 and returned in 1684.

Robert's brother was the William Penoyer of Harvard fame.

In the records there is reference to Anne Rich marrying Thomas Penoyer in 1686. Descendants:

A. Elizabeth - bc1652, m Richard Lounsbury.
B. William - b1654, m Mary ____. Mamaroneck, NY.
C. Thomas - b1658, d1724, m1 1685 Lydia Knap (bc1670, d1710, d/o Moses), m2 Mary ____.
  1. Abigail - b1686, m Joshua Reynolds.
  2. Samuel? - b1687, d young?
  3. Mary - b1688, d1732, m1707 Benjamin Weed.
  4. Millicent - b1691, m1710 Jonathan Hoyt.
  5. Mercy - b1693, d1734?, m1714 Eliphalet Holly.
  6. Samuel - b1696, d1761, m1720 Theophila Selleck (b1695, d/o Capt Jonathan).
  7. John - b1698, d1775, m1 1725 Abigail Ferris (b1702, d1737, d/o Joseph), m2 1738 Elizabeth Bishop (b1706, d1777, d/o Joseph).
  8. Reuben - b1702.
  9. Martha -.
  10. Lydia - b1710.
D. Mary - b1660, d young.
E. Martha - b1664, m 1680 Henry Rich.
F. Abigail - b1666, d young.

PETTIT, John - b1608, d1662, m Mary ____ (d1657).

John Pettit was born in Wilford, Essex, the son of Henri (a Huguenot), probably. He and his brother Thomas came to America, to Ipswich about 1630 to 1632. He was in Roxbury in 1634 and later in Long Island with his brother. He was in Stamford by 1652 and had a house on the west side of South Street. Did he marry a Debro (Deborah) who died in 1658? The second John died with very young children, some of whom Jonas Weed, Jr. took into his household. There may have been more children of the first John between 1638 and 1652. Was Deborah his daughter? In 1658 there is a reference to a William Pettit in the Town Meeting Records.

Jonathan Pettit held many positions in Bedford, NY, and died there. Descendants:

A. John - b1638, d1676, m1665 Sarah Scofield (bc1640, dc1684, d/o Daniel), she m2 Stephen Sherwood.
  1. Sarah - b1666 m John Finch.
  2. John b1668, d1715, m1 1693 Mary Bates (d1702, d/o John), m2 1707 Ann Gold (d1720, d/o John).
    a. Jonathan - b1693, d1772, m1 Mary ____, m2 1715 Hannah ____.
    b. John - b1695, d1758, m1729 Mercy Bishop (b1709, d/o John).
    c. Sarah - b1697, m1723 David Weed.
    d. Samuel - b1699, d1729, m Elizabeth Tomlinson.
    e. Ebenezer - b1701.
    f. Ann - b1708.
    g. Mary - b1711.
    h. Mercy - d1712.
  3. Solomon - b1672, d by 1695.
  4. Mary or Mercy - b1674, d1714, m1697 Jeremiah Beard.
  5. Bethia - b1676, d1715, m1 1699 Theophilus Miles; m2 1705 Josiah Tibbals.

B. Deborah - b1652, d1657.

C. David - b1654, d1657?

D. Jonathan - b1656, dc1709, m Elizabeth Finch (b1669, d/o Isaac?). Bedford, NY.
  1. David - d1726.
  2. Jonathan - d aft 1713.
  3. Elizabeth - b1690, m1714 Nathaniel Scofield.

References: Virkus, *Compendium of American Genealogy.*

POND, Nathaniel - b1675, d1716, m1 c1697 Elizabeth Slason (b1672, d1711, d/o John), m2 1711 Sarah Ferris (b1675, d1716, d/o Daniel Weed, wd/o Lt David Waterbury, wd/o Benjamin).

Nathaniel Pond came to Stamford in 1696 and was a blacksmith. He was previously in Branford, CT. He had a house just east of the Noroton River (now in Darien) which still stands.

Only Josiah, Naomi, and Thankful are mentioned in Nathaniel's estate proceedings.

Descendants of POND, Nathaniel:

A. Abigail - b1698, d by 1716.
B. Elizabeth - b1699, d1706.
C. Josiah - b1701.
D. Hannah - b1703, d1706.
E. Naomi - b1705.
F. Thankful -.
G. Nathaniel - b1712.
H. Israel - b1714, d1715.

POTTER, William - bc1609, d1684, m ____.

William Potter was in Stamford by 1650, and his house was on the corner of North Street and the North Street extension to Mill River. He also had had a house on the east side of North Street that was sold to Thomas Lyon by 1650. When William died, he left five pounds to the Church, and the silver cups still in use in the Congregational Church were bought with this gift. He also left his house and land to the three Bishop sons. Later this houselot was turned over to John Davenport for his parsonage. He also left bequests to the eleven children of his son-in-law, John Mead.

There was a William Potter who came to America in 1635 on the *Elizabeth*. As his age was given as twenty-five, this may well have been the Stamford man. He was in Roxbury, MA in 1646. Descendants:

A. Hannah - b1635, mc1657 John Mead.

REYNOLDS, RENOULDS, John - b1612, d1660, mc1630 Sarah _____ (b1614, d1657). Greenwich.

John Reynolds married Sarah in Ipswich, England and presumably they came together to America on the *Elizabeth*, in 1634, though only Sarah (20) is listed. John was a freeman in Watertown, MA in 1635 and was chosen to divide the common lands. He was in Wethersfield in 1636 and was one of the first group of settlers in Stamford in 1641. He lived on the west side of South Street. By 1650 he had moved to Greenwich. Descendants:

A. Jonathan - bc1631, d1673, m Rebecca Husted (d by 1664, d/o Angel).
  1. Rebecca - b1656.
  2. Jonathan - b1660.
  3. John - b1663.
  4. Sarah - b1665, m Joseph Mead?

Descendants of REYNOLDS, John (continued):

5. Elizabeth - b1667, m1687 Joshua Knap.
6. Joseph - b1669.

B. Elizabeth - b1634, d1703, m1654 Peter Ferris.
C. John - b1638, dc1701, m1 Naomi Latimer?, m2 1668 Judith Palmer.

References: Marion H. Reynolds, ed., *The History and Descendants of John and Sarah Reynolds 1630-1923*: The Reynolds Family Association, NY., 1924. James Savage, *A Genealogical Dictionary of the First Settlers of New England*, Vol. 2, p. 525.

RICH, RITCH, Henry - d1712, m1 1680 Martha Penoyer (b1664, d/o Robert), m2 Sarah June (wd/o Peter?). Greenwich.

Henry Rich was in Stamford in 1678 and in 1680 married Martha Penoyer over the objections of her guardian. He bought a home lot in 1681 on the west side of Mill River on the south side of the road. In a year or two he had moved on to Greenwich.

The records mention an Anne Rich who married Thomas Penoyer in 1686. Descendants:

A. Thomas - bc1682.
B. Elizabeth - bc1700, m Samuel Banks.

ROCKWELL, John - b1621, d1673, m Elizabeth Weed (b1637, d1676, d/o Jonas). Rye, NY.

John Rockwell is believed to be the son of John Rockwell and Wilmot Cade of Windsor, CT. He came to Stamford late in 1641 and had a home on the west side of West Street. He moved to Rye, NY about 1670 and died there. Little is given in the Stamford records about his family. Rockwell Ridge in Darien is named for him. Descendants:

A. Sarah - b1653, m ____ Webb.
B. Hittabel - d1656.
C. child - d1658.
D. Hittabel (or Mehitabel?) - m1 1679 John Keeler, m2 by 1725 Zarubbabel Hoyt.
E. Jonathan - c1665-1731
F. Thomas - c1667-1712.
G. Joseph - c1670-1714.

References: Edwin Hall, *Ancient Historical Records of Norwalk, Connecticut.*

SCOFIELD

Daniel and Richard Scofield (22) came to America in 1635 on the *Susan and Ellen*. They were born in Rochdale, England and settled first in Ipswich, MA. Daniel came to Stamford late in December 1641 and his brother followed him in the early 1650s. Their homes were on the west side of West Street. Daniel was very active in town affairs and was marshal in 1658. Joseph Scofield died of injuries in King Philip's War. Did Nathaniel marry a Susannah Waterbury in 1713? Descendants:

A. Daniel - b1595, dc1670.
  1. Sarah - bc1640, d1684, m1 1665 John Pettit, m2 Stephen Sherwood.
  2. John - b1647, d1699, m1677 Hannah Mead (d/o John).
    a. Sgt Samuel - b1678, d1768, m1711 Hannah Weed (b1687, d1739, d/o John).
    b. Sgt John - b1680, d1758, m1 1703 Mary Holly (b1680, d1740, d/o Samuel), m2 1743 Mary Mead (wd/o Caleb).
    c. Ebenezer - b1685, d1725, m1712 Ruth Slater.
    d. Nathaniel - b1688, d1769, m1714 Elizabeth Pettit (bc1692, d/o John).
    e. Mercy - b1690, d young.
    f. Mary - b1694, m1709 Henry Lounsbury?
    g. Susanna - b1698, m1720 Caleb Smith.
  3. Daniel - bc1650, d1714, m Abigail Merwin (bc1652, d/o Miles).
    a. Daniel - d1746, m1701 Hannah Hait (b1676, d1710?, d/o Joshua or Benjamin?).
    b. Mary - m1 169- Jonas Weed, m2 1707 Samuel Hoyt.
    c. Abigail - d1734, m1701 Lt Samuel Weed.
    d. Joseph - bc1676, d1726, m1709 Unice Scofield (b1678, d1743, d/o Clement Buxton, wd/o Samuel).
    e. Samuel - d1707, m1704 Unice Buxton (b1678, d/o Clement, she m2 1709 Joseph Scofield).
    f. Sarah - bc1685, d1718, m1704 Samuel Bates.
    g. Elizabeth - d by 1727, m1708 Daniel Weed.
  4. Joseph - d1675 or 1676.
  5. Mercy - b1657, m1682 Samuel Camp.

B. Richard - b1613, d1670, m Elizabeth _____, she m2 1671 Robert Penoyer.

Descendants of SCOFIELD (continued):

1. Richard - b1652, dc1745, m1689 Ruth Brundage (d/o John).
   a. Jeremiah - b1691, m1714 Abigail Weed (b1695, d/o Jonas).
   b. Joshua - b1693, m1712 Ruth Youngs (b1696, d/o John).
   c. James - b1696, dc1783, m1723 Elizabeth Weed (d/o Joseph).
   d. Jonathan - b1698, m Ruth Brown.
   e. Hannah - b1700.
   f. Deborah - b1703.
   g. David - b1706.
2. Hannah - b1653, m1 1672 or 1673 Joseph Webb, m2 aft 1684 John Finch.
3. Elizabeth - b1655, d1703.
4. Jeremiah - b1658, d bef 1671.

References: Charles Arthur Hoppen, *Washington Ancestry, and Other Colonial Families.*

SEELY

Obadiah and Capt. Nathaniel Seely was born in London, the sons of Robert Seely, who came to America about 1630 on the *Arabella.* They first lived in Watertown, MA, in Wethersfield in 1631, and then they moved to New Haven.

Obadiah was a carpenter and built John Miller's house. He lived on the east side of South Street, presumably in Miller's house as he married the widow after Miller's death in 1642. His sons Cornelius and Jonas moved to Bedford, NY, and Cornelius had a tavern there in 1699. Jonas returned to Stamford.

Capt. Nathaniel Seeley's children were born in Stamford, but moved to Fairfield at an early age.

Obadiah - bc1628, d1657, m aft 1642 Mary Angell? Miller (b1625, wd/o John). Descendants:

A. Obadiah - bc1646, d1680, m Esther Stevens (bc1654, d/o Thomas), she m2 Moses Jackson.
   1. Obadiah - bc1670, d1745, m1692 Susannah Finch (d1710, d/o Samuel).
      a. John - b1693, d1756, m1720 Abigail Bishop (b1696, d1757, d/o Stephen).
      b. Nathaniel - b1695, d1757, m1 1722 Elizabeth Holly (b1698, d1742, d/o John), m2 Hannah ____.
      c. Mercy - b1698, d1715.

Descendants of SEELY, Obadiah (continued):

d. Obadiah - b1701.
e. Susannah - b1705.
f. Elijah - b1707.
g. Preserved - b1711.

2. Benjamin - bc1673, d1696.
3. Abigail (prob) - m1703 Joseph Finch.

B. Cornelius - bc1650, dc1710, m1674 Priscilla Osborn (bc1650, d/o Capt Richard). Bedford, NY.

1. Cornelius - bc1675, m Mary Jones (b1677, d/o Joseph).
2. Sarah - b1676.
3. Elizabeth - b1678, m Joseph Hunt.
4. Capt Joseph - bc1685, m Martha _____.

C. Jonas - b1653, d1703 or 1705, m1 Mary Slason (d/o Thomas?). Bedford, NY. m2 c1689 Mary Waterbury (bc1660, 1738, d/o Thomas Wicks, wd/o John).

1. Sarah - b1684, d1727, m1707 Jonathan Holmes.
2. Samuel - b1687, d aft 1722, m1709 Charlotte Popino.
3. Martha - b1690, d1710.
4. Jonas - b1692, d1710.
5. Susanna - b1694, d1710.
6. Ebenezer - b1697, d1767, m1 1719 Mercy Dean (d/o John), m2 Eunice Davenport.
7. Nathaniel - b1699.
8. Eliphalet - b1701.

D. Habakuk - d1658.

Capt Nathaniel - b1629, d1675, m1 c1649 Mary Turney (bc1631, d/o Benjamin), m2 1674 Elizabeth Gilbert (d/o Jehu Burr, wd/o Nehemiah Olmstead, wd/o Obadiah Gilbert). Descendants:

A. Nathaniel - bc1650.
B. Robert - bc1653, d1690.
C. Benjamin - b1657.
D. Joseph - bc1659.
E. John - bc1661, d1710.
F. Mary -.
G. Sarah -.
H. Phoebe -.
I. Rebecca -.

SELLECK

Jonathan and John Selleck were the sons of David Selleck, called a soap boiler; of Dorchester, MA. They may have come from Wales and were in Boston by 1643. There was a third son, David, and all three sons became involved in maritime concerns. Jonathan and John married Richard Law's two daughters and became prominent and rich citizens of Stamford from 1670 on. Jonathan lived on the east side of South Street, and John lived opposite him on South Street.

Maj Jonathan - b1641, d1713, m1 _____, m2 1665 Abigail Law (d1711, d/o Richard). Descendants:

A. Capt Jonathan - b1664, d1709, m1685 Abigail Gold (d/o Maj Nathan)
   1. Nathan - b1686, d1772, m1 1708 Susannah Hooker (d1709), m2 1710 Mary Sands (d1712), m3 1713 Sarah Sands.
   2. Abigail - b1685 or 1688, d1706, m1705 Dr Jacob Moen.
   3. Jonathan - unm.
   4. Theophila - b1695, m1720 Samuel Penoyer.
   5. Abigail - b1707, d1772.
   6. Gold John -.
B. David - b1666, d bef 1713.
C. John - d1694, m Martha Gold (bc1668, d1712, d/o Maj Nathan), she m2 1695 Rev John Davenport.

Capt John - b1643, d aft 1689, m1669 Sarah Law (d1732, d/o Richard). Descendants:

A. Sarah - b1670, d by 1705, m1698 John Potter.
B. David - b1672, d1707.
C. Nathaniel - b1678, d1712, m1700 Sarah Lockwood (bc1675, d/o Gershom or Jonathan), she m2 1714 Benjamin Hickock, she m3 1725 Samuel Kellogg.
D. John - b1681, d1706.
E. Susanna - b1683, d1745, m1704 John Holly.
F. Joanna - b1686, m1705 Jonathan Bates.

References: Henry S. Gorham, *Bates, Selleck and Allied Families*; *Lester Card Manuscript*.

SIMKINS, SIMKINGS, Vincent - d1653, m Mary Ackerley (d/o Henry), she m2 c1657 William Oliver.

Vincent Simkins was with the first group of settlers from Wethersfield in 1641. He lived on the north side of East Street. His son Daniel moved to Bedford, NY, and his son John also left Stamford shortly after his father's death.

Descendants of SIMKINS, Vincent:

A. Ens Daniel - d1699, m1 Sarah Webb (b1653, d/o Richard), m2 aft 1694 Elizabeth Webb (d/o Thomas Hine, wd/o Joshua).
  1. Vincent - Bedford, NY.
  2. Elizabeth -.

B. Jonathan? - d1657.

c. John -.

References: James Savage, *A Genealogical Dictionary of the First Settlers of New England Settlers*, Vol. 3.

SLASON, SLAWSON, George - b1616, d1695, m1 ____, m2 1680 Mary Jennings (d1697, d/o ____ Williams, wd/o Joshua).

George Slason and his brother Thomas were born in Southwark, England, the sons of Richard. George probably came to America on the *James* in 1636. He was first of Lynn, Mass. and then went to Sandwich in 1637 where he was married. George and Thomas, who was also in Sandwich and then in Plymouth, came to Stamford in 1642, but Thomas soon returned to Plymouth. George lived on the east side of South Street. He was a leader in Stamford. His two sons, John and Eleazer, both moved to Bedford, NY in 1680-1681 but returned to Stamford. John's wife Sarah was murdered by her brother. Descendants:

A. John - bc1641, d1706, m1 1663 Sarah Tuttle (b1642, 1676, d/o William), m2 by 1679 Elizabeth Benedict (d/o Thomas), m3 aft 1690 Hannah Gibbs (b1642, d1706, d/o John Punderson, wd/o John)
  1. John - b1664, d1745, mc1692 Mary Holmes (d1745, d/o Stephen). Norwalk.
    a. Sarah - b1693, d1713, m1710 John Bell (prob).
    b. John - b1695, d1788, m1722 Rebecca Brush (bc1700, d1745, d/o Jacob).
    c. David - b1697, m Mary Daly.
    d. Martha - b1699, d1747, mc1720 Lt Samuel Knap.
    e. Elizabeth - b1703, d1733.
    f. Hannah - b1705, dc1775.
    g. Mary - b1707, d1760.
    h. Rebecca - b&d1710.
  2. Sarah - b1667, d1744, m1700 Ebenezer Bishop.
  3. Jonathan - b1670, d1727, m1 1699 Mary Waterbury (b1680, d1710, d/o John), m2 1711 Rose Stevens (b1683, d1727, d/o Obadiah).
  4. Elizabeth - b1672, d1711, mc1697 Nathaniel Pond.

Descendants of SLASON, George (continued):

5. Mary - b1680, m1707 Joseph Slason (gs/o Thomas).
6. Thomas - b1682, d1710, m1709 Sarah Stevens (b1687, d/o Joseph), she m2 1712 Jabez Smith.
7. Hannah - b1686, d young.

B. Eleazer - b1643, d1698, m1 by 1665 Mary Chapman (bc1650, d1678?, d/o John), m2 1679 Susannah Belding (b1651, d/o William).

1. Eleazer - bc1672, m1711 Hannah Webb (b1679, d1723, d/o Joseph).
2. Martha - bc1675, m1692 John Smith.
3. James - b1681, d1759, m1702 Mehitabel Ambler (bc1676, d1737, d/o Abraham).
4. Susannah -b1683, d1707, m1700 Samuel Hoyt.
5. Ebenezer - bc1688, m Ann ____.
6. Nathaniel - b1696, d1787, m1719 Margaret Belding (b1701, d1780, d/o William).

C. Hannah - bc1640s, m1 by 1600 John Gold, m2 1714 Dea Samuel Hoyt.

SMITH, Henry - b1619, d1687, prob m1 Hannah ____, m2 1665 Ann Andrews (d1685, wd/o Francis).

Henry Smith, according to H. Stanley Finch, was the son of Thomas Smith of St. Mary Adermanbury, England, but no sources for this are given. He was with the first group of settlers from Wethersfield in 1641 and lived on the east side of West Street. He married, secondly, Ann who had three children, Rebecca, Ruth, and Abraham. He left his home to his son John and his grandson, John Knap.

There is a Sarah Smith who is unaccounted for. She married Jonas Hoyt in 1705 and then married Thomas June in 1714. Was she a daughter of John or was she of another Smith family? Descendants:

A. Hannah - bc1640, d1685?, m1 c1660 Caleb Knap, m2 c1674 Thomas Lawrence.

B. Samuel - bc1646, d1658.

C. Daniel - b1648, d1740, m1677 Hannah Knap (b1660, d1721, d/o Joshua). Greenwich.

1. Joshua - d1706.
2. Daniel - bc1680, d1757, m1 1706 Rebecca Butler (d1751), m2 Mary ____.
3. Sarah - d1727, m1702 John Bates.
4. Joseph - d1755, m1708 Mary Cornell.
5. Jabez - d1716, m1712 Sarah Slason (b1687, d/o Joseph Stevens, wd/o Thomas).

Descendants of SMITH, Henry (continued):
6. Caleb - m1720 Susanna Scofield (b1698, d/o John).
7. Nathan - m Hester Green (b1696, d/o Benjamin).
8. Benjamin - m Hannah Husted (d/o Angel).
9. Mary - m1723 Charles Webb.
10. Hannah - m ____ Weed.
11. Moses - b1703.
12. Ezra - b1705.
13. Ruth - d1740, m1729 James June.

D. Rebecca - m1672 Edward Wilkinson.
E. John - d1711, m1679? Elizabeth Scofield (b1655, d1703, d/o Richard).
1. Hannah - d1703.
2. Jonathan - m1704? Temperance ____.
3. John - b168-, d1724, mc1708 Phebe Green (b1686, d aft 1756, d/o Benjamin).
4. Samuel - mc1712 Mary ____ (d1715).
5. David - m1738 Rachel Hoyt (d/o Samuel).
6. Ebenezer - bc1690, d1763, m1723 Hannah Whitman (dc1782).
7. Nathaniel - bc1693.
8. daughter - d1703.

F. Mary - d1658.
G. Abigail -.
H. daughter - d1661.

STEVENS, Thomas - d1658, m Ann ____ (she m2 Francis Holmes).

There was a John Stevens who came to America on the *Hopewell* in 1634 and lived in Hingham, MA. This may have been the John who came to Stamford by December of 1641; little more is known of him.

Thomas was probably a son or brother of John. There was a Thomas on the *Abigail* in 1635 who was twelve years old. Thomas was in Stamford by 1650 and lived on the north side of East Street.

His sons Benjamin and Joseph went to Bedford, NY; Benjamin moved on to Danbury, CT, but Joseph returned to Stamford. Descendants:

A. Obadiah, bc1644, d1702, m1678 Rebecca Rose (b1657, d1729, d/o Robert).
1. Thomas - b1679, mc1705 Sarah ____.
2. Ephraim - b1680, m1711 Hannah Clark (bc1687, d/o Robert).
3. Rose - b1683, d1727, m1711 Jonathan Slason.

Descendants of STEVENS, Thomas (continued):

4. Rebecca - b1686, m Benjamin Kellam?
5. Elisha - b1688, m1715 Mary Youngs (d/o John).
6. David - b1691, m1719 Jerusha Hoyt (b1698, d/o Joshua).
7. Nathan - b1694.
8. Deliverance - b1697, d by 1741, m1724 Elizabeth Youngs (d/o John).
9. Obadiah - b1702.

B. Ephraim - bc1646.

C. Thomas - bc1647, d1706, mc1680 Mary Green.

D. Benjamin - bc1648, d169-, m Hannah ____ (d1730). Bedford, NY & Danbury, CT.

E. Joseph - bc1650, d1717, m1680 Sarah Buxton (d/o Clement).

1. Joseph - b1681.
2. Unica - b1683.
3. Sarah - b1686, m1709, Thomas Slason.
4. Mary - b1691.

F. Esther - bc1654, m1 Obadiah Seely, m2 Moses Jackson.

THEALE, THELE, Nicolas - bc1615, d1658, m1 c1640 Elizabeth Charles or Carles (d1660, wd/o Joseph?), she m2 1660 Thomas Uffit (Ufford).

Nicolas Theale and his wife Elizabeth were in Watertown in 1638 and their two children were born there. Elizabeth had two former children: Catherine who married John Archer and Mary who married Thomas Newman. Nicolas was in Stamford by 1645 and lived on the north side of North Street by Mill River. The bridge there was named Theale's Bridge. Joseph held many positions of importance in Stamford and was made captain of the train band after he moved to Bedford, NY in 1680. He later moved to Rye, NY where he was justice of the peace. Descendants:

A. Joseph - b1640, d aft 1710, m1 ____, m2 c1695 Rebecca Hull (bc1633, d/o Rev John Jones, wd/o Cornelius). Bedford, NY.

1. Ebenezer - bc1678, d1747, mc1700 Hannah Ann Brown.
2. Elizabeth - b1680, m1710 Daniel Purdy.
3. Hannah - b1682, m1702 John Merritt.
4. Joseph - b1684.
5. William - b1686, m1714 Sarah Depew.
6. Mary - b1688, m1708 Joseph Merritt.
7. Anne - b1690, m1709 Solomon Lane.
8. Martha - b1693, m David Purdy.
9. Phebe - b1696, m1717 John Miller.

Descendants of THEALE, Nicolas (continued):

10. Sarah - b1698, m1719 John Ogden.
11. Eleanor - b1701.
12. Mary? - b1702.

B. Elizabeth - b1643, m1 1659 William Ratcliffe, m2 1687 Zachariah Baldwin.

TURNEY, Joseph - d1713, m1 ____, m2 1691 Mary Hoyt (bc1646, d1724, d/o Francis Bell, wd/o Joshua).

Joseph was probably a nephew of Benjamin Turney. He was in Stamford by 1680. In his will he left his negro girl to his wife. He was a hatter and lived at the east end of town north of the Eastfield. Descendants:

A. Edward - d1706.
B. Thomas - m1685 Mercy Stevens (d/o James). London, England.
C. daughter - d by 1698?, m by 1695 Joshua Hoyt.
D. Mary - m Joseph Ferris.

References: "Ancestry of Benjamin Turney," *The American Genealogist*, Oct. 1936.

USHER, Robert - d1669, m1 ____, m2 1659 Elizabeth Jagger (wd/o Jeremiah).

Robert Usher was in New Haven in 1644 and had land in Stamford by 1650. He was a man of some prominence and was the brother of Hezekiah Usher of Boston. Descendants:

A. Robert - Dunstable, MA.
B. Elizabeth - b1660.

WARD, Andrew - bc1597, d1659, m Hester (Esther?) Sherman (b1606, d1666, d/o Edmund). Fairfield.

Andrew Ward was born in Homersfield, Norfolk, England, the son of Richard or Andrew. He was married in Dedham, Essex. He came to America in 1630, probably with John Holly and Francis Bell. He was in Watertown until 1635 when he moved to Hartford where he was a magistrate of the court. He was one of the original group of settlers in Stamford in 1641 and was one of the first men chosen for townsmen; later he was a magistrate. In 1647 or 1648 he moved to Fairfield, CT. He was also in Hempstead, L.I. for awhile. Descendants:

A. William - m Deborah Lockwood.
B. John -.

C. Hester -.
D. Sarah - m Nathaniel Burr.
E. Abigail -.
F. Andrew -.
G. Samuel -.
H. Edmund -.
I. Mary - m John Burr.
J. Anna - m Caleb Nichols.

WATERBURY, John - b1621, d1658, m1 Sarah ____, m2 1658 Rose ____ (bc1618, d by 1688), she m2 1659 Joseph Garnsey.

John Waterbury was baptized in Sudbury, England; he was the son of William. William and Alice came to America on the *Arbella*, in 1629-1630. There is no mention of John until about 1639 when he was an innkeeper in Watertown, MA. He went to Wethersfield in 1645-1646 and was in Stamford by 1650. He first owned a home on the south side of North Street and then bought Thomas Morehouse's house on the east side of South Street. The Waterburys were well off, John having been a merchant. All three of his sons were active in town affairs just as their father had been. Both John and David served in King Philip's War. Lt. David's son John was known as "river John" as he lived by the Noroton River.

A Susannah Waterbury married Nathaniel Scofield in 1713. Was she a daughter of John? Descendants:

A. Rachel - b1638, m1659 John Holmes.
B. Sarah - b1646, d1712 or 1714, m1666 Zachariah Dibble, div in 1672, m2 Nicolas Webster, m3 by 1705 Edward Trehern.
C. John - b1650, d1688, m by 1679 Mary Wicks (bc1660, d1738, d/o Thomas), she m2 c1689 Jonas Seely.
  1. Mary - b1679, d1710, m1700 Jonathan Slason.
  2. Sgt John - b1682, d1744, m1 1707 Sarah Holmes (d1709, d/o Stephen), m2 1710 Hannah Cross (b1688, d1756, d/o Nathaniel).
  3. David - b1684, d1710, m1707 Waitstill Green (b1685, d1730, d/o Joseph), she m2 1713 Stephen Bishop.
    a. Thomas - b1687, d1758, m1 1716 Elizabeth Holly (b1693, d1719, d/o Elisha), m2 Elizabeth Boardman (d1730, d/o Joseph Gibbs, wd/o Israel), m3 by 1738 Hannah Hoyt (b1701, d1762, d/o Samuel Finch, wd/o Joseph).

Descendants of WATERBURY, John (continued):

D. Jonathan - b1653, d1703, m Unice (d/o Clement Buxton?, she m2 1707 Richard Higgenbotham.
  1. Sarah - b 1677, m1700 Benjamin Mead.
  2. Unice - b1679.
  3. Rose - b1681, d by 1702.
  4. Rachel - b1684, d by 1702.
  5. Jonathan - b1685, d1765, m1714 or 1718 Sarah Mead (b1691, d/o Jonathan).
  6. Abigail - b1688, d1729, m1708 John Newman.
  7. Joseph - b1691, d1751, m1719 Hannah Fountain (d/o Aaron).
  8. Benjamin - b1694, m1727 Mary Mead (b1704, d/o Jonathan).

E. Lt David - b1655, d1704 or 1706, m1 c1680 Sarah Newman (b1659, prob d/o William), m2 1698 Sarah Weed (b1675, d/o Daniel), she m2 Benjamin Ferris, she m3 1711 Nathaniel Pond.
  1. John - b1682, d1736, m1710 Susannah Newkirk.
  2. Elizabeth - b1684, m1702 Isaac How.
  3. Sarah - b1685, d1727, m1704 Jonas Weed.
  4. Ruth - b1699, m ____ Bouton.
  5. David - b1701.
  6. Ebenezer - b1704, d1721.
  7. Marcy - b1706.

References: *Deeds of Suffolk County, Massachusetts,* taken by Colin Campbell.

WEBB, Richard - bc1623, d1676, mc1645 Margery ____.

There were two Richard Webbs, one of Norwalk, who seemingly had no heirs. The Richard Webb of Stamford may have come from Dorset, England. He was first recorded in 1651 in Stamford when he bought a house near the mill which he later took over. He may have had Quaker leanings. Descendants:

A. Joseph - bc1648, d1684, m1672 Hannah Scofield (b1653, d/o Richard?), she m2 John Finch.
  1. Joseph - b1674, d1743, m1698 Mary Hoyt (b1673, d1750, d/o Benjamin).
  2. Mary - b1677, m1697 Daniel Weed.
  3. Hannah - b1679, d1723, m1711 Eleazer Slason.
  4. Sarah - b1681, d1706.
  5. Margery - b1683, d1737, m1716 Joseph Lockwood.

B. Richard - bc1650, d1656.

C. child? - d1656.

Descendants of WEBB, Richard (continued):

D. Joshua - bc1656, d1694, m Elizabeth Hine (d/o Thomas), she m2 Daniel Simkins. Bedford, NY.
1. Richard -.
2. Ebenezer -.
3. John -.
4. Susannah -.

E. Caleb - bc1658, d1704, m Sarah ____?
1. Mary - William Hill.
2. Joshua -.
3. Sarah - m1718 Nathan Holly.
4. child - d1704.
5. Margery - m1722 David Holly.

D. Samuel - b1662, d1736 or 1737, m Hannah Jagger (bc1668, d1729, d/o John).
1. Waitstill - b1691, m1713 Joseph Holly.
2. Lt Samuel - b1692, d1735?, m1720 Abigail Slason (b1700, d1760).
3. Mercy - b1694, m1713 Francis Brown.
4. Mary - m1722 John Bates.
5. Charles - b1697, d1730, m1723 Mary Smith (d/o Daniel).
6. Mary - 1699.
7. Nathaniel - 1700.
8. Benjamin - 1705.

E. Sarah - b1653, m Daniel Simkins.

References: Harrison E. Webb, "Richard Webb of Stamford, Connecticut," *The American Genealogist*, pp. 194-197.

WEBSTER, Nicolas - d1687, mc1673 Sarah Dibble (b1646, d1712 or 1714, d/o John Waterbury, div from Zachariah), she m2 by 1705 Edward Trehern.

Nicolas Webster was in Stamford about 1673. Nicolas moved to Bedford, NY in 1680 but returned to Stamford in 1685. He lived in the eastern part of Stamford. Descendants:

A. John - bc1674, d1716, m1702 Sarah Jagger (bc1677, d1760, d/o Jeremiah), she m2 James Slason.

B. David - bc1676, d1732, m1 1706 Abigail Holly (d1707, prob d/o John), m2 1709 Mercy Morehouse (d/o Jonathan).

C. Rachel - m1 1708 Henry Atwood, m2 1732 or 1733 Nathan Sturges.

WEED, Jonas - bc1598, d by 1676, m Mary Hoyt (dc1690).

Jonas Weed was probably from Yorkshire, England. He came to America on the *Arbella* in 1630. He was a freeman in Watertown, Mass., in 1631 and then went to Wethersfield, CT in 1635. He was in Stamford in 1642 and lived on the north corner of the road to the mill and "River Street." His son Jonas was called "of Noroton Corners," and his son John's oldest son was known as Jonas Weed, shoemaker. His son Samuel went to Bedford, NY in 1680 and then on to Danbury, CT. His son Daniel went to Rye, NY about 1677, to Bedford from 1680 to 1685, and then returned to Stamford.

The name Weed is often confused with Wood in reading the early records because of the way they formed their e's. Descendants:

A. Mary - bc1635, mc1657 George Abbott.
B. Elizabeth - bc1637, d1676, m John Rockwell.
C. Dorcas - bc1640, d1692, m1660 James Wright.
D. John - bc1642, d1690, m1 by 1664 Joanna Westcott (bc1640, d/o Richard), m2 Mary Abbott (d1714), she m2 Josiah Firman.
  1. Jonas - b1667, d1706, m169- Mary Scofield (d/o Daniel), she m2 1707 Samuel Hoyt.
    a. John - b1698.
    b. Miles - b1701.
    c. Sarah - b1703.
    d. Nathan - b1705.
  2. Daniel - b1669, m1697 Mary Webb (b1677, d1714?, d/o Joseph).
    a. Joseph - b1698 m Rose ____.
    b. David - b1700.
    c. Joanna - b1702.
    d. Daniel - b1705.
    e. Ebenezer - b1708.
    f. Sarah - b1710.
    g. Samuel - b1712.
  3. John - bc1672, m1702 Mary Beauman or Beaumont (d1743).
  4. Lt Samuel - bc1675, m1701 Abigail Scofield (d1737, d/o Daniel). Norwalk.
  5. Joseph - b1679, d1711, m1701 Rebecca Higginbotham (b1682), she m2 1716 Jonathan Crissy.
  6. Isaac - b1682, d1754.
  7. Mary - b1684, m Joseph Lockwood.
  8. Hannah - b1687, d1739, m1711 Sgt Samuel Scofield.

Descendants of WEED, Jonas (continued):

E. Daniel - bc1643, d1697, m Ruth ____, she m2 1705 Peter Ferris.

1. Sarah - b1675, d1716, m1 1698 Lt David Waterbury, m2 1706 Benjamin Ferris, m3 1711 Nathaniel Pond.
2. Abraham - b1680, d1711, m1706 Susanna Bell (b1686, d1756, d/o Jonathan), she m2 1715 Thomas Talmadge.
3. Lt Daniel - b1685, d1762, mc1708 Elizabeth Scofield (bc1688, d by 1727, d/o Daniel).
4. Capt Ebenezer - b1692, d1675, m1713 Mary Bell (b1689, d/o Jonathan).
5. Capt Nathaniel - b1696, d1750, mc1719 Mary Reed (b1695, d1792, d/o Thomas?).

F.Samuel - bc1645, d1708, m Mary ____. Bedford, NY & Danbury, CT.

G. Jonas - bc1647, d1704, m1676 Bethia Holly (b1655, d1713, d/o John).

1. Jonas - b1678, d1753, m1704 Sarah Waterbury (b1685, d1727, d/o Lt David).

H. Benjamin - b1681, dc1748, m1707 Mary Penoyer (b1688, d1732, d/o Thomas).

1. Jonathan - b1684, d1728, m by 1716 Mary Green (b1681, d/o Joseph).
2. Abigail - b1695, m1714 Jeremiah Scofield.

I. Hannah - bc1650, d1711, m1670 Benjamin Hoyt.

J. Sarah - bc1654.

K. child - d1656.

References: Charles Arthur Hoppen, *Washington Ancestry and Other Colonial Families*; Julia Frame Bunce, *Some of the Ancestors of Rev. John Selby Frame and His Wife, Clara Winchester Dana*, p. 141; Paul W. Prindle records.

WESTCOTT

Richard Westcott was in Wethersfield by 1636 and moved to Fairfield, CT about 1645. Four of his children, Joanna, Abigail, John and Daniel, moved on to Stamford by the early 1660s. Daniel held a number of important positions and was a sergeant in King Philip's War. In 1692 he became involved in the witch trial case. John went to Westchester in 1669 and then to Bedford, NY in 1680, where he was an original proprietor and continued residing. Daniel also had land in Bedford, but he left Stamford in 1697, and he died in Caesaria, NY. While in Stamford, John and Daniel lived west of Mill River.

Descendants of WESTCOTT:

A. Joanna - bc1640, m by 1665 John Weed.
B. Abigail - bc1642, d aft 1713, m1669 Moses Knap.
C. Richard - bc1644, m Ruth Belden.
D. John - bc1646, d1704, m1667 Ruth Hyatt (bc1650, d aft 1710, d/o Thomas). Mamaroneck & Bedford, NY.
  1. Richard - b1668, m Rachel Holmes (b1669, d/o John). Bedford, NY.
  2. child - b1670, d young.
  3. child - b1672, d young.
  4. child - b1674, d young.
  5. John - b1679, d1743, m1702 Rose Holmes (bc1678, d/o John). Bedford & Wilton.
  6. Thomas - b1686, m Elizabeth ____.
E. Sgt Daniel - bc1648, d1704, m Abigail Gaylord (b1653, d/o Samuel).
  1. Joanna - m ____ Foster.
  2. Abigail - m ____ Lummus.
  3. Samuel - m Elizabeth Coley (b1680, d/o Peter). New Jersey.
  4. Daniel - m Elizabeth Foster?, of New Jersey.
  5. Ebenezer - m Barbara ____.
  6. Mary -.

WHITMORE, John - d1648, m1 ____, m2 c1639 Joanna Jessup (wd/o John).

John Whitmore was in Wethersfield and was among the first settlers of Stamford in 1641. After his murder by an Indian in 1648, his children must have moved away as there is no further record of them in Stamford. His second wife moved to Newtown, L.I. Descendants:

A. Thomas - bc1615.
B. Ann - bc1620.
C. Mary - bc1623.
D. Francis or Frances - bc1625.
E. John - bc1627.

INDEX

This index references all names found in the historical text, as well as buried names found in the genealogies.

Stamford 1641-1660

This map shows the early home lots as given in the land deeds, and as recorded in 1650. The 1650 date is not the date of acquisition but the date when many of the existing homelots were recorded. Most of the home lots were designated as 1 1/2 acres, but the map can only give an approximation as to size and shape. All features are drawn as accurately as possible in view of the existing data.

1 John Coe; Elias Bayly; 1651 Nicholas Knap
2 1650 William Newman
3 John Finch; William Potter; 1652 Thomas Lyon; c.1659 William Ratcliffe
4 Samuel Sherman; 1654 John Chapman; 1654 Samuel Dean
5 1650 Thomas Lyon
6 1650 Richard Hardy
7 1650 Henry Accorley; 1653 John Finch II
8 1650 Edmund Lockwood; 1658 John Green
9 1660 Vincent Simkins; 1660 William Oliver
10 1650 Thomas Stevens; 1658 Ann Stevens
11 1650 Simon Hoyt?
12,13 1650 Nicholas Theale; 1658 Joseph Theale
14 1650 Jeffrey Ferris
15 1650 Robert Bates
16 1650 John Finch; 1653 Richard Ambler
17 Daniel Finch; 1648 Richard Ambler
18 1650 Jeremiah Jagger; 1658 Elizabeth Jagger; 1659 Robert Usher
19 1650 John Waterbury; c.1654 Richard Mills
20 1650 William Potter
21 1650 John Bishop; Daniel Scofield II?
22 Matthew Mitchell?; 1650 David Mitchell
23 Richard Denton; Robert Lockwood; 1650 John Bishop
24 John Coe; Henry Jackson; 1650 George Stucke?; Jonathan Lockwood?
25 1650 Jeffrey Ferris
26 1651 Peter Brown; 1658 Thomas Brown
27 1653 Jonas Weed
28 1650 Jeffrey Ferris; Mill Lot
29 1650 Thomas Newman; John Mead; 1659 Robert Penoyer
30 1650 Robert Rugg; 1651 Richard Webb; Edmund Lockwood; 1656 Ann Accorley
31 1650 Daniel Scofield
32,33 William Mead?; 1650 Joseph Mead
34 Robert Emory; 1657 Richard Law; 1658 Jonathan Law
35 1650 Richard Law
36 Thomas Colgrove; Elias Bayly; 1651 John Bassett; 1652 John Waterbury; 1652 Ealse Marshall; 1652 Robert Penoyer; 1654 Stephen Clawson
37 Jeremiah Wood; Edward Jessup; James Steward; Robert Bassett; John Waterbury; John Rockwell; 1657 Garret Rivers & Aron Anderson; Henry Disbrow; 1658 Jonathan Lockwood; 1658 Abraham Frost
38 1647 James Steward; 1658 Richard Law
39 Edward Jessup; 1647 Clement Buxton; 1658 Unica Buxton Brown
40 William Newman; 1647 John Holly
41 1650 Henry Smith
42 1647 John Reynold; 1652 Jeffrey Ferris; John Pettit
43-45 1652 Thomas Hyatt; 1657 Cornelius Jones
46,47 1649 Obadiah Seely; 1657 Obadiah Seely II
48 1649 George Slason
49,50 1649 Thomas Morehouse; 1650 John Waterbury; 1658 Rose Waterbury
51 1649 John Chapman; 1655 heirs of John Chapman
52 1651 Thomas Hunt; c.1658 Francis Brown
53 1650 Francis Bell
54 Henry Olinson; 1651 James Lareson
55 1650 John Eliot
56 1650 William Newman; 1658 Francis Holmes
57 1650 William Graves

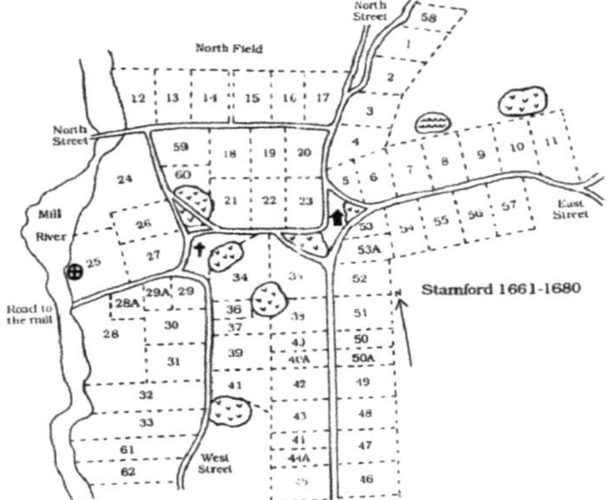

Stamford 1661-1680

1 Richard Ayres
2 Samuel Finch
3 Heirs of Daniel Scofield; 1680 Daniel Scofield II
4 Samuel Dean
5 Joshua Hoyt
6 Richard Hardy
7 Isaac Finch
8 John Green?; 1680 John Green
9 John Holmes
10 Thomas Stevens & Obadiah Stevens; 1680 Obadiah Stevens
11 Samuel Hoyt
12,13 Joseph Theale
14 Peter Ferris
15 Robert Bates; 1680 heirs of Robert Bates
16 Richard Ambler; 1680 Abraham Ambler
17 Richard Ambler
18 Robert Usher; widow of Robert Usher; 1680 John Jagger
19 Joseph Alsop of New Haven; John Miller
20 William Potter
21 Heirs of Daniel Scofield; 1680 John Scofield
22 William Newman; 1680 Thomas Newman
23 John Bishop
24 Edmund Lockwood
25 Richard Webb; 1680 heirs of Richard Webb
26 John Pettit; 1680 heirs of John Pettit
27 Jonas Weed
28 Richard Webb; 1680 heirs of Richard Webb
28A John Thompson; Richard Webb
29 Thomas Laurence; 1680 John Judson
29A 1680 Town Land (formerly occupied by Thomas Laurence)
30 Daniel Simkins; John Austin; Samuel Dibble; Nicholas Knap; Moses Knap
31 Richard Scofield
32 Daniel Weed
33 John Weed
34,35 Richard Law
36 Stephen Clason; 1680 Joseph Garnsey
37 Timothy Knap; Robert Usher; Matthew Bellamy; George Slason or 1680 Eleazer Slason
38 John Selleck
39 Clement Buxton
40 John Holly
40A 1680 John Holly Sr.
41 Henry Smith
42 John Holly; Samuel Holly?; 1680 Samuel Holly
43,44 Cornelius Jones
44A 1680 Joseph Jones
45 Frederick Hermison; Joseph Garnsey; George Slason; 1680 John Gold
46 Heirs of Obadiah Seeley; 1680 Obadiah Seeley
47 Heirs of Obadiah Seeley; 1680 Jonathan Miller
48 George Slason
49 Heirs of John Waterbury, d.; 1680 Jonathan Waterbury
50 John Waterbury
50A David Waterbury; 1680 Jonathan Waterbury
51 Francis Brown; John Judson; 1680 Francis Brown
52 Francis Brown; Philip Minthorne; Jonathan Selleck
53 Francis Bell
53A 1680 Jonathan Bell
54 Jonathan Selleck; John Slason
55 William Crissy
56 Francis Holmes; 1680 Stephen Holmes?
57 William Newman; 1680 Daniel Newman?
58 Nicolas Knapp?
59 John Bates
60 John Jagger; 1680 Jeremiah Jagger
61 Caleb Knap
62 Daniel Weed; 1680 John Austin

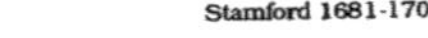

Stamford 1681-1700

Stamford 1681-1700

By this time many inhabitants of Stamford lived to the east, the north, and the west of the center of the village.

1 Abraham Finch; John Finch (no house)
1A Abraham Finch
2 Samuel Finch
3 Daniel Scofield
4 Samuel Dean
5 Samuel Dean?
6 Samuel Hardy; Thomas-Wood; 1700 Samuel Weed
7 Isaac Finch
7A 1700 Samuel Blackley
7B 1700 Isaac Finch
8 Benjamin Guen; Joseph Stevens; Thomas Newman; Elisha Holly
9 Elisha Holly
10 Obadiah Stevens
11 Samuel Hoyt
12,13 Jonathan & John Selleck; Peter Ferris; 1700 Joseph Ferris
14 Peter Ferris; Peter Ferris Jr.
15 John Bates; 1700 John Bates Jr.
16 Abraham Ambler d. 1700
17 Richard Ambler d. 1700
18 Heirs of John Jagger; Jonathan Jagger; 1700 Simon Chapman
19 Jonathan & John Selleck; Benjamin Hoyt
20 Sons of John Bishop; Ebenezer Bishop; Town land for parsonage; 1700 John Davenport
21 John Scofield
22 Daniel Weed; 1700 heirs of Daniel Weed
23 John Bishop; 1700 Benjamin Bishop
24 Joseph Lockwood
25 Heirs of Richard Webb; 1700 Samuel Webb
26 John Pettit, d.; John Pettit; 1700 Jonas Weed, Jr.
27 Jonas Weed; 1700 Jonas Weed, Sr.
27A Thomas Newman; Joseph Stevens; John Arnold; Moses Knap, Jr.; Henry Kimball; Daniel Weed, Jr.; 1700 Jonas Weed, Jr.
28 Heirs of Richard Webb; 1700 Samuel Webb
29 John Judson; Town House; Ebenezer Bishop; 1700 John Pettit
30 Moses Knap
31 Richard Scofield; 1700 John Smith
32,33 John Weed; 1700 heirs of John Weed
34,35 Jonathan Law
36 Joseph Garnsey; Zachariah Roberts; 1700 John Finch, Jr.
37 Joseph Stevens
38 Widow Sarah Selleck
39 Clement Buxton
40 John Holly (no house)
40A Jonathan Holly; 1700 John Holly, Sr.
41 John Smith
42 Samuel Holly
43 Cornelius Jones, d. 1690; 1700 heirs of Cornelius Jones
44 Joseph Jones, d. 1690; 1700 heirs of Joseph Jones
45 John Gold?
46 Obadiah Seeley
47 Jonathan Holly
48 George Slason; 1700 Jonathan Waterbury
49 Jonathan Waterbury
50 Heirs of John Waterbury; widow Mary Waterbury
51 Francis Brown; Joseph Brown
52 Jonathan Selleck
53 Francis Bell; Jonathan Bell
53A Jonathan Bell
54 John Slason
55 John Crissy; 1700 John Bishop
56 Stephen Holmes
57 Daniel Newman; 1700 Thomas Newman
58 Jeremiah Andrews; John Finch; 1700 John Pettit
59 John Bates, Sr.
60 Jeremiah Jagger; 1700 heirs of Jeremiah Jagger
61 Caleb Knap
62 John Austin; 1700 heirs of John Austin
63 Increase Holly
64 Francis Brown (moved to Rye in 1686); Joseph Brown

www.ingramcontent.com/pod-product-compliance
Lightning Source LLC
Chambersburg PA
CBHW050142170426
43197CB00011B/1934
* 9 7 8 1 5 5 6 1 3 3 9 4 7 *